William Morrow & Company

THE GOD
OF THE
BEGINNINGS

○ ROBERT ARON *author of*
Jesus of Nazareth: The Hidden Years
Translated from the French
by Frances Frenaye

New York 1966

In memory of my parents.
May their souls repose in peace.

Acknowledgments

I should like to thank all those who have helped to check the historical facts of this book: particularly two Christian scholars, Monsieur Jacques Guitton of the French Academy and the Benedictine Father who previously advised me on *Jesus of Nazareth—The Hidden Years*; two scholars versed in the Jewish tradition, Chief Rabbi Schilli of the Rabbinical School of Paris and Monsieur Emmanuel Levinas; and also Monsieur André Parrot of the French Institute and Monsieur Jacques Cauvin of the National Council of Scientific Research.

The research for this book was done jointly by Robert Aron and Simone Raymond-Weil.

Titles of books and authors mentioned in the text will be found in the Bibliography.

Contents

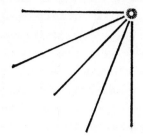

I *Introduction*

Two remarks are pertinent at the outset of this work, one about its subject and the other about its documentation.

This *God of the Beginnings* is not a general history of the origin of religious feeling, of all the gods humanity has known or still knows. It does not claim to deal with all the religious traditions that have at different times and in different places held the allegiance of men. However profound their interpretations of the mystery of human fate, however great their contributions to civilization, there will be no treatment of Buddhism, Hinduism or even the religion of Islam. We shall limit ourselves in these pages to the history of the God of the Bible, to Whom western culture, even if under occasional protest, owes its existence and survival—in other words to the God Who is a part of history, and to the portion of this history relevant to our Judeo-Christian religious and humanistic tradition.

The prehistory of this God and His first manifestations will be the compass of our domain. We are neither ignorant nor disdainful of all that lies outside. But no history of God can be isolated from our experience of it. And our experience, no matter how incomplete and tentative it may be, lies within the tradition of the Bible, as it has come down to the western world.

It is within this tradition that the documentation for this book has been sought. In part, quite obviously, it comprises the Bible itself, whose inspired books make the primary contribution to our knowledge of God. The second source is "tradition," that is to say, the commentary man has contributed over the ages to the understanding of the Scriptures. This "tradition" consists of the exegesis and interpretation of the Old Testament by generations of learned Jews. For centuries the lives of these men were shaped solely by the Word of God; they had no occupation but to study it, and no goal but to live by it. To live by it they composed—thought by thought, sentence by sentence and story by story—the great collections of the Talmud and the Midrash. The first of these was more concerned with drawing from the sacred books the rules of life and their modes of application; the second sought to bring to its interpretation a poetic or philosophic commentary which would make the rules more comprehensible and attractive to later generations.

When, in the present book, we speak of "tradition," we refer to the rabbinical tradition, as it is expressed in the Talmud and the Midrash, between the third and the twelfth centuries of the Christian era. For some it may be a surprising discovery to learn that Jewish religious thought did not wither away after the coming of Christ but continued to be fruitful. We ask such readers not to be dismayed: to pursue with us the supplementation of the familiar Bible stories by the wealth of fables heretofore unfamiliar to them but often stimulating and provocative.

The third source—for both pre-biblical and biblical religion—

is the contribution of the discoveries of contemporary archaeology. Recent explorations and excavations have thrown light on the circumstances under which biblical events actually took place. The books which relate such archaeological discoveries are indispensable adjuncts to a study of the early history of God.

To recapitulate, the research for this book drew upon three main sources:

First, upon the manifestation of God's will and purpose as they are expressed, through the vicissitudes of history, in the Book which He inspired;

Second, upon the commentaries, explanatory or critical, made by men, the assent or dissent that human intelligence added to the Scripture;

Third, upon the historical and geographical facts, known today, which form the framework of the sacred story.

From the interweaving of these three kinds of documentation perhaps the history of the God of the beginnings may emerge reinvigorated and closer to our own times.

Everything has been said, yet there will always be something to say, as long as there are men on earth to seek, in every generation, a new meaning in the Word. The history of God, like that of man, always remains to be written; it is a paradox that defies resolution. Transcending the world yet in the world, transcending man yet bound up with his vicissitudes, it writes itself simultaneously into eternity and into the ceaseless motion of the passing hours. It is both outside our destinies and within them, dominating and directing them and yet affected, in its unrolling, by our free will. Do we not find, even in the Bible, frequent dialogues and exchanges between the God of Israel and His human partners? Dizzying and troublesome paradoxes, but necessary ones—perhaps it was in order to learn to live with them that this book has been written.

There was a time when, upon our call, in answer to our need, the history of God was expressed by the revelations in which the

Eternal manifested Himself to His creatures, by a sacred story, filled with miracles and celestial interventions, with promises and commandments, which left no room for doubt except on the part of atheists and nonbelievers. Although impregnated with the supernatural it was as precise and easy to assimilate as any other historical account, written by man for man.

Today, at a time when revealed religions are undermined by atheism, meditation on the Bible, particularly on the crude and archaic texts of the Old Testament, needs to have a new light thrown upon it. The light of faith, which drew its certitudes from the Scriptures, is not sufficient. In the shadow of doubt, under the stimuli of the idolatrous seductions of science and technology, the history of God has to make itself known to a world which in large part no longer knows the Eternal and furnish new reasons for interest and perhaps for faith.

What is important today in reading the Bible is not the exactitude of a story which in certain books is only a step removed from legend, not merely the inspired character attributed to it by believers. What matters is the human effort to which it testifies, the development of religious feeling in a succession of generations. Through a welter of anecdotes, likely and unlikely, the Bible records the restless progression toward God by our forebears, in an uninterrupted sequence of mortal aspirations. Our contemporaries are concerned not so much with the God revealed in the biblical tradition as with the problems that provoked this revelation, the human and material difficulties that God had to overcome, and which are strangely similar to those that assail and disorient our own world. The history of God, merely on the level of history, is more alive than ever.

Even if it is beyond our human powers to prove the existence of God, it may be counted a considerable achievement to prove and describe men's faith in His existence. Failing an authentic portrait of Him Whose face no man may know, let us trace a picture of the would-be painter, of the man, believing or unbelieving, who cannot help searching for his place in relation to the Eternal, who cannot escape God. The history of God—the history of men before God and God as men came to conceive Him—from what angle, in what sequence shall we approach it?

In the biblical tradition everything takes place as if the unit for measuring time were the bimillenium, as if it required two thousand years for a religious evolution to begin, develop and complete its cycle, as if every religious period fitted into this exact span. Two thousand years, approximately, according to the accounts of the Bible, made up the original period of monotheism, from the creation of the world to the birth of Abraham. Another two thousand years, beginning with Abraham, the father of all believers, and ending with Jesus, was the extent of the exclusively Jewish period, marked by the further emergence of the One God and the expression of His moral law. And finally, the two thousand years which saw the extension of monotheism, through Christianity, to all the nations of the earth, up until the present day, when its supremacy is besieged by idolatrous and atheistic philosophies. Perhaps modern times are preparing and awaiting a new bimillenium, a new Covenant.

Among the thousands of prayers which have risen to heaven through the ages many have lost their significance. Our contemporaries, refusing to believe in God, cannot accept the words formerly addressed to Him; their spiritual aspirations call for a new vocabulary or a new silence. But in the immense repertory of prayers there is one, very old and very pure, which has no reason to be discredited. A Jewish prayer whose simple words have come down to our century without offending its taste for historical truth and objectivity.

"*Elohe Abotenu*, God of our fathers"—who can find fault with these words? Believers or nonbelievers, the God Whom we do or do not worship is our fathers' God, the God Who reigned supreme in their unquestioning faith and conscience—which means that we have, in history, at least one point of contact with Him. This one prayer which we can all say, some of us wholeheartedly, others with nostalgia, which in an accent sacred or profane has the same meaning for us all, contains the uniqueness of the God of the Bible, the God inscribed in history.

Indeed, in relation to this fundamental prayer, to believe or not to believe becomes a secondary problem. What matters is to know that our forebears believed, that their belief maintained them in their humanity, that it shaped us and that we reap its benefits even if we do not share it. These two words, *Elohe Abotenu,* should be the watermark of every page of this book; they alone give it its true dimensions and unshakable foundation. May they give us the feeling of reality, the certainty, our epoch so sorely needs to save it from confusion.

We must not overreach ourselves, however. At the least we shall try to prove that God has always existed to those who deny that He exists today.

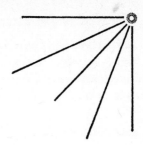

2 *The God of Prehistory*

How are we to imagine him, this god before God? Can we speak of a god of the infinite time before that recorded by the Bible when, as the first chapter of Genesis tells us, the earth was *tohu bohu*, "without shape and void"? Does he fit in with the figure of God the Creator? Prehistory tells us how to answer these preliminary questions.

"*Bereshit bara elohim* [In the beginning God created] . . ." At the official threshold of history, the first stage of our faith, this phrase apparently forbids us to push our research any further back than the D-Day of Genesis. But only apparently. For just as God cannot be confined to any idea or image which man makes of Him, so no passage from the Bible can be limited to its literal meaning. Maimonides, the master of medieval Jewish philosophy, proclaims in the following words the hidden meaning of Holy Scripture:

"Men are divided into three categories. The first and second are composed of narrow-minded individuals who see only the literal aspect of the rabbinical fables; the only difference is that one category listens to them ingenuously while the other makes fun of them. The third and smallest category is composed of persons understanding enough to admit that these stories have an occult meaning and that the scholars' teachings, even if they seem improbable, contain, in parable form, a deep significance and that their study leads to the perception of a higher truth."

Thus the first Bible story, with its train of commentaries and fables, is not so simple as it seems; it is an apologue or, better yet, a mystery. Apart from its commonplace meaning, which is accessible to positivist spirits, it has a quite different significance for the small number of initiates who in their hidden sanctuaries transmit truths, incomprehensible to the multitude, from one age to another. The true history of any faith is based less on revelation than on initiation. One leads to the other, but the real process takes place and is transmitted in shadowy whispers before it breaks, with some solemn pronouncement, into the light of day. Like any initiation myth, the story of Genesis must not be spread abroad but rather transmitted from mouth to ear, from heart to understanding. Among the mysteries to be expounded with circumspection, according to one of the rabbis of the Talmud, who was perhaps in his own way an initiate, is the creation story, which he says must not be told to more than one person at a time.

Thus Genesis is not an absolute beginning, a creation *ex nihilo*, following a pre-established schedule. It does not mark the chronological starting point of time but only the indefinite, albeit essential, moment when God leaned toward the world and inscribed Himself in its history. It is, as we have said above, an apologue, which rabbinical tradition has told us over and over we must not mistake for reality.

From all eternity, before the *"Bereshit bara,"* the Midrash tells us, there was an unseen previous element. There was the Torah, the Law, which Moses was to reveal when he came down from Mount Sinai. For thousands of years the Torah existed, lingering in the mysterious shadows, near God's side, until He should have completed the universe and the human creature in which it was to be manifested.

In this broad perspective the myth of Genesis takes on a meaning. It is not a clap of thunder in the silence of the night, a ray of light and hope in the dark nothingness. It is the setting in motion, by transcendent will inaccessible to man, of the elements, both good and bad, which were to determine his destiny. According to the rabbis, God wanted man to be of all creatures upon earth the closest to Him. He placed man at the intersection between two hierarchies, in appearance conflicting but more likely complementary: earth and matter on the one side, heaven and spirit on the other. It is as if He wanted man to be the most spiritual of material beings and the most material of spiritual beings, the first earthly and the last heavenly creature.

Foreshadowing and joining up with the story of Genesis, prehistoric religions, which we may now bring in without breaking the Law, afford us a humble and elementary means of seeing the Creator in a new perspective, of distinguishing features which we have never perceived before.

From now on our search will be in the realm of what the world calls "material" reality, as if any reality could be totally material in nature. The detailed precision and apparent coldness of our story, the profanely scientific objectivity of our search for manifestations of the sacred, have the sole aim of pinning down the circumstances in which the Spirit breathes, in which God appears in the world which He created and in the history which He began.

In 1912, when the French archaeologists Count Begouën and his sons stumbled into the sanctuary of the cave of Tuc d'Audoubert in the region of Ariège, they knew that no one had set foot there since prehistoric times. Access to this dark place, already difficult enough in the Pleistocene period, had been blocked by further obstacles during the thirty thousand years that it remained empty. At the entrance the Begouëns found a channel, dug out by a subterranean stream. Crossing it in a boat, they came to a cliff which overhung a number of large rooms ornamented by superb limestone deposits; in one corner a vertical shaft almost forty feet high led them to a corridor and then to a narrower low-ceilinged passage, on whose walls were incised drawings from the Aurignacian period, between twenty-two and twenty-eight thousand years before our era. At this point the way was obstructed by a row of stalagmites, which had been formed over the centuries by dripping calcareous water. It was certain that since they had formed no human being had gone any farther. The explorers had to cut their way through the natural barrier of calcium to a continuation of the corridor and to another chamber where on the clay floor they found scratches of bear claws and piles of animal bones. There were the imprints of human feet as well, "the feet of the cave dwellers who had slaughtered the animals." From this point the narrowing corridor led to the end room of the cave which, as Count Begouën says, might have been "the sanctuary where the tribe kept its fetishes or idols, perhaps clay bison." For bison were the subjects of the wall drawings.

Just as, in an era of persecution, our revealed religions celebrated their mysteries in crypts or grottoes, some of which are used for religious services even today, so our more distant ancestors were moved by a primeval stirring of faith to hide themselves from an indifferent or hostile nature in uncomfortable but well-protected places. "We can imagine," writes the Rev. Théodore Mainage, somewhat anachronistically, "men prostrate in supplication before these painted or drawn or sculpted images, which apparently put them in contact with mysterious tutelary or malevolent powers."

In such primitive shelters paleolithic man already had a feeling for the supernatural which almost qualifies him as a believer. In caves or in hidden clearings throughout the sparsely inhabited lands of Europe, Africa, and central Asia the wind of the spirit was blowing, not in great storms but in sporadic gusts, in chance places where it had to combat the blind forces of nature and animality. This animality was evident not only in the wild beasts which pawed the floor of the sanctuaries and imperiled the lives of their captors; it was inherent in man himself, in this favored species which, in order to assume an attitude of prayer, had to free itself from the chains of bestiality.

It seems as if some inner force impelled our species to raise itself up and direct its eyes toward inaccessible mysteries. A long-ago ancestor, common to both monkeys and men, left the ground, which abounded in enemies of every kind, and lived in trees, where it underwent a fundamental evolution in posture and means of locomotion.

First the hand became free. Ceasing to be a front foot, serving to hold up and balance the body, to grasp tree branches and find in them its support, it began to reach out for any object which inspired desire or attention. It went after fruits, closed around them in order to take them from one place to another, and clutched its offspring protectively. Soon the thumb branched out from the other fingers and came to face them. Thanks to the thumb, a hand could collect stones and finally hammer them. This was the beginning of craftsmanship.

At the same time man began to pull himself upright. Since the hands were no longer used for support, the whole body seemed to swivel on the hips until it finally became vertical. The bodily posture which was to be that of civilized man was born directly from that of an animal. Movement was freer and individual liberty increased. The range of man's sight was greater, and by looking around him he could see logical connections between events and things.

This development of the hand and the straightening up of

the body had an effect on the brain, which now found itself in a new position. The head in general underwent a change. Now that the hand conveyed food to the mouth, there was no reason for the face to protrude. The teeth no longer had to snatch at something; they had merely to chew it. The lower part of the face receded, while the upper part fell into line, giving more prominence to the eyes and more room to the brain cavity. Stereoscopic vision demanded a new effort from the brain and stimulated its activity. Instead of simply registering sensations to produce reflexes, it became the organ of new faculties such as attention, co-ordination, and eventually imagination. In short, the brain passed from a passive to an active role. Perched on top of the body and relating external vision to more complicated internal operations, turning at will toward the faraway horizon or the sky above, it acquired the faculties not only of imagination but also of thought and prayer.

It took thousands of years for the primitive man who had sought out an impenetrable cave in which to address inarticulate prayers to a rudimentary notion of divinity to arrive at a more definite form of worship. Over the same period another evolution was taking place, alternately completing or nullifying the effects of the one of which we have spoken above. Man was not aware of it in his flesh and bones, for it took place outside, in the surrounding nature, whose travail had repercussions upon him. Between these two developing processes, that which he bore within him and that which pressed upon him from the outside, man developed a conscience and acquired a belief.

In the early Pleistocene period or Ice Age there were continuous variations of climate which brought about changes in the contours of continents and in living conditions. For thousands of years there were violent shifts of temperature and the advance or withdrawal of glaciers. Masses of water congealed around the slopes or summits of mountains; the level of the ocean was lowered a hundred yards when the weather was cold and raised by the same amount when it was more temperate.

How many plains and river valleys were swallowed up in the course of this immense to-and-fro movement, how many habitable areas were alternately opened to and shut upon primitive peoples, how many rudimentary sanctuaries, like the legendary church of Ys, were submerged by a tidal wave or came to light when it receded!

The encroachment of the glaciers and their retreat did not take place all at once, but rather by degrees. The Pleistocene period is marked by four major glacial epochs. During the first one man did not yet exist; he appeared and developed in the three epochs, broken by two intervals, that followed. The last of these glaciations, which ended some ten thousand years ago, coincided with the six hundred centuries during which primitive man left the greatest number of traces of his religious awakening. His dwelling place, the site of his earliest sanctuaries, could not be established until the ice had melted and the ground reappeared. He moved into valleys dug out by the movement of the glaciers or the melting of the ice, some of which was still piled up threateningly on the overhanging mountains before it ran down their slopes in swollen streams. The ground was scored by glacial striae, which bore witness to the violence of a hostile and incomprehensible nature. In other words, the landscape was by no means peaceful; it too had a prehistory which was anything but reassuring and demanded considerable powers of adaptation. Excavations carried out half a century ago at Schweizerbild, in Switzerland, uncovered a Magdalenian site built on the rolled and crushed pebbles of the last glacial period. On this unstable soil we see petrified all the fears and anxieties of the years that went before. Here, while man's inner resources, his endurance and audacity, were mysteriously developed, he found himself the prey of external circumstances, frequently terrifying, over which he had no control. He was, as always, in the pincer grip of two conflicting forces: the obscure premonition of his own genius and of the destiny for which he had been held in store on the one hand, and on the other the ferocious pressure of the outside world, which was quite unaware of his existence and ready to wipe it out.

It was under these circumstances that Neanderthal man, still mired in animality, began to develop. He was characterized by a beetling forehead, the protuberance of the brow ridges, the powerful cast of his jaws, and the absence of a chin. Later came *Homo sapiens*, represented by various races, including the man from Grimaldi of negroid type, with a straight forehead and prominent jaw, and that of the Cro-Magnon, with a high and bulging forehead, normal brow ridges, a definite chin, and a prominent straight nose. Because both of these had ample cranial capacity they may be said to have ushered in the era of man.

Brains still developing from a structural and physiological point of view evolved the beginnings of ritual manifestations, not necessarily religious in origin, but often corresponding to family usages. Burial customs provide the most definite clue to these. The early nineteenth-century excavations at Grimaldi in Italy and at other places revealed that ritual elements now distinguished true burial from mere grave digging. The body was not shoved underground simply for fear of some malevolent influence or in order that animals should not be attracted to it and attack the survivors. Neanderthal man dedicated genuine monuments to his dead. Instead of laying their bodies in natural cavities or in an area of friable earth, he used his elementary flint tools to dig out a safe resting place in the floor of his cave dwelling. Other signs of the attention paid to the dead are the ritual position in which the body was laid out, the stone cushion under the head, the piece of flint lengthening the nose, the impregnation of the body or the earth around it by a coloring substance, the presence of weapons, tools, objects of clothing, and other "grave furniture" intended for use in the next world. Thus these crude tombs hollowed out in the floors of caves thousands and thousands of years ago contained the germ of the tradition which was to inspire the pyramids and other monumental mausoleums.

It seems, then, as if primitive man believed in a future life. The existence of tombs such as we have described above and the care taken of the bodies buried in them bear witness to this belief, to a spiritual outlook in which bodily appearances— whether living or dead—are not the only reality.

The respect shown to the dead not only indicates faithfulness to their memory and belief in their survival but may also have been accompanied by a certain fear. In other words, funeral rites served to stave off the evil influence that a dead man could exercise on the living. Even in our own day and age there are people who fear ghosts or go in for superstitious practices intended to conciliate the dead. In prehistoric times such tendencies to occultism could have far more easily held sway in places where primitive rites were celebrated.

As the prehistorian, J. Murphy, puts it, paleolithic man was subject to dreams and hallucinations centered about the dead. It is probable that these nocturnal visions, in which the departed seemed to live, practically unchanged, in a world not unlike ours, inspired his belief in a future life and another world.

When we consider the fears evinced by waking man and the nightmares which assail him when he is asleep it seems obvious that the first manifestations of the human mind have highly emotional origins and derive in great part from the terror of death. But they come also from man's active and lucid wish to understand and survive. Man must have belief in survival; in prehistoric times he could not imagine that death was the end. Indeed, he could not conceive of or explain death at all except as the result of incantations, magic spells, or other such occult practices by which evil spirits sought to drive him from the world. It was natural that the purpose of the earliest rites should be to protect him against these spirits.

If the prehistoric cave drawings are of animals it is not because primitive man was a figurative artist and for this reason chose them as models. In order to stay alive he had constantly to be alert in their presence. Either he lay in ambush so as to kill them for food or else he was on guard lest they attack him; in both cases his life depended upon them and he knew that a moment of inadvertence might result in his death. The subjects of the cave drawings, whether game animals or wild beasts, are symbolic of the herds of their kind which the artist hoped to enlist on his side in the terrible struggle against hunger and death. And if he hid his drawings so far under the ground, concealing the approach to them from the uninitiated, it was because they belonged to the category of sacred objects which have in all ages been isolated and surrounded with mystery.

The instincts of self-preservation and self-defense were tied up, then, with the origins of spiritual life. Another factor was the urge to understand. Intelligence was, indeed, one of the most efficacious weapons possessed by this frail and vulnerable creature called man, who before he ever ruled over the world was in danger of being crushed by it. He survived the glacial era because he was intelligent enough to find caves in which to sit it out and to discover the means of making fire. Above all intelligence taught him the relationship between cause and effect which guided him through the maze of the apparent anomalies of the universe. Actually it was his feeling for the sacred which, thousands of years before our rational mechanics, wove the fabric of his understanding of the world. The fabric had rough edges, but this mental awareness of the sacred was not only the forerunner of man's spiritual life but also of his knowledge, to the extent that we may almost call it "prescientific." The powers which primitive man brings into play are not, then, so very mysterious. "They are forces," writes Emile Durkheim, an outdated but intuitive sociologist of the beginning of the century, "obviously different from those which the modern scientist conceives and teaches us to employ. They behave differently and cannot be disciplined in the same way. But to anyone who believes in them they are no more unintelligible than are weight and electricity to the physicist of today."

We might imagine that man's mental effort to understand the universe was provoked by the fear of sudden and unexpected events, by the natural cataclysms to which humanity is so frequently subjected. In other words, that man's first look at nature and his first attempt to explain it came out of his bewilderment and anxiety in the presence of terrifying phenomena.

Actually nothing of the sort is true. What drew the attention of prehistoric man, what led him to question himself and find a supernatural answer, was not fear but the need of certainty, not the abnormal but the normal. He was astounded not so much by the fact that the regular course of natural phenomena was interrupted by cataclysms as by the fact that such phenomena existed. Epidemics and accidents were less disconcerting than old age and natural death, tempests than tides, eclipses than the regular succession of day and night, thunder and lightning than seasonal rains and daily dew.

Friedrich Max Mueller says that when men first looked at the world nothing seemed to them less natural than nature. Nature was for them the great surprise, the great terror, a permanent marvel and miracle. It was only later on, when they discovered their constancy and invariability, that certain aspects of this miracle were considered natural, inasmuch as they were regular, foreseeable, and intelligible. It was this vast domain opened up to feelings of surprise and fear, this marvel, this immense unknown as opposed to the known, which gave the first impulse to religious thought and religious language.

This awareness of the universe did not proceed, as it would in our day, by means of a rational, dialectic reasoning process, which in the presence of repeated phenomena would seek to establish a chain of cause and effect and to identify its author. To primitive man God was above all a presence; in the beginning there was the sacred one. Our largely secularized Western minds find it difficult to understand the primitive mentality which saw everywhere elements of the sacred and the religious. Ideas were unnecessary to a perception of divinity; the directly perceived presence of God was sufficient. The whole world was sacred; in it there was no element of the profane. In modern life the religious element is set apart and can be perceived only by a particular logical mechanism, or else in a state of intermittent mystical exaltation, open only to a small number of initiates. It is only incidentally that religion arises out of man's weakness and infirmity. More truly it proceeds out of the strongest and most virile elements of his nature, out of the exhilarating sensation of playing a part in a secret universe.

This pursuit of the divine presence, manifest in embryonic form in prehistoric drawings, is still to be found today among primitive peoples, for whom the purpose of prayer is to produce favorable interventions. Here, for example, is the invocation of a North American Winnebago Indian:

"My son, when you grow up, see that you are of some benefit to your fellow men. . . . Our grandfather, the fire, he who at all times stands in the center of our dwelling, sends forth many kinds of blessings. Be sure that you make an attempt to obtain his. . . . Remember to have our grandfathers, the war chiefs, the spirits who control war, bless you. . . .

"Try to be a leader of men. . . . For that the blessings of all spirits are necessary. . . .

"If you are blessed by the spirits and if you then blow your breath upon people who are ill, they will become well. Thus will you help your fellow men. . . . So shall you travel on your journey through life, along the virtuous road taken by all your fellow men, and your actions and behavior will never become the butt of your neighbour's sarcasm."

In this rudimentary phrasing, which perpetuates a primitive invocation, there appears, still bogged down in superstition, that belief in some sort of bond, both material and sacred, which even an unbeliever owes to religion.

From the beginning, then, man committed himself to a religious attitude. He was impelled by fear of the brutal world around him and by his need for certainty, by his weakness and strength alike. As Claude Levi-Strauss puts it, he mingled the rational and the irrational. "So-called primitive peoples devised a reasonable way of fitting irrationality, in its double aspect of logical contingency and affective turbulence, into rationality."

Hence the apparent complexity of primitive religions. Nothing either isolates them in the world or limits them to the interior of the human spirit. Just as man's life is not divided into two parts, one sacred and one profane, so in the universe there is no separation of material and spiritual forces. As Alfred Loisy says: "The world was crawling with spirits." Every supernatural element spilled over, by a process of contagion, onto the nature around it. If a tree, dedicated to the memory of one of the departed, was considered sacred, then every bird that perched on one of its branches was sacred in equal measure and similarly protected. Around a sacred animal a whole network of supernatural bonds shone through the primitive world, reaching out to any man whose name recalled that of the animal, to other animals that had racial affinities with it, to plants which provided animal nourishment, and to the rocks which marked the place of ceremonies.

And so not only was the sacred everywhere but it was multiform as well. By reason of its contagious quality it acted, eventually, upon the great universal rhythms which mark the slackening or outbursts of cosmic life. In a universe obsessive in character, which threatened his weakness, primitive man managed to fit himself into the network of live forces and to give his own answer to the insoluble questions raised by the world.

"Plants die every year," writes Durkheim; "the question is,

will they be reborn? All animal species are snuffed out by either natural death or violence; will they in due time return? Rain is especially capricious; there are long periods when it seems to have disappeared forever. These abrupt lapses bear witness to the fact that the sacred beings on whom plants, animals, and rain depend pass through the same critical stages; they too have their moments of weakness. But man cannot look on indifferently at these sights. In order that he may keep on living it is necessary that universal life continue to live. The gods must not die. So he tries to bolster them up, summoning to their aid all the forces at his disposal. The blood in his veins has fertilizing qualities, so he sheds it. Among the sacred rocks of his tribe he searches for the latent seeds of life and sows them in space."

Everything is bound to man and needs him, in order to escape from the natural fatalities that weigh on the universe. From the first moment when man conceived of the sacred and learned to serve it he became a factor of progress. He achieved understanding of the sacred, which was the beginning of intellectual endeavor, and the ability to stimulate and direct its mechanism, which was the beginning of practical activity. It was to the awakening of his feeling for the sacred that man owed these two fundamental advances, from which all others derive. Already, in other words, he owed them to God.

The man of prehistory acquired a whole battery of weapons and practices to be used upon the mysterious forces around him. He dispersed his enemies by the use of terrifying noises, flames, or blinding colors. He conciliated hostile powers as one would quiet an animal, by offering them food and sacrifices. He even used a rudimentary sort of music when, as far back as paleolithic times, he made instruments out of reindeer bones, when he clapped his hands or beat two sticks of wood against one another, or with a primitive drumbeat called up the spirit of war, which had to be won over before he went into combat.

The rites which prehistoric man associated with hunting also had a sacred basis; some of them were so complex as to reflect a long-standing tradition. In the Stone Age he practiced ritual dances, wearing a mask and a disguise. Sometimes, by mimicking the animal he was after, he achieved the double purpose of camouflaging himself and propitiating the spirits.

Cave drawings tell us that even the cave dwellers of the Ice-Age used masks. They have left representations of them, set apart like still lifes, on the rocky walls. In other places we see the masks being worn in a ritual dance, or at the very moment when the wearers take them off, putting aside their sacred attributes and returning to the status of ordinary, barefaced men.

Contemporary anthropologists are wont to divide these primitive practices into various categories and to build up contradictory theories about them. Too glib a distinction is made between religion and magic. Religion, according to some hypotheses, came first, while magic was only a utilization or degradation of the sacred. Other scholars, in an even more abstract classification, distinguish among animism, or the worship of spirits, naturism, or the worship of natural forces, and totemism, the parent of the other two, in which every human group is regarded as having a relationship with an animal.

There are those who impose modern classifications, such as theism, pantheism, polytheism, and monotheism, upon the primitive mind, thus opening up a still inconclusive debate about the unity or multiplicity of religious ideas. Here there is too much effort to systematize something which was essentially complex and uncertain. Prehistoric men were not prehistorians, and there is no need to compartmentalize their religious conceptions. The independent nineteenth-century thinker, Hartmann, was right in saying: "Religion, at its beginnings, was indifferent to theism, pantheism, monotheism, and polytheism; it presented, rather, a balance among all these elements."

The most varied aspects of religious feeling were, in the beginning, all bound indiscriminately together, and so, in spite of our tendency to catalogue them, they still are today. Instead of constructing intellectual hypotheses on a raw material which could never have been fitted, in its time, into dialectics, let us attempt, quite objectively, to see how it has come down to us.

Paleolithic religion can still be found. Various uncivilized peoples who still exist represent, more or less exactly, the various phases of primitive evolution. "Contemporary primitives," says Mainage, "restore life to the archaeological remains of the Quaternary period." How, we may ask, is this restoration effected after so many thousands of years? By means of a syllogism which experience proves to be valid:

At the same time that prehistoric peoples were beginning to conceive of the supernatural they were readying themselves for practical life. With flint and other stones they built up a repertory of techniques for making tools and arms which demanded just as much ingenuity as our modern inventions. One after another, in the course of the ages, sharp-edged wood chips, bone fragments, scrapers, points, bone harpoons, ax blades, and other cutting tools were milestones of technological progress, in step with the process of spiritual evolution. Doubtless there was a relationship between them. Consequently the use of certain rudimentary tools allows us to reconstruct the religious customs that go along with them. In some of the primitive tribes still in existence we find tools and weapons identical with those used in prehistoric times. And we deduce, therefore, that the present-day religious beliefs of these primitives are the same as those of their long-ago predecessors at the same state of tool or weapon development. If we see javelins in use among certain primitive tribes and find also a certain set of beliefs regarding a god or gods and a future life, we can be reasonably sure that these beliefs were elaborated at the same time as the invention of the javelin. There is no absolute proof, but there is a strong probability. "It's just as if . . ." This phrase, so widely employed by would-be impartial commentators on current events, provides us with a bridge between prehistoric times and their continuation in our own. As for prehistorians, the discovery in Africa, America, or Australia of the actual practices with which they first became acquainted through archaeological findings cannot but satisfy and further stimulate their curiosity.

In North America, beginning with the sixteenth century, travelers and explorers blazed a trail to the study of prehistory by scrutinizing the customs of Indian tribes which had remained at a primitive level of civilization. The first white men to set foot in the uncharted regions of the New World found there very old cults unsuspected in Europe. It was an extraordinary intellectual adventure, this discovery of a world countless centuries older than their own. These men of ardent faith were amazed to find that many "savage" ceremonies prefigured the rites and prayers of the sophisticated religions practiced in Europe. In the process of exploration Europeans discovered supreme beings, gods with different names and different forms of worship, but who inspired the same religious fervor. The exploration of the land was at the time an exploration of the past and took on the character of a religious inquiry.

In 1586 a mathematician called Thomas Heriot, who was acquainted with the language of the Indians of Virginia, undertook to describe their beliefs. "They believe," he said, "in a number of gods whom they call 'Mantoac' and whom they divide into different categories. At the same time they admit the existence of a supreme god, who has been present since the beginning. He made the other gods to serve as his instruments first of creation and then of government and after them he made the minor gods of the sun, moon, and stars. The souls of good men find happiness among these gods; the souls of the wicked burn in the *popogusso*, a great ditch where the sun goes to rest." Here we have not only the belief in a supreme being but also a notion of heaven and hell.

At the beginning of the following century, in 1611 and 1612, two other travelers, William Strachey and Captain John Smith, related that the supreme being was called Ahoni and the avenging spirit Ohi. In 1623 and 1624 we have news of the Indians of Massachusetts. Governor Winslow tells us that a certain Kiehtan made the other gods and also a man and woman who were to be the parents of the human race. The Indians say that in the beginning there was no king but Kiehtan, who lived in a place far above the western sky where all good men go after death and enjoy their hearts' desires. The wicked come to this same place and knock at the door, but Kiehtan turns them away and lets them wander in endless misery and disgrace. The Massachusetts Indians have never seen Kiehtan, but they hold feasts in his honor; they sing his praises and call upon his name in order to obtain victory over their enemies and abundance of worldly goods. They recognize another powerful being whom they call Hobomock and who is none other than the devil. Him they implore to heal them of their wounds and diseases. When these are not too serious they take them for passing troubles and imagine that Hobomock sent them because they have in some way displeased him. When there seems to be no hope of a cure they see them as inevitable and say that they were sent by Kiehtan. In neither case do they pray to Kiehtan to heal them.

Belief in a supreme god with minor deities around him, in an evil spirit, the prehistoric Satan, reference to the creation of man and woman, to the efficacy and limitations of prayer . . . we wonder if the seventeenth-century explorers felt a shock of recognition when they came across these familiar evidences of religious feeling among intellectually underdeveloped "savages."

And here, from the lore of the Sioux, are some curious analogies with Genesis. "Their supreme being is called Napi, an immortal man who existed before death came into the world. All his creations—birds, animals, and men—understood when he spoke. He made man and woman out of clay, but the foolishness of women brought on death." This primitive story lacks only the serpent and a few other details to tally with that of the Bible.

In Australia explorers did not come upon primitive religions until the nineteenth century. In 1829–30, in Wellington Valley,[1] an ethnologist called Henderson was the first to report the natives' ideas of a supreme being. Here he found two parallel myths. The first was that of a creator made unhappy by the revolt of his creatures. "Piame created Mudgegong, who turned into an evil spirit and changed all Piame's children into wild beasts, except for two of them, who became the ancestors of the present inhabitants. Piame sleeps now, in the north. Once, when he woke up and turned over, there was an earthquake and a flood tide, and when he wakes up again the flood tide will return."

Here we have war among the gods, such as there was on the Greek Olympus, but there are also resemblances to the Bible, such as the evil spirit and the flood.

The second myth is closer to the European tradition. A supreme being, Baiamé, who lives beyond the clouds, is the creator. And here is what the natives said about him. (1) He lives very far away, toward the rising sun. (2) He has stayed there, in a sitting position, for a very long time, and he will never die. (3) He does what he pleases. Whatever he desires or orders comes about. When he wants to eat bread or fish, they must come to him. (4) He is very good and does no one harm. He loves the good dark-skinned people.

The resemblance of these myths to those of the Bible make it seem as if European missionaries had passed this way. If this were true all our previous reasoning would collapse. The accounts of primitive tribes would be as misleading as much of the news we read in the daily papers. Nothing would have happened as if . . .

But dates prove that this is not true. Henderson's trip to Wellington Valley took place three years before the arrival of the first missionaries. The earliest mission was opened in 1832, and the priests did not understand enough of the natives' language

[1] The Rev. Wilhelm Schmidt (see Bibliography) is the source for the quotations from Henderson and Archdeacon Guenther concerning Wellington Valley.

to learn what their religious beliefs were. A dictionary of the "Wirradhuri" dialect was not published until 1839. Even then the priests had to win the natives' confidence before they were told of the local initiation ceremonies and the creed that went with them.

"I must not forget to tell you," writes Archdeacon Guenther, "that from time to time, every three or four years, the natives hold a curious ceremony. Several tribes gather together in what must be the remnant of a religious rite. Baiamé or his son had sent a canticle to the ceremony of which I was told, and all those present sang it. There was a solemn procession, and certain mysterious figures, painted on fragments of human skin, together with other objects, were displayed. I did not succeed in learning all the details of the ceremony because the natives are very secretive about it. My informant insisted that I should not quote him."

Indeed, accounts given forty years later by two other explorers state that indiscretions of this kind are exceedingly dangerous. When young men are initiated into the mysteries of their religion they are enjoined "under penalty of death not to reveal them to women, children, or foreigners. Whenever a native reveals something to a white man he does so in whispers, in an isolated place and trembling all over. And even then he does not disclose the whole mystery."

All this gives us some idea of the difficulties that missionaries encountered in their effort to find out something about the local religion. We must realize, also, that the traces of many other primitive beliefs were lost when various segments of the native population died out.

Here is the account given by the Rev. Wilhelm Schmidt of the destruction of the tribes of Tasmania:

"The first colony was established in 1803. The natives went on living in peace and quiet and maintained a normal relationship with the colonists. But in 1825 they waged a merciless war against one another, which went on until, between 1831 and

1836, G. A. Robinson persuaded the remaining two hundred of them to submit to the law and to let themselves be interned on Flinders Island. At this point their tribal life may be said to have ended. In 1847, J. Milligan assumed jurisdiction over the natives. By 1854 there were left only three men, eleven women, and two children. The last male Tasmanian, Billy Lannee, died in 1865 and Truganini, the last of four women and of the Tasmanian race, died in 1871."

The death of Truganini marks the end of a whole primitive population and also of a religion which endured from prehistoric times almost to our day. In certain historical junctures god and man seem to be one, and religions prove themselves to be as mortal as civilizations.

Only fragmentary notions have come down to us of primitive beliefs. But nonetheless enough is known to contribute usefully to our picture of prehistoric religion. The beliefs of primitive man do not have the logic and dialectical unity of the religions of today. They have no catechism or theological system and are utterly lacking in respectability; in them are manifest the most extravagant vagaries of the human soul, unrestrained by any concern for verisimilitude or even common decency. They abound in anomalies, monstrosities, and perversions. For through the ages even religious yearnings have been corrupted by excesses of cruelty and eroticism.

The origins of certain primitive gods are mingled with those of stars or animals. Among the first images of god were the sun and moon, also such diverse creatures as the falcon, the cow, the emu, and the kangaroo, all of them peopling an Olympus which seems very much like a zoo. In this bizarre pantheon we find, for instance, a fly-eater, a sort of lizard which created man with a knife. Another god showed his power by whirling tops. Two malevolent deities had knives for arms and used them to kill men before they ate them. Another was one-legged, having lost his other limb in falling from heaven to earth and letting his hatchet drop on it, at which point a jagged bone grew in its place. In other words, primitive man endowed his deities with the most grotesque products of his imagination. Everything grimaces in a sort of delirium, inspiring alternate terror and admiration. We are far from the mystery, silence, and meditation which form the familiar atmosphere of the religions we know. We must not imagine the primitive man of either yesterday or today as absorbed in devotions or given to silent prayer. He was quite unable to concentrate; he gesticulated and prayed with his whole body, so that his prayer was almost more organic than cerebral.

In his illuminating study of the ancient rhythm of words and prayers, the Rev. Marcel Jousse points out that as man sought to make himself understood in language there was no barrier between the different parts of his body; they expressed themselves, all at once, in the words that he was pronouncing. "We think with our hands," he writes, "as well as with our brains; we think with our stomachs; one thing cannot be separated from another. Psychology is the science of the whole man, not just a science of the mind as has for so long been erroneously believed."

This is even more true of primitive man. "What is commonly called the 'sign language' of the Indians," he says, "is not something so very special. This sign language, the mimicry of deaf mutes, and the language of all other peoples make up a single language, the mimic language of humanity, of which each one of them is a dialect." It was in this "mimic language," expressed not only with the lips and tongue but also with the hands and the whole body, that primitive prayers were formulated, long before the rudiments of syntax lent importance to articulated words. Here is the source of the primitive gesticulation which we incline, perhaps arbitrarily, to confuse with dancing. Hence also the multiplicity and confusion of the first religious ideas, which were not compelled to find logical expression in definite words or coherent sentences.

In an awareness which was not yet divorced from animality,

primitive man translated his thoughts and words into gestures. Because we have given up this mimicry and gone in for intellectual formulas, our efforts to describe and understand his beliefs are inevitably arbitrary. But we must go on trying, not so much in order to comprehend religions so different from our own but rather in order to distinguish the various stages of the history of God.

Man, being both a cerebral and a visceral creature, is called upon to formulate his concept of divinity not only with his brain but also with his body. And the body, by its very nature, has many other functions besides a religious one. Its reception and retransmission are subject to interference and disorder.

In every race we find intimations of monotheism—that is, the belief in a supreme being, the father and creator of all things, who in some way rules over the world, and alongside him a "quantity of obscure and fantastic myths," as the Rev. Wilhelm Schmidt put it, and a sort of spiritual chaos. This mixture of mythology and monotheism seems to be an enduring composite of man's faith and has not disappeared from even the most highly developed religions of our own day. We may, somewhat arbitrarily, distinguish four essential stages in its evolution.

First, at least theoretically, was the stage of *mana*. At this stage the human mind did not attempt to distinguish matter from spirit. "Even in the thoughts of the lowest type of savage," writes the sociologist Washburn Hopkins of Yale University, "there is no body without conscious power and no mind without body." Even today there are Samoans, Finns, and Africans who are unable to distinguish that which is in mind and that which is in matter. At the origin of this concept there was the notion of a mysterious power spread through everything on earth—objects, beings, and natural phenomena—to which sociologists have given a name derived from a Melanesian root, *mana*.

Mana was an emanation of God, an impersonal force which was known or felt by its effects rather than by personal acquaintance. Even in our day Indian jungle tribes in South America try to conciliate this diffuse, indefinable, but omnipresent and active "will" to which they attribute everything unforeseen and incomprehensible. The astonishment stirred in primitive man by his first contacts with animals, his terror in the face of natural phenomena whose power overwhelms him, and the horrors of death were variously localized manifestations of this mysterious power. His belief in *mana* was not a form of pantheism, for in this phase he had as yet no notion of divinity. It was, rather, a sort of pan-spiritualism which partook of both magic and religion.

At the second stage *mana* was localized and divided in the animals, vegetables, and minerals over which it was formerly spread out indiscriminately and without any definite character of its own. From this universally diffused spirit were born the spirits of rivers and seas, of trees and plants and all growing things and finally the spirits of animals and men. Sleep, ecstasy, sickness, and death were all familiar spirits arising out of primitive *mana*.

In the third stage these spirits spread through the world and set it in motion; they charged it with good or evil powers, just as in a magnetic field steel shavings are charged with magnetism. At this point, as Monsignor Schneider says, "primitive man believed in myriads of personal spirits which filled the universe, stimulating and regulating its every activity." Of these spirits "the highest and most powerful usually abode in lakes, rivers, caves and on mountaintops, rarely making an appearance." Others were more accessible to man; they contracted with the familiar objects around him a union like that between body and soul.

Man now knew that he lived in a haunted universe, in a world which spirits opened or closed before him, making it lucky or unlucky. At the beginning of the fourth stage came a belief basic to all religions, primitive or advanced, the belief in two categories of spirits, or two single opposing spirits, the spirits of good and evil, of which the first led man to heaven and the second to hell.

Primitive tribes in southeastern Australia believed in an evil spirit which sojourned in a forest or in the Milky Way and sallied forth in the night like a gigantic warrior, killing those whom he met on his way. His unfortunate victims went to the isle of the dead, in the northeast, where soon afterward lightning destroyed them. Another opinion was that "good" men went to dwell forever in heaven, while "bad" men were devoured by evil spirits.

Amid this array of spirits, which gradually took on separate functions as members of a primitive pantheon, amid these superstitions which marked the initial phases of religion, it is strange and touching to see the origins of beliefs which we have inherited and which still speak to us of the supernatural. We see in outline what the Rev. Wilhelm Schmidt calls "the shadow of a supreme being."

We have already found, among the natives of America and Australia, myths which seem to foreshadow certain Bible stories. But there exist elsewhere even more definite beliefs that point to the stories of the Creation, the Flood, and Jacob's ladder. The natives of the Andaman Islands off southern Asia are pygmy Negritos, who before knowing any European missionary had conceived the belief in a supreme being. They called him Puluga, and he had many of the attributes of the God of the Bible. The sight of him was forbidden to man; he was eternal, "never born and immortal." He was also the creator; with the exception of the powers of evil he made everything in the world, and all living beings, including men, were his creatures. He was omniscient and knew all the secrets of the heart; he was angered by sin, whether falsehood, theft, murder, or adultery. He prescribed religious commandments and punished the violation of dietary regulations and the practice of witchcraft. He was merciful, feeling compassion for sufferers and often condescending to help them. Finally, he judged men's souls and punished them in the next life for their sins.

It is regrettable that Puluga, who is in many respects a forerunner, should have had a conjugal life so bizarre as to exclude him from this honor. He was married to a woman called the "mother shrimp" or the "mother eel," by whom he had many daughters and a single son, who served as messenger and conveyed his wishes to the celestial spirits. In good weather he ate and slept, for which reason there was no thunder or lightning, but when men angered him he visited a storm upon them. One of his actions is particularly significant: provoked by men's sins, he sent a great flood which swallowed them all up.

Other gods were equally ahead of their time. A tribe from the country around Melbourne had a creation story strikingly like our own. The supreme being, Pundjel, "long ago made two men out of clay. He was pleased with his work and danced around their bodies. Then he took eucalyptus fibers and made them into hair, curly for one man, straight for the other. Again he danced with pleasure. He gave each of them a name, polished them all over, then lay on top of them and breathed into their noses and mouths and navels. After he had blown very hard they began to stir. He danced around them again, then caused them to talk and finally to stand up, and when they stood up it was not as children but as men."

For another Australian tribe the first living being was a bat, who in order to take a wife had to transform himself into a man. In his new incarnation this curious god foreshadowed another episode of the Bible. First, by rubbing a stick against a tree he made fire. Then he set up traffic between heaven and earth, like that of Jacob's ladder. All mankind climbed up a rope to the sky, leaving only one man on earth, who was the ancestor of all the living.

Such myths, then, in spite of their oddities, are the prototypes of certain biblical stories and have definite elements of biblical religion. Sifted and stripped down to their essentials, they are entirely familiar to us. Among these same unconscious archetypes we find the first indications of the essential belief in immortality and the first words of prayer. Among the songs of the Arondas, a tribe of southeastern Australia, there are many which convey nothing to our ears but others have a famiilar ring. We find, in Tasmania, an invocation which points to the Old Testament proclamation of God's oneness, the *Shema*, which Jesus Christ, in line with Jewish tradition, recognized as one of the essential points of the Law (Mark 12:29). The natives' name for the supreme being and creator was Tiggana Marraboona, and by breaking down these words we find that *tiggana* means an extremity of the body, either the head or the heel, *marra* means one, and *boona* means eminent. In primitive language this is surely the equivalent of "the One extreme and eminent," and we are justified in comparing it to the Jewish *Shema*: "The Lord our God is one Lord" (Deuteronomy 6:4).

Certain terms which we find used in primitive religions foreshadow those of the Christian Lord's Prayer as well. Many tribes used to call their supreme being "Father" or "Our Father." Among the Indians of New Mexico, Awana Wilma was addressed as "the creator and preserver of everything" and the "father of all." The supreme being of the Pawnees was Ti-ra-wa, the "spirit father," known also as A-tuis-ta-ka-wa, "our father everywhere."

Similar appellations were current among the Australians. The supreme being was the "chief of the country of heaven," a title which corresponded to that of the chief of the local tribe. Just as the latter was known to the tribesmen as father, with no implication of blood ties, the father in heaven was so called out of respect rather than from any feeling of actual relationship. Thus the reference to "Our Father" in the prayers of today.

There are, then, in primitive cults, many foreshadowings of modern religions. In the vast mass of beliefs and incantations there are precious hints of the biblical religion which was to come. The biblical account of the six-day creation of the world was preceded by thousands of primitive geneses. But between the imperfect prototypes and the definitive story there is an essential difference concerning the problem of evil, which plays so important a part in the conscience of man. All cults admit the presence of evil. But whereas in our revealed religions evil is separate from the supreme being and inimical to him, in certain primitive beliefs it is one of the elements of his make-up.

"Bundjil, the god of an Australian tribe on the Yarra River, made the first man, Karwein, and the two women who went along with him. . . . Subsequently Bundjil himself coveted the two women and took them away, only to return them later. . . . Meanwhile Karwein had called upon Waung, the crow, to help him. He came, with a number of other birds, and in the course of a battle Karwein was wounded in the heel. Bundjil changed him into a crow, appropriated the two women, and had a great many children by them."

That is the story of a god addicted to women.

In other cults there were two spirits, one good and one evil, but the victory of the former was not always sure. In Tasmanian legends the evil spirit was subordinate to the good but sometimes escaped his control. During the night he visited vexations upon man, and during the day he sent thunder and lightning upon him. The supreme being, desiring to re-establish the balance which his obstreperous subaltern had apparently upset and to show forth his power by night and by day, did not make the mistake of engaging in battle on enemy ground or of having recourse to brute force. Rejecting demagogy and propaganda, he chose to assert himself by more subtle means. He turned to mystery and incantations, addressing himself not to ordinary men but to a small number who were able to understand him. For their benefit he held secret ceremonies and rites of initiation.

This idea of initiation was to become a cornerstone of religion, a decisive element of the supreme being's entrance into history. From the very beginning the practices of ordinary men were no more than approximations. The faith of initiates was the key to the mystery, the secret of truth, and at the same time it brought about God's affirmative answer to the problem of evil. Here is the evidence provided by an initiation ceremony among the Kurnas, a tribe in Australia, which culminated in the proclamation of a primitive moral code.

The candidates "had their heads wrapped in blankets, in such a way that they could not see. They sat on the ground, while sixteen boards were beaten to produce a terrifying clamor. After this they got up and turned their faces toward the sky. The blankets were taken off their heads, and the chief, pointing with his spear to the stars, called out three times: 'Look there!' Then, having given them to understanding that they must reveal nothing to their mothers and sisters or any noninitiates, he made a moving speech in which he revealed the primitive traditions, the secret doctrine of Munnganngana, 'a great initiate . . . who had lived on earth and taught the Kurnas arts and industries. . . .' After that they were introduced to laws which imposed upon them: (1) to listen to old men and obey them; (2) to share all their goods with their friends; (3) to live in peace with their fellows; (4) not to have intercourse with young girls or married women; (5) to observe the rules concerning food unless the old men gave them dispensation."

This decalogue, or rather pentalogue, is elementary by comparison with that which Moses brought down from Sinai. But it makes clear that, from the beginning, an initiation was the necessary preamble to the supreme being's demonstration of superiority over the forces of evil. There had to be recourse to a mystery, which was made manifest to a group of selected young men, before the insertion of God into the universe could be shown in its full moral significance.

After the first word of Genesis, "*Bereshit* [In the beginning]," it became obvious that the purpose of the creation of the world was to show forth God's Law. It is strangely comforting that in the days of rudimentary and inarticulate religion primitive man designated an egoist as "a man not initiated into the mysteries."

Man's love for his fellow man . . . the mystery of creation and of initiation in the knowledge of God.

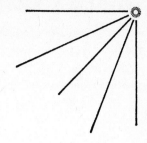

3 *The Pre-biblical God*

Pre-biblical times begin some five thousand years before Abraham—that is, seven thousand years before Christianity and nine thousand years before our own day. They mark an essential phase in the history of man, the passage from a nomad state to a sedentary one. The tribal way of life began to give way to civilization.

In the neolithic age man took to living in dwellings of his own construction. Heretofore, according to the *Prometheus* of Aeschylus, which is a repository of ancient Greek legends, men lived in isolation and often underground "like frail ants." Now, abandoning caves and glades, they started to build huts, some of them on stilts, and even houses of a kind, made of sun-dried bricks, on clayey ground or stone foundations, with a plaster coating. At the same time stone and flint tools became easier to handle and more efficient.

The crude flint "archaic ax" (of the sort that Boucher de Perthes discovered in the 1830s, and with which he opened up the entire field of modern prehistory) evolved in neolithic times into an almond-shaped tool, flattened on both surfaces so that it was lighter and more manageable. Subsequently, axes became rarer, as the era of the reindeer began, and tools were made of bone: points with cleft or solid bases and sharpened bone awls co-existed with stone burins, scrapers, and blades of many shapes. Later, arrow and spear points marked the technical apex of that civilization, and eventually its decline, as if the perfection of a technique had weakened the men who used it and, as Théodore Mainage says, "men, exhausted by a prolonged effort, had passed into a period of being ripe for invasion"; ripe, too, for the burgeoning of a new civilization, which was to endure until our own time.

This period brought the beginning of the population explosion whose effects we are still feeling. But the earth was inhabited not only by man but by God as well. Men achieved the first economic revolution, more radical than any that was to come after; they domesticated vegetables and animals and began to raise them. The first revolutionaries were tillers of the land, whose production made life more secure. They lived first in villages and then in towns, where the dwindling preoccupation with food and lodging favored the development of the mind. Social organization, art, and culture were on the rise. At the same time the idea of God spread over the earth. From this time on God was earth's principal inhabitant, the greatest single influence over mind and manners. As Jean Brunhes asks in his *Géographie humaine*, what sort of world should we have if divinity had not come to dwell in it, what would earth be without God? It would not only be desanctified, without spiritual or moral uplift, even of a secular variety; it would also be empty and amorphous. What would our countryside be without church towers and spires, Japan without its 322,000 sanctuaries, Cambodia without its 1000 Khmer temples? Can we imagine Jerusalem without its Christian and Jewish shrines, ancient Egypt without the places of religion which serve also as refuges for the peasant, Assyria without its temple-fortresses?

Earth's greatest inhabitant was an extraterrestrial being, "not of this world." Soon we find three sorts of buildings which testify to religious aspirations. First, obviously, temples and sanctuaries; second, the abodes of the dead, which in ancient civilizations took up more place than those of the living; third, men's private dwellings, in which even today there are cultural ornaments and furnishings and in which religious rites are practiced. In certain places even their location and orientation were determined by religious considerations.

Long before the advent of biblical monotheism religion guided man in the choice of his home. It taught him to distinguish between favorable and unfavorable alignment of the walls and to choose the best place for opening doors and windows. In the Far East a sorcerer, wielding the great Chinese compass, determined the houses' orientation; among the Indians of Bolivia all the huts faced the east and doors were cut on this side. In this case, private dwellings followed the same rule as the cathedrals of today.

Even the building of a house took on a ritual or religious character. Among primitive peoples, as in our own day, the laying of the cornerstone was ceremonial. "Among the Kabyles," Pierre Deffontaines tells us, "the first stroke of the pick was made by the oldest worker and the first stone had to come from the tomb of a venerated hermit." The building of a Madagascan house began at the northeast corner, the corner of the ancestors; wheat grass, a symbol of vitality, and a piece of quartz, a symbol of resistance to life's trials, were put into the ground.

Cultural or magical factors went into the foundation of a city as well; the first forms of urbanism had a religious inspiration. In India and Africa villages were built around a center dedicated to protective deities, which could be seen and worshiped from every individual dwelling. Sun worship determined the plan of certain Hottentot settlements. Such supernatural considerations played a part in the fields also. The historian Marc Bloch has pointed out that the primitive outlines of French fields followed an obscure religious pattern. In many religious traditions, including that of the Bible, we find that a god or God is the master of the land. The human owners have only temporary use of a domain which belongs permanently to a heavenly proprietor.

We have seen that religion played a part in population shifts and in urbanism; it was also a determining factor in primitive migrations. The first moves that men made toward empty regions were in a ritually determined direction: to the east, the seat of the promised land whence rose the sun, or to the west, reputed to be the land of the dead. This primitive symbolism may be compared to that of Gothic cathedrals, in which the south door was dedicated to the glory of the New Testament and the north to the more remote glory of the Old. For the Huastecan Indians of Mexico, east and north were fertile regions which produced light and life, while west and south were sterile, given over to demons and death. The migrations of primitive peoples were determined fully as much by motives of this kind as by geographical or economic considerations.

The religion which, in the thousands of years before Abraham, taught man to spread himself out over the earth also taught him to situate himself in time. Time was very different at the beginning from what it is today. It was not the regular and irreversible chronology by which we place past, present, and future events. To us time is a matter of nomenclature and spacing, which we perceive by detailing its various stages and of which we become a part by making our actions coincide with its intervals. Man's adaptation to time is marked by his punctuality. To primitive man time as a whole was as vague as it was definite and vivid in every one of its moments. He felt and lived it intensely, but he could not imagine what Charles Blondel calls "this sort of uniform straight line along which events are situated." His way of acting upon time was more often than not magic, and consisted of an active divination which transformed events. When he was preparing himself for combat victory was already won; as soon as a sign or omen announced the death of the enemy he was dead. A Zulu chief said to his men: "You won't even see an army. I tell you I have already killed this one and that; you have only to capture the livestock. There are no more men; there are only women."

Such confusion between what is believed to exist and what does exist is closer to mythology than to science, to superstition than to religion. When religion took shape, when divinity appeared no longer as an element of disorder and imprecision but set itself among the causalities which govern the universe and permitted us to understand it, one of its first effects was upon the notion of time. All religions insert their practices in time and thus afford the faithful a means of apprehending and experiencing its regular unrolling. The regular observance of a day of devotion created the unit of the week, and the succession and return of religious observances gave names to the seasons.

In every country religious development had the same effect of awakening a consciousness of time. In ancient Greece every city, such as Delphi or Olympia, had priests who established its feast days and its calendar. In Rome the college of pontiffs played the same role, and in Israel the Sanhedrin designated the exact moment of the birth of the moon, which was the beginning of the unit of the month. The Egyptians, with their two New Years, one civil, one religious, the Incas with their two calendars, one based on the moon and the other on the sun, proceeded from astronomical but at the same time religious calculations. The day of rest and worship may have varied from one religion to another, but in every one its regularity broke up time and life into units. All over the world the priestly class were the discoverers and organizers of time. And today every hour rung out by a church bell is an echo of these first affirmations of faith and reason.

This contribution made by divinity to the way of life and thought of succeeding generations began seven thousand years ago, at the advent of the pre-biblical era. The God of the Judeo-Christian tradition was just starting to enter man's awareness, and from the very start He superimposed principles of order and perspectives of the future upon the original chaos.

Palestine, where the first patriarch, Abraham, settled, had been, since the paleolithic age, a passageway between Asia and Europe. All around this Promised Land, with its special vocation, other peoples participated in the restless searching which foreshadowed the time of the Bible. The Mediterranean basin was already a geographical and historical whole where civilization was on the march and beliefs were shaping. The coastal zone of Palestine proper, two great fluvial plains, that of the Nile in Egypt and of the Tigris and the Euphrates in Mesopotamia, the peninsula and the archipelago which make up Greece, were the cradles of the great ancient religions which, before the coming of Abraham, were the first civilized though imperfect manifestations of faith. The religions of Babylonia and Assyria, the religion of the Hittites, the pre-Hellenic religions, the Egyptian religion, the religion of Canaan, marked the first installation of the divinity in the cities of man. God began to inhabit the earth at the same time that religion enlightened man's soul and his reason. His habitation varied according to regions and diverse types of society, according to the character of different races and even of climates, adapting itself to earthly conditions. Thus it was that between the neolithic age and the beginning of the Christian Era ancient Greece provided the example of an uninterrupted religious tradition independent of the Bible. First the island of Crete originated a polytheistic cult. The first religious forms appeared around the year 3000 B.C., and in 2000 B.C. the first sanctuaries, followed by palaces where gods in human guise met the kings of the earth. In 200 B.C., when Indo-European conquerors came upon the scene, they adopted the gods of the primitive pantheon and gave them the vigor and prestige which we see reflected, in a secular form, in the art of today. Greece remained outside the biblical tradition and had no effect upon its development; its religious line ran parallel to that of the patriarchs and Jesus and neither contributed nor owed anything to it.

It seems as if, before God chose a people to which to confide His Law and a man with whom to strike a Covenant, He made a number of trials of human possibilities. He tried out the grandeur and servitude of great empires, the material wealth and spiritual poverty of fertile lands, the achievements of warriors and lawmakers. In every climate and nation he began by adapting Himself to the local laws and customs. In pre-biblical times religion accepted political necessities and compromised with profane interests without having an existence of its own. It was only with the nomadic people of Israel that the divine purpose wholeheartedly manifested and imposed itself.

Before the essential moment of God's Covenant with Abraham, other religions showed signs of a trend toward monotheism but were hindered by all sorts of obstacles which prevented its achievement.

We must examine both their positive and their negative properties if we are to understand the unique quality of the God of the Bible.

The religion of Babylonia, from its first appearance in the fourth millennium B.C. until the nation was taken over by the Persians in 539 B.C., represents, in its every phase and as a whole, a syncretism of all that the human mind of those times could encompass of the supernatural. A syncretism between the two sorts of peoples which came together in Mesopotamia: on the one hand the Semites and the Akkadians (divided in turn into Babylonians and Assyrians) and on the other the Sumerians.

During the third millennium, immediately preceding the biblical era, and the millennium that followed, Semites and Sumerians clashed with one another on behalf of their respective cults,
alternately calling in foreign peoples and suffering the invasion
of savages.

Before and during this two-thousand-year conflict, which began under the dynasty of Ur in the third millennium, Babylon
ran through all the stages of religious history, each one of which
left its mark. It began with naturism, the adoration of natural
forces and phenomena in the guise of mountains, rivers, or animals. Little by little this cult extended from the divinity itself to
the objects or beings which were supposed to be its mainstays
or receptacles. Then it passed to anthropomorphic beliefs, in
which natural divinities were humanized and gods created in the
image of man, this after an intermediate stage in which gods
had an aspect half animal and half human.

Gods whose power was originally limited gained stature and
extended their power to the universe. Chaldea conceived a creator god who had a double masculine and feminine personality,
while at his side other gods assured the ripening of grain, the
fertility of the harvest, and the bursting forth of water. Soon, as
the population grew and clustered in urban centers, the gods left
the countryside and were worshiped in cities. Every city had its
patron god; under the Hammurabi dynasty, in the first half of
the second millennium, Marduk became the god of the new
capital, Babylon, while Assyria, conscious of its identity as a
state, adopted a single god, Assur, for the whole country.

An entire Babylonian pantheon was built up out of the tutelary deities first of the cities and then of the regions. Once more
syncretism came into play. In the days when Babylonia was split
up into tribes it was natural that the dispersion of divinity
should match that of political power and the religion be polytheistic. But as the country was knit more closely together religious rites were co-ordinated. The gods of cities conquered and
absorbed by the central power did not disappear with these

cities' loss of independence; they lived on beside the national gods, the gods of the conquerors. But a hierarchy, based on conquest, was established in the pantheon. The gods of the annexed cities did not abdicate but were demoted to the rank of subalterns of the conquering god. The religious hierarchy was patterned on the political hierarchy and on the organization of the state.

It came about that the priest became king and the king became god, taking his place, after death, in the national pantheon. And the relative positions of the gods varied with political fluctuations.

Professor A. H. Sayce writes that the tutelary gods followed the fates of the cities of which they were the protectors. The rise of a city brought with it the supremacy of the god to which it was dedicated; the city's decline entailed the decline of the god as well. The gods of conquered cities became vassals of the god of the conquerors; when the kings of Ur ruled over Babylonia the moon god of this city was supreme. Similarly the rise of Babylon made for the predominance of its god, Merodach, who became the Bel or lord of the pantheon.

This feudal conception of religion, this division of a multiplicity of gods into two categories—the lords and the vassals—was not such as to favor the moral development of religion or progress toward monotheism. As customs became more refined, as human intelligence unified the confused mass of early experiences, the Babylonian cults were torn by two conflicting processes: on the one hand the continuation of the early dispersion and confusion, on the other the affirmation of principles of order and morality, which eventually prevailed, if not within the country itself at least in the neighboring region of Canaan.

Transitional, evolving, and prophetic, the religion of Babylonia contains, in its disparate rites and beliefs, both that which was fated to endure and that which was fated to disappear, that which was to make for the progress of humanity and that which was temporarily to block and warp its development. It answered man's moral and rational aspirations on the one hand and his taste for distractions and his need of phantasms on the other. The Babylonian pantheon was a sort of crossroads, where multiple deities came and went, their cults alternately according and conflicting with each other, in the same pattern as that of the relations among men, of whom they were the idealized images and projections.

Among these gods the most powerful were obviously those of the universe. The world, born of chaos, consisted of four different kingdoms: sky, earth, water, and the lower world, under the rest, which was the kingdom of the dead. Each one of these domains had its own divinity. The god of the sky, An or Anum, was the leader of the pantheon and had for a wife the goddess Antum. The god of the earth, Enlil or Ellil, was an important figure whose name came from a word meaning "lord." He was invoked under the titles of "lord of breath, of spirit" or "king of the country" and imposed his law upon all the inhabitants of the world. He wielded a great net in which he caught liars. His orders were irrevocable, his jurisdiction without limit and beyond appeal. He it was who, to punish men, brought the flood upon them.

The third god of the visible world was Ea or Enki, the god of waters. The Sumerians and the Akkadians imagined that below the earth there was a sheet of fresh water on which it floated, a sort of immense reservoir feeding the rivers above. Ea's importance derived from the fact that he was able not only to dry up the world but also to throw it off balance. And because of the role which water plays in the practices of purification and divination he was the god of magic, to whom initiates turned, with formulas and gestures passed down from generation to generation, to combat evil. At the same time he was the lord of wisdom, intelligence, and understanding. Because this last property was located in his ears, these were reputed to be large and open. He was the master of the arts of making pottery, gold, and other kinds of jewelry, and the procreator of men, whom he had shaped with his own hands.

The fourth god, Nergal, was lord of the underworld, or the "land of no return," originally a solar deity. His father, Enlil, had given him charge of all living things, both animals and men. Later he turned into a destructive flame and went down to the realm of shadows. He was a moralizing god, who combated heresy. The Bible refers to him (II Kings 17:30) as an enemy whose worshipers were to be cast to the lions.

These four great gods, along with their subalterns, were lords in the feudal sense of the word. They had kingly courts with ministers and attendants, wives, children, and household servants. Beside them, reflecting their powers, were other categories of gods, with special prerogatives. First, three astral deities, corresponding to the sun, moon, and the planet Venus. The moon god enjoyed priority among them, because night precedes day. He was the father of the sun god and of Venus, his sister.

The moon god, Sin, was the master of the month. He was also called Nanna, the man of the sky. He was worshiped in a many-tiered tower, of which we shall speak later. An archaic plaque represents him as seated on a throne receiving the libation poured out to him by a naked priest. He had varied appearances, according to the phases of the moon. When the month was coming to an end he manifested himself as a bearded old man whose wise counsel guided gods and men. The fragment of a prayer addressed to him runs as follows:

> When your word sounds in the heavens the Igigi bow down;
> When your word sounds on earth the Anunnaku kiss the ground.

The sun god, Shamash, was second in the hierarchy. He was "the one who gives life" and "the one who revives the dead."

He was also the god of justice, who punished wrongdoers. In this capacity he was accompanied in the heavens by six judges and in his earthly temple by a mayor of the palace, two war horses, two porters, a hairdresser, and six harpists.

The planet Venus was an intrusive goddess, who perpetually trespassed on the domain of her brother. The Sumerians called her Innina, the lady of the heavens, the Akkadians Ishtar, which was equivalent to Astarte. Ishtar had two powers which often go together, love and war. As goddess of the evening she was the patroness of love affairs and sensual pleasure; as goddess of the morning she presided over battles and bloodshed. In both incarnations her favorite weapon was a bow and arrow, with which she spread alternate joy and terror.

Alongside these principal objects of the astral cult there were minor gods corresponding to other stars: the Pleiades, the planets, and the fixed stars such as Sirius and Orion. Their renown was less and their powers not so widespread. Although they did not have a large number of devotees they wielded influence over initiates. Astrologers and soothsayers turned to them for knowledge of the mysterious forces which rule the life of the world.

The Babylonian pantheon did not stop there. There were other nature gods who in different periods and different dynasties had a role to play. In the time of Abraham the god of lightning, Adad, enjoyed great power. He ruled over rain, winds, and floods. In his dominion over these last he was associated with Nin-Urta, the god of hurricanes, who also presided over war and hunting. There were gods of fire, the most popular Gibil, to whom the following prayer of thanksgiving was addressed:

> *Gibil, the mighty, who is exalted in the land,*
> *The hero, son of Apsu, who is exalted in the land,*
> *Divine Gibil, with your pure fire*
> *You bring light to the house of darkness;*
> *You rule the fate of everything that has a name.*
> *You are the smelter of copper and lead,*

The purifier of gold and silver,
You are the one who turns aside the attack of the evil man
    in the night.

There were river gods, whose cult reflected the prosperity
brought to the country by the Tigris and the Euphrates and by
all rivers:

You are the river, creator of the universe;
When the great gods made you
They put all good things on your banks . . .
You judge human judgment;
Great river, sublime river, river of the sanctuaries.

Among the nature gods were those that presided over fertility,
food, and drink and were celebrated in rural and agrarian festi-
vals. Such was Tammuz, god of vegetation, whose fame spread
as far as Egypt. Dumuzi was the fisherman god; Ezinu, god of
wheat; Gestin, goddess of wine; and Shakkan, god of livestock.
Nisaba, the grain goddess, had special characteristics; she was
represented in the guise of a young woman "holding a pure reed
and the tablet of the propitious star in her hand and bearing
good counsel." She was the intellectual of the nature gods' pantheon, the goddess of writing, astrology, and mathematics;
thanks to her, man discovered and perfected the art of agriculture and passed from savagery to civilization.

For all these Mesopotamian gods—the four leaders, the astra
gods, and the gods of nature—adapted themselves to the transformation of primitive society and in spite of their cosmic or
rustic origins associated themselves with progress. As the tribe
became the city and the city became the nation the gods became
urban and national gods. Coming out of caves and groves, they
dwelt in the sky and water and then in temples and palaces,
where like the great of this world they had servants to wait upon
them. In the Mesopotamian plains there came into being two

familiar attributes of the religions of today: pomp and hierarchy.

The Mesopotamian temple was a majestic building. In a special section there were clusters of sanctuaries dedicated to the gods of the city and their satellites. There were a podium or tribune, called *parakku,* a main room, the *ashirtu* or *eshirtu,* where the rites took place, and around it chapels whose exact use is unknown and must not be too superficially compared with a modern counterpart. This temple, which served at times as a fortress, was built of solid and expensive materials: marble, alabaster, lapis lazuli, cedar, gold, and silver. Stone, asphalt, and plaster were brought to the site in boats. The king himself went to "the mountain of cedars, where no man has set foot," in order to cut the precious wood. Stonecutters, blacksmiths, and jewelers were called upon to decorate the sanctuaries. Such splendor, which the Bible ascribes to the Temple of Solomon in Jerusalem, was common, in Mesopotamia, to all the monarchs of the time; the kings of Babylon, Assyria, and Sumeria rivaled one another in lavish gifts. As Shamshi Adad I, the king of Assyria, who restored the temple of Enlil, tells us: "The roof of the temple I made out of cedar, and within I raised cedar doors, encrusted with gold and silver."

The importance of the god worshiped in a temple of this kind was pointed up not only by the costliness of the building materials but also by the number of its annexes. Like a nobleman's castle, the temple had its "commons"—gardens, stables, a library, and storehouses and cellars which provided for the material needs of the officiants, a "house of learning" or academy for their intellectual fare, and a cloister, called *gagû,* which served as lodgings for the priestesses or sacred prostitutes.

Other parts of the temple area had particular functions, some of which are mysterious to this day. One of these was the *akitu,* reserved for the celebration of the New Year, another a special sanctuary, the *gigunu,* a sort of holy of holies, upon which no eye could look and which was perhaps the god's tomb. Above all there was a building whose grandiose dimensions cannot fail to strike the imagination, the ziggurat, a many-tiered tower which inspired one of the most popular Bible stories, that of the Tower of Babel.

The ziggurat of Babylon, one of the most monumental of all Mesopotamia, was the skyscraper of its day, nearly three hundred feet high and having seven or eight stories, depending on whether or not the ground-floor terrace is to be counted among them. It was made of raw bricks with a layer of baked bricks on the outside and mud for mortar. "And they had brick for stone, and slime had they for mortar" (Genesis 11:3). Inside, a network of pipes drew off the rain water, which otherwise would have crumbled the bricks.

What was the purpose of this tower? The question is much discussed, but one thing is sure, it had a religious function. According to Herodotus, there was a chapel at the top, with a bed where a woman, chosen by the god, came to spend the night with him. According to Diodorus of Sicily, it was an observatory, whence the priests studied the astronomical phenomena which influenced the life of man. The Bible, which has a point of view of its own to maintain, says ambition drove men to build something of such huge proportions. And other authorities have it that it was a place for sacrifices. In any case its sacred character is confirmed by the rites which so-called fundamental texts tell us were performed there and also by the fact that a treasure was buried underneath it. "Gold, silver, and precious stones from the mountains and the sea I buried at its base," says King Nabopolassar.

From this place of prayer hymns and supplications were addressed to the deity; some of them have a biblical tone and foreshadow those which passed over to the Jewish and Christian religions. Here is a New Year's prayer addressed to Marduk: "My Lord and my God, my Lord and my Master, is there any Lord beside him?" And here is the prayer addressed to the same deity by Nebuchadnezzar II: "Beside you, O Lord, who is there?

The king who is pleasing to you you keep on the straight path.
. . . You created me and set me to reign over all peoples. By
your grace, Lord, make your lordship propitious. Let the fear of
the Lord be in my heart, grant me what you will, you are the
author of my days."

The sacred tower of Babylon was then, beyond doubt, a sanctuary, one of those which men have raised in all ages, but we
may doubt that the cult to which it was dedicated was monotheistic, since every city that had a ziggurat worshiped there its own
patron god.

When the Bible came along it branded, from a monotheistic
point of view, such a construction as idolatrous and made of the
Tower of Babel one of the most prodigious and significant
myths of the human race. This metamorphosis is an example of
the Bible's great originality, of the new turn which it marks in
human affairs. The biblical Tower of Babel is a faithful counterpart of the ziggurat, built out of the same bricks and mud and
rising to the same miraculous height. But in spite of these material similarities there is an essential difference between the historical Mesopotamian structure and that of the Bible story.
First, there is all the difference inherent in the passage from
polytheism to monotheism, from the adoration of "false gods,"
as the Bible calls them, to that of the true and only God. But
above all the Bible shows forth, on this occasion as on many
others, its preoccupation with morality. Its stories, like those of
the Midrash, are not to be taken literally but rather for the
teaching which they contain.

The Babylonian ziggurat was a monument which typified the
faith of the pre-biblical religions, highly evolved from a material
point of view but ingenuous in spirit. The Tower of Babel, on
the contrary, teaches one of the noblest and most enduring les-
sons which Judeo-Christian thought has given to the Western
world. As we have seen in the prayers quoted above, the Babylonians had in mind only to build a majestic and opulent sanctuary dedicated to Marduk, whereas in the biblical story the tower

symbolized the overwhelming pride of man, which made him try to be equal to God.

A Babylonian monument has turned into a biblical myth. In the interval between the two God struck a Covenant with Abraham, the moral law was incarnated, and the Bible began. From this first example we can see how the pre-biblical religion of Babylonia, in spite of its crudity, paved the way for the Judeo-Christian tradition and holds an important place in the religious history of mankind. Other Babylonian stories have contributed to the Bible as well. The Creation of the world, the Flood, the drama of Job, are all Babylonian myths to which the Bible gave new meaning.

In the religions of Assyria and Babylonia, as in the Bible, the world was born out of chaos. *Enuma Elish*, a poem from the time of Abraham, depicts chaos in the guise of the monster Tiamat, who procreated the first gods. Soon he regretted this act and plotted to destroy them, but the gods were warned of his design and entrusted their cause to one of their number, Marduk, with the promise that he should be their leader if he were victorious in the encounter. Marduk accepted and girded himself for combat. "Get ready," he said to Tiamat, "we're going to fight." After his victory Marduk cut Tiamat in two, like a fish, making one half of him into the sky and the other into the earth, then, as had been agreed, he was acclaimed by the other gods as their leader.

Subsequently came the creation of man, contributed by the Babylonians to Marduk and by the Assyrians to Assur. The god shaped figures out of clay and then breathed life into them, just as in Genesis 2:7 ("And the Lord God formed man of the dust of the ground, and breathed into his nostrils the breath of life; and man became a living soul"). Once more a pre-biblical story furnished material to the Bible. But the latter went beyond its original by introducing from the very start the problem of man's relationship to his Creator. In the Mesopotamian account, as we have seen, man does not seem to be created in the image of his Maker; he was born as the result of a mythological combat among the gods whose purpose was to determine whether or not the creation of the world was worth while: a stake which may have had value for the immortals but does not add to the dignity of man.

The Babylonian myth of the Flood likewise gains new significance in the Bible. Here too we have a combat among the gods, in which man is the stake but bears no responsibility. After man had been created and his descendants had peopled the earth, the gods, for undefined reasons, were sorry and decided to destroy him. Only one of them, Ea, dissented. He confided his resolve to save man to his servant Utanapishtim, the counterpart of Noah, who set about constructing a ship under Ea's instruction. Into this ship Utanapishtim took his family, his gold and silver, domestic and wild animals and, with prudent forethought, men skilled in such a way as to be able to deal with the dangers of the voyage and those of disembarkation. The rains came and lasted for six days and six nights; indeed the cataclysm took on such proportions that the gods repented their action. Ishtar, their queen, cried aloud: "May that day turn into mud whereon I voiced evil in the assembly of the gods and ordered the destruction of my people." At these words the other gods, sitting in a circle, wept with her. "Did I make my people," Ishtar went on, "in order that they should fill the sea, like fish?" The rising flood justified her fears and the gods themselves fled in terror to the sky, at whose doors they lay like beaten dogs. Fortunately Utanapishtim, seconded by Puzur-Kurgal, a skilled pilot, sailed on. On the seventh day the storm abated and the waters fell. Utanapishtim wept to see the damage they had left behind them, and meanwhile the waves carried his ship to the summit of Mount Nisir. For seven more days the refugees remained on the ship, before Utanapishtim proceeded to act in a way very much like that of his successor Noah.

"I brought out a dove and let her go. She flew away, only to return, because there was no place for her to alight. I brought out a swallow and released her, but she returned for the same reason. Then I brought out a crow. The crow found that the waters had dried up; he paddled through the mud and crowed and ate his fill, but never came back. Then I went out, with all my people."

In Mesopotamia a crow played the role of Noah's dove. Can we say from what we know of this bird that he was equally suited to it? In any case, the drying of the waters set the stage for the next act of the drama, which is quite different from the corresponding episode of the Bible and far less meaningful. In the Bible the sequel to the Flood was marked by a Covenant between God and man, between God and all mankind rather than with just the survivors. This is the Covenant of which the rainbow was the permanent guarantee, the covenant which preceded that with Abraham. We shall see later on its importance in the history of God.

In the Mesopotamian myth the end of the Flood benefited only those who survived it. When the ship came to land the gods flocked down "like flies" to be present at the sacrificial thanksgiving offered by Utanapishtim. They were still arguing among themselves as to whether the sins of a few men had justified so enormous a punishment. This debate touched upon the problem of evil but found, in the Babylonian story, no broad solution. Only concerning Utanapishtim and his wife were the gods in agreement. Ea mounted the ship, blessed them, and declared: "Before this Utanapishtim was a mere man; now he and his wife shall be gods, like ourselves."

No greater reward than admission to the company of the gods could have been given. But how paltry a triumph it is if we compare it to the promise of the rainbow, which encompassed not only Noah but also his descendants! It had neither moral significance nor universal value.

The content of the Babylonian religion had to be re-elaborated and reinterpreted before it could get into the Bible. This conclusion, which we have drawn from the Flood story, is confirmed by the transformation of the myth of the good man unjustly punished, the myth of Job, as it passes from one tradition to another.

The book of Job may be considered the apex or culminating point of the Old Testament, when for the last time God talks directly to man. He deals with man's doubts in the face of an adverse and unjust fate, and resolves the problem of evil by giving him an answer devoid of facility or superstition and one which clarifies the relationship between man's freedom and God's will. The whole relationship of man to God is quite different in the Bible from what it was before, because the idea of God underwent a change as it passed from the Babylonians to the Hebrews.

"The Mesopotamian God," writes G. Contenau, "was a jealous, tyrannical, and venal master." He did not create man in his image but rather for his use. Man's greatest virtue was obedience, not to morality but to the arbitrary and contradictory whims of the deity. He was not made to show forth or accomplish the moral law, but to be a sort of satellite to the god and to carry out the most ignoble of his purposes. As long as man followed this subsidiary vocation he was entitled to protection, but when he failed the god turned away from him and delivered him over to evil spirits. The question was not whether man was innocent or guilty but whether his loyalty or disobedience to the god entitled him to reward or punishment. This was a cynical and purely empirical conception of morality. The plight of the "suffering servant" in the Babylonian tradition has none of the passionate interest of that of Job in the Bible. His health and fortune were taken away from him without any conscious evildoing on his part to justify the deprivation. But he did not complain to the god or invoke a question of morality. If he suffered it was because evil spirits or sorcerers—whom he hoped to overcome or whom he hoped the god would overcome on his behalf —tormented him. Just as the Babylonian flood was the result of a quarrel among the gods which was visited upon humanity, so a just man suffered from evils which he was powerless to combat and which had no reason for being other than a discord among supernatural forces.

More and more we become aware of the differences between the religion of Babylon and that of the Bible. Most obvious, of course, is the passage from polytheism to monotheism. But even more important is the passage from a belief in blind forces and magic to the belief in a moral law. Babylon handed down to the Hebrews myths and customs which they adopted and transformed by giving them an entirely new meaning. Babylon's contribution was mythological and strictly formal; there was nothing of the essential character of the Judeo-Christian tradition, neither the solemn proclamation of the uniqueness of God nor the affirmation of a moral law. In Babylonia we find the framework in which the God of the Old Testament was to appear, but a framework empty of the spiritual content which the Old Testament was to supply. In the river valleys of Mesopotamia we find some of the premises of the religion of Israel, but the picture of God is sketchy. The idolatrous gods contribute certain external elements to it, but they manifest nothing of God's real nature or function. The budding tradition did not know in what direction it was going or to what it would lead.

In another river valley, this time in Egypt, the religious evolution which paved the way for the Bible developed in quite a different way. No Egyptian myth was adapted so faithfully by the Bible as those of Babylonia. Egypt furnished less of a framework but it made a greater spiritual contribution. In the midst of idolatries there was an inkling of monotheism and the basis of a moral law. It seems as if, in order finally to show us the Eternal One, the God of Israel, the Bible effected a synthesis of the sporadic efforts put forth in the river valleys by peoples of idolaters, seeking to bring unity out of chaos.

:

We shall not, as we did for Mesopotamia, make a complete roll call of the Egyptian gods. Whether of naturalistic or historical origin, whether worshiped in territorial subdivisions such as the *nomes* or throughout the country, they had a typically prebiblical variety, whose exact make-up changed from age to age. Their forms included those of wild animals—the lion, the crocodile, the serpent—and of domestic ones as well. Others were anthropomorphic; it even happened that there were two sorts of incarnations in the same single god or family of gods. Geb, for instance, had a human aspect which did not prevent him from co-existing and getting along with the goddess of the sky, Nut, who had also the form of a cow. Some gods had human bodies and animal heads; one such goddess was a dolphin and another a scorpion.

This confusion in the appearance of the gods extended to the roles attributed to them. Khnum, the creator of men, fashioned them like a potter, on his tower. His mate, Heket, was the patron of women in childbirth; Anubis was the god of embalmment, Osiris the god of the dead, Thoth the god of science, Ptah the patron of craftsmen, Seshat the goddess of writing.

The Egyptians also deified natural forces, first among them the Nile, which created the riches and unity of their country, and in equal measure the sun. Several great gods represented the powers, good or bad, which the Egyptians encountered outside themselves: Horus was associated with both the sun and light, Seth incarnated the desert and also storms, Osiris was in the beginning a god of vegetation who ruled over the growth of crops and their harvesting.

This scattering of the divine power, this proliferation of gods, this wide distribution of beliefs and human aspirations made for an infinite variety of the forms of polytheism and for a number of state religions. In prehistoric times Horus, who was identified with the sun god, was the official deity of the royal family and the kingdom, but palace revolutions undermined his power to the advantage of his rival, Set, the god of Upper Egypt. After a period of dual reign Horus recovered his hegemony, until a new dynasty installed another god called Ptah at his side. These events date from some twenty-eight hundred years before Christ.

Sun worship, personified by Ra, predominated toward the middle of the third millennium, and after Ra came the legendary Amon. The invasion of the Hyksos around 1785 B.C. marked the end of Amon's cult and the beginning of that of Set, who was resented by true Egyptians as a collaborator with the invaders. Two centuries later, after the Hyksos had been driven out, Amon reappeared and the sun became once more an object of worship.

But during this prolonged civil war among the gods, this religious poliferation which lasted over thousands of years, not only in the highest spheres but also on a local level, in the midst of all this idolatry, there was laid the groundwork for the great religious events of the Bible. Many facts testify to this religious evolution which, no matter how gross were its forms, was nevertheless a forerunner of the Judeo-Christian tradition.

First of all, pre-biblical Egypt, though it had no monopoly in this regard, has left many attestations to a belief in the survival of the dead. We have only to look at the carefully planned and elaborate rites of the funeral:

"These began with the transportation of the sarcophagus from the mortuary to the tomb. The road was a hard one; first it was necessary to cross the Nile and then to follow winding paths to the necropolis, in the desert. Several boats were employed to cross the river, one for the sarcophagus and the canopic jars, others for the statue, the rest of the funeral equipment, and the mourners. On the far side the sarcophagus was placed on a sort of sledge pulled by oxen. Along the way special priests perfumed the mummy with incense and recited the dead man's praises; sometimes the cortège was preceded by dancers. At the tomb the mourners took leave of their dear one and the priests performed the important rite of opening the eyes and mouth so that he could make use of the food brought to him and exercise

his vital functions. . . . There was also a rite called 'the breaking of the red vases,' whose meaning is obscure but which had a
definitely magical character. Once the ceremony was over the
sarcophagus was lowered into the vault, the entrance was sealed
off with stones and rubble, and the dead man was left to his new
life."

This other life was as painstakingly staked out as the funeral.
According to the famous Book of the Dead, a collection of sayings which facilitated the passage to the beyond, the dead man
found all the pleasures and pains of this world in the next. He
wished to maintain his body, to save it from rotting away, and to
conserve his memory of the past. . . . He was afraid of losing
his personality and his place; he prayed and practiced magic
rites, just as when he was alive, to preserve them.

The funeral customs we have described above bear witness to
a definite and detailed belief in an afterlife. The Egyptian religious spirit was not content with halfway measures or empirical
practices. Its religious monuments were uniformly magnificent,
whether they commemorated this life or the next.

Egyptian temples, in the centuries preceding the calling of
Abraham, were grandiose architectural complexes. Let us recall
the temple to the sun of the fifth dynasty, in the middle of the
third millennium B.C. This was connected with the royal city by
a gentle ramp leading up to a porch at the foot of the walls.
Inside there was a rectangular courtyard around which were
storerooms and the priests' lodgings. An obelisk stood on a pyra-
midal base, at the foot of which there was an offering table. The
lack of statues or decorations pointed up the majestic proportions of the architecture.

The temples of the New Empire, a thousand years later,
abounded, on the contrary, in works of art. A wide alley, called
the path of the gods and flanked by sphinxes, led to a great
portal with a tower on either side. Beyond the portal was a
courtyard with an arcade around it, where the crowd looked on
at processions. A vestibule, called the hypostile, surrounded by

columns with ornate capitals, was reserved for ceremonies at which only a small number of initiates were present. This led to the apartments of the god, to which only the king had access. Here the sumptuous decorations included military paintings, celebrating the victories of the god and the king, and religious compositions which portrayed traditional rites.

The heaviness of the Egyptian temple was such that we may wonder if it did not stifle religious feelings and spiritual aspirations and delay the advent of a purer religion. Too often, in the history of God, pomp and ceremony have clouded the vision of His spirit. But in spite of such obstacles, here in the Nile Valley, which had so many exchanges with the land of the Bible, there was traced the first zigzagging path toward the belief in a single God and the proclamation of the Law. By idolatrous ways Egypt led to the coming of biblical times.

At the end of the third millennium—that is, a relatively short time before Abraham—a Heracleopitan king formulated some ambiguous teachings which seem to be based on the existence of a single god in the Nile Valley:

"One generation gives way to another, and the god who knows nature hides himself. . . . Honor the god in his own way, honor him who is made of copper and precious stones, as water takes the place of water. No river can hide itself, it escapes through the dike that masks it. . . ."

This single god of thousands of years ago, who may have represented no more than the river spirit, seemed to have been the object of spiritual rather than ritual worship. The terms in which the king counsels his subjects—"The good behavior of a virtuous man is more acceptable than the sacrifice of an ox by an evildoer"—might come from the mouths of the prophets Isaiah and Jeremiah.

We have seen some of the hints of things to come that can be detected in Egypt, long before the covenant with Abraham. There are others, still more explicit. From the end of the Old Kingdom, about the middle of the third millennium, some individuals more highly developed than the rest, perhaps initiates, conceived of an all-powerful and disinterested judge, sitting above the other gods. This belief must have been latent in various cults for a period of a thousand years. For fourteen hundred years before the Christian Era Amenophis IV, who changed his name to Akhenaten, openly professed monotheism. He replaced Amon, one of the mysterious and fearful gods whom men sought to placate with their offerings, by Aton, a kindly god who protected the poor against the tyranny of the rich. This god's religion was optimistic, based upon the joy of living and acknowledgment of nature's beneficence. The hymn which Akhenaten wrote to this god's glory celebrates a universal creator. All things that live and breathe—men, animals, and plants—show forth his grandeur and share his great works; thanks to a preestablished harmony, man's freedom is written into the plan of the universe as God conceived and created it. There was still lacking, of course, the direct and personal bond which the Bible was to set up between God and His creatures. Men did not know God, even if they did His will; between them there was an intermediary in the person of the king.

In spite of the mythological and feudal elements in Akhenaten's ideas, the fact remains that Egypt produced the first form of monotheism. And in the writings of a scribe called Amenemope we find a moral law, expressed in almost biblical terms.

"Do not say," he counseled his son, " 'I am without sin.' No one is perfect in God's hands. Poverty, under God, is to be preferred to the riches of a storehouse; a few grains of wheat, when the heart is content, are better than riches in the midst of care. Do not seek out riches . . . for every man's hour is fixed by fate; keep evil words from your tongue and you will be beloved among men."

The essence of this text anticipates that of both the Old Testament and the Gospels. The covenant with Abraham was in the air; in different but converging ways the idolatrous religions of Mesopotamia and Egypt foreshadowed the Bible. They fore-shadowed it, but they were capable of giving it birth. The single God who was dawning upon man's conscience was still in a ru-dimentary stage; none of the river valleys, neither the Tigris, the Euphrates, nor the Nile, was the promised land where He was to make Himself known, none of the great pre-biblical empires could hear and announce His word. It took a minor country, open to invasion, and a nomad people, to draw a universal meaning out of local idolatries, as if the God of Israel and Jesus were mistrustful of the pomp and riches of this world.

". . . In all places where I record my name I will come unto thee, and I will bless thee" (Exodus 20:24). This assurance which God gave to Israel after the promulgation of the Law on Mount Sinai responded to the customs of the land of Canaan, where His people went to dwell and to lay the foundations of His worship.

The land of Canaan, or Palestine, was never a pilot country, a country of builders, where grandiose monuments focused the prayers scattered over the earth and in the hearts of men. There were no ziggurats, no pyramids, no great temples of any kind. This very lack, according to Claude Tresmontant, is the genius of Israel. Israel has left no monuments at all; it is represented in museums only by spades and a few other primitive tools.

In Canaan, it is on the earth itself that man, at every time and every place, has left his imprint; God manifested Himself through every landscape. From paleolithic times Palestine was a passageway between the highly developed regions of southern Asia and the then backward ones of Europe. A hundred and fifty thousand years ago, in a glacial era, men took refuge in caves near Mount Carmel. Judging by the skeletons which have survived, they were modern men, of the *Homo sapiens* type, which had come from a mixture of a primitive civilization with one more developed. It seems as if it were foreordained that

Canaan should never lose touch with elementary realities and yet should at the same time transform them by the work of the spirit.

Centuries and millennia went by, working here as everywhere toward the future. There was no leap ahead and no regression, but rather a continual process which took root in the earth and adapted itself to natural conditions. At Jericho, in the neolithic age, a primitive people, practicing agriculture and the raising of livestock, came to settle. They left remains which testify to their religious feeling, clay statuettes representing groups of men or domestic animals. In some places there are rocks which served for building tombs or sanctuaries.

Canaan's vocation arose from intimacy with the land, from confidence in nature, in short out of a constant familiarity between the sacred and the human. Of course throughout the ages the accidents of history did at times upset this harmony. The discovery of traces of fortifications shows that, before the arrival of the Hebrews, Canaan had been involved in foreign wars and suffered invasion. Other remains, dating from the Bronze Age— that is, from the fourth millennium B.C.—bear witness to pronounced social inequalities, which may have been a source of conflict. The co-existence of elaborate houses and shacks point to a division of the population between patricians and slaves.

But these were passing occurrences, due to the flux and reflux of various peoples, which did not permanently interfere with the real genius of the country. Outside the great waves of invasion there were vast empty spaces, such as the mountains of Ephraim and Judah and the region of Galaad, where religious rites were unaltered. Amid areas of shifting sand and hence of changing contours there were rocks which, throughout the ages, served as places of prayer. One of these is the sacred rock, dating from pre-Canaan times, which is now the base of the Mosque of Omar; others include the natural caves, such as that of Guezer where, at the end of the neolithic age, the Canaanites practiced a primitive form of worship which has left interesting and touching remains. Prehistoric dolmens and menhirs lasted until the arrival of the Hebrews, who reconsecrated them to the offering of prayers which have survived until our own day.

The land of Canaan was, then, a simple place but one imbued with holiness. Here, in all ages, man felt himself surrounded by ill-defined, mysterious powers, which he sensed were related to nature, although he was unable to pin down their exact personality. While Babylonia, Egypt, and Greece had, at this same time, hierarchies of gods and sanctuaries pertaining to them, Canaan was characterized not by polytheism but by polydemonism. The life of its inhabitants was bathed in an atmosphere of the sacred, in which magic was mixed with religion, but where rudimentary cults, scattered by the accidents of space and the vicissitudes of time, had a fervor and intensity which inspired myths and tended toward unity.

This unity was not one of beliefs or rites but stemmed from the sacred atmosphere in which the whole country was enveloped. This unity dwelt in the twilight which, according to folklore, incited spirits to come out of their retreat and people the hostile shadows of the night. It was in the sacred rocks, particularly those to which nature had lent a human appearance. These were thought to be the habitations of gods, spirits, or other invisible powers, and attracted caresses, sacrifices, incense, and offerings of various kinds. It was also in holy things and in places known to have a sacred character. Water was held to be divine on account of its quivering and its importance to the life of plants, animals, and men. Trees were peopled with spirits; soothsayers questioned them and found omens in the rustle of their leaves. Mountains were, as high places, the recipients of sacred emanations and dispensed lucky or unlucky influences from their summits.

Sacred things had a way of becoming sacred places, without abdicating any of their natural character. Around them stretched a measured space filled with invisible powers stemming from a tree, a rock, or a spring. This marked-off space did not give property rights to either the god or his ministers, but an awesome fluid circulated around it, which could be channeled by rites or prayers.

Thus the developing religion of Canaan remained in contact with nature; its monuments were gardens, shrines, and woods, far from any human habitation. The sacrifices offered there were often as cruel as any primitive immolation; not only animals but men and even children were their objects. Holy days were connected to the passage of the seasons and the fruits of the earth. At the beginning of winter there was a ceremony of mourning for the death of vegetation; a harvest festival was later transformed into the Jewish day known as the Feast of Tabernacles, and finally there was a celebration of spring which turned into Easter. At the beginning of every month there was an observance of *neomenia,* or the advent of the new moon.

These ceremonies were anything but passive. The priests and the faithful abandoned themselves to a sort of sacred delirium, dancing around the altars, shouting to attract the spirits' attention, and even lacerating themselves in order that they might sacrifice their blood. They also practiced divination, questioning the dead, drawing omens from the clouds, or consulting the entrails of animal victims. By so doing they delved into the mysteries of the earth and unveiled the supposed mysteries of the nature in which they lived so intensely and which they considered their great inspiration.

The religion of Canaan deified created things without knowing their creator. The few gods who stood out amid this indistinct mass were personifications of natural phenomena. The principal figure of this crude pantheon was Baal, the god of the tempest; at his side there were fertility goddesses, among them Astarte, who was at the same time a virgin and the creator of all life. Around them the sun, fire, lightning, and wheat were possessed of spirits of their own, called baals.

Out of this sanctified nature and this welter of spirits no monument, nor even the record of one, has come down to us.

The religion of Canaan left no traces behind it. But in this land which was the cradle of Western man's greatest spiritual adventure there emerged two practices which are still valid today. The consecration of a sacred place required a tree, hence the grove which the patriarch Abraham, the first man dedicated to God, planted in Beersheba. Even more significantly the Canaanites adopted the position which was to become traditional for prayer. Face to face with the nature whose mysteries and powers they revered, they fell to their knees and raised their hands to heaven.

This religiosity, this feeling for the supernatural, might have crystallized around a temple, imitating those of Egypt, or a ziggurat inspired by those of Babylonia. It might equally well have given rise to a mythological pantheon like that of Crete. The Canaanites were not ignorant of the religions of other countries; as navigators and traders they exchanged goods with peoples on every side. From Babylonia they drew many of their spiritual ideas, importing all kinds of lore and myths; with Egypt their exchanges were commercial, and they imported statuettes of the gods, which they reproduced on a large scale and sold in the market. From Greece they imported ceramics and bronzes. All around the Mediterranean the standard of living was uniform because of such trade and the mass manufacture and sale of identical objects in every country. The Egyptians, Babylonians, and Cretans were all capable of creating and perfecting commercial wares, whereas the Canaanites were more passive and imported or reproduced them. It would have been quite natural for them to import their religion also from these greater and more enterprising powers. They did nothing of the sort, and it is one of the miracles of history that the country's religious development should have stemmed from a poor, ingenuous, and undeveloped people.

In one of the poetical commentaries on the Bible which the rabbis set down in their Midrash it is told that when God decided to entrust His Law to one of the nations of earth He looked for the strongest and most enduring among them. He addressed Himself, therefore, to the great empires and cities, in the belief that with them His Law would be secure. He turned to Babylonia and Egypt, to Greece, rich in its past and confident of its future, perhaps even to Etruria, which was foreshadowing the triumphal destiny of Rome. But at every palace gate, on every temple porch He was rejected. One did not wish to be burdened with the Torah because its commandments might interfere with its trade, another could not adapt it to wars of conquest and the capture of slaves, still another could not reconcile it to the search for sensual pleasure. God had begun to doubt that He would ever be able to put such a cumbersome burden upon man's shoulders when He finally called upon the poorest and most miserable of peoples, that of a nomad nation in which wealth and comfort had not blunted the taste for spiritual adventure. He called upon Israel, and this people, having nothing to lose, accepted the challenge. When the Israelites came to Canaan they brought with them a spiritual ferment which was to guarantee their endurance, even though the others had cast it aside.

This ingenious and humorous story reflects the truth of history. From a religious point of view Canaan owes little to the Mesopotamian countries which furnished it with legends and material goods. The primitive and wandering Hebrews brought it the means with which to go beyond its early crude beliefs and to ensure itself a place in history, to become the cradle of humanity's great spiritual tradition. The nomadic Hebrews, made sensitive by their wanderings to the vicissitudes of nature, had a feeling for the sacred equal to if not greater than that of their sedentary contemporaries. They were not rooted in the land, and their only frontiers were those they bore in their hearts. If they worshiped spirits, these became attached to them and followed them on their march.

The Hebrews, like the Canaanites which whom they were to co-exist, perceived in the universe the presence of occult powers which had to be conciliated. All the phenomena of nature were explained by the direct intervention of spirits. In order to exorcise these spirits religion was accompanied by magic, which Adolphe Lods defines as "belief in the possibility that man can exercise a constraint upon invisible powers, on gods, demons, spirits, and the souls of things." All sorts of magic practices had asserted themselves with these wanderers: the evil eye, the consultation of arrows, imprecations before combat, oaths, vows, and ordeals or trials of God's judgment.

A nomad had always to be on the alert; the powers and spirits of nature accompanied and surrounded him, either to protect or to destroy. Without confidence or love, but simply to court favor with them, he venerated the spirits of trees, caves, mountains, and water. A tree was thought to be the abode of a spirit because of the life force manifest in its trunk and foliage; as it grew its branches had the same suppleness as the limbs of an animal; when it was cut down it grew again. Its leaves groaned under the impact of a storm and rustled in a quiet breeze. Certain trees seemed to bleed when they were cut, another testimony to some hidden life which must have been that of a spirit. Mountains were held sacred not because of their height but, as Adolphe Lods points out, because they were filled with divine energy. The stars influenced human life.

Other spirits besides these localized ones played a part in the nomad's life. Caravans, crossing the desert on their way from Palestine to Egypt, were attacked by demonic winged serpents called seraphim. Later on, shorn of their wings and sedentary, they became the seraphim that hymn the glory of God in His temple. But at the time when the first wandering Hebrews entered Palestine sacrifices were not offered up in any temple or sanctuary. The victims' blood was spilled on a sacred stone or tree or in a spring or cave. There was no material or human intermediary between the sacred and man. Religious observances fitted the hard facts of the nomad's existence. A feast for the new moon, which might bring a change in the weather, another for the milking of the sheep. Easter, originally a celebration of the first fruits, brought the sacrifice of the first-born of the flock, whose blood served as a protection against epidemics.

As they wandered through strange lands, to seek sustenance and secure their safety, the Hebrews never felt themselves to be alone; the universe was peopled by spirits; the world was haunted, and they came upon the immaterial presences already known to the sedentary people of Canaan. But these supernatural inhabitants acquired, for them, a new characteristic; they were interested in man and ready to form an alliance with him. Spirits were no longer obscure forces, guided by the blind determinism of their inhuman caprices; they distinguished between those whom they helped and hindered. They were freed from their pedestals and attached themselves to the human communities—families, tribes, or clans—which accepted their guidance and accorded them worship.

Herein lay the strength of the Hebrews who emigrated to Palestine. The rigors of life in the desert compelled them, more than the sedentary natives, to group themselves together. Their communities were of medium size, large enough for mutual aid but not so large as to exhaust the resources of the land where they settled. These social units were equally free of the loneliness of isolated men and of the mushroom growth of great cities and nations. Family and blood relationships drew their members together, and gradually these family clans gathered into tribes. The tribes included auxiliary formations which shared the same kind of life, recognizing the same chief and granting him the power to choose their god. Membership in the clan or tribe was obtained through a rite of initiation. When he reached a certain age the child was instructed in certain articles of faith and received the imprint in his flesh of circumcision. This blood brotherhood not only united men among themselves but also bound them to the god chosen by the leader of their clan or tribe. Every such leader, later to be known as a patriarch, chose a personal god who became that of his followers. Alliances or covenants were struck up, which obliged the god to protect and man to worship him.

It was thus that there came into being an idea which the great pre-biblical empires never fully formulated, that of a contract between God and man, of an intimacy and almost a kinship between them, an embryonic idea of the Covenant. This idea was to have a decisive bearing on the development of monotheism and the advent of God upon earth; it was to bring the Bible into being and to situate God in history.

Recent study seems to indicate that the conception of a direct bond between God and man was about to flower in Canaan at just the time of the Hebrew emigration. There remained, of course, numbers of what Genesis (35:2–4) calls "strange gods," idols inherent in nature rather than related to man. But, contemporaneously with Abraham, Canaan did conceive of one god, dominant over all others and worshiped in diverse places. He was called by the unique name of El, which testified to His ubiquity, but was endowed with attributes which adapted themselves to the various circumstances under which He manifested Himself and to the various aspirations to which He responded.

These attributes, writes André Parrot, varied according to the stress placed upon one aspect of Him rather than another: *El t-olam* (El everlasting); *El-el'yon* (El the most high); *El-shaddai* (El of the mountain, or the Almighty); *El roi* (the El that sees me). We have here not monotheism, strictly speaking, but a preliminary stage, monolatry, which developed in an idolatrous land. This El, the forerunner of the one God, was there to greet the Children of Israel when they came to the Promised Land.

The arrival in Canaan of the nomad Hebrew tribes, the penetration of a land dedicated to the sacred by a people destined to conceive the idea of the one God, was a decisive moment in the history of mankind. As the German historian Heinrich Graetz puts it:

"One spring day a few tribes of shepherds crossed the Jordan and made their way into the narrow strip of land bordering the Mediterranean, the land of Canaan. . . . The place to which they came was to be called the 'Holy Land,' and the day of their coming was to mark an historical epoch. Faraway nations could not have imagined the importance of the arrival of the Hebrews or Israelities in this place, and even the native peoples were unaware of its fateful effect upon their future."

Thanks to God's presence among them, these feeble and primitive tribes survived mighty empires. Their rudimentary beliefs, devoid of intellectual pretension, were to shape the centuries to come.

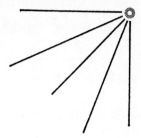

4 *The God of Genesis*

We have seen that the rudimentary beliefs of primitive and pagan man had something of a sacred character and certain elements of mystery. Now we shall see these premonitions develop into monotheism.

We have come to the God of the Old and New Testaments, the God of the patriarchs and prophets, of Abraham, Moses, and Jesus, the God who, according to Nietzsche, was about to die, the God perpetually threatened but perpetually reborn, the God of whom Saint Augustine says that we seek Him in order to find Him and find Him only to seek Him, in short the living God, with all that this term implies of mystery and risk, of grandeur and hesitation.

We are passing from one level to another, from that of pure

history to that which is interpreted and aggrandized by the author. We are in biblical times, whose story is the herald and servant of faith, having the single purpose of manifesting God and at the same time of enlarging and glorifying the figure of man.

It is through that inspired book, the Bible, but also through the commentaries encrusted upon it, the writings of the Jewish tradition over the centuries, the Talmud, the Midrash, and later the Cabala, through both God's word and man's commentary that we glimpse the decisive moment of the great adventure.

Generations of doctors of Israel were, until the coming of Christianity, the only persons to have guessed at the existence of the living God. They spent their entire lives commenting upon His words, interpreting His Law, and filling in the details of His story. Let us hope that we may reap the inheritance of their hunger for holiness, of their haunted preoccupation with God.

"In the beginning," the Bible tells us, "God created the heaven and the earth [*Bereshit bara elohim et ha-shamain ve et ha-haretz*]." For three thousand years religious feelings of the deepest kind have been attached to this simple and grandiose sentence. Its ten words include, or at least suggest, everything. To start with, the fact of monotheism. The verb *bara* (created) is singular and its subject *elohim* (God) is plural, a grammatical anomaly which has challenged exegetes and theologians. Is the plural one of majesty or of abstraction, or has it no particular implication? This is the debated question. At first sight, without splitting hairs, we may say that this juxtaposition of a singular and a plural signifies that all spiritual forces converge in the oneness of God. This is the first mystery, in which the scriptural text reflects the deepest feelings of any man in search of God.

Included also is the universe, but this is not merely God's raw material, the passive object upon which He exercised (according to the literal meaning of the word *bara*) His craftsman's ingenuity. From the beginning heaven and earth played an active role in the preparation and fulfillment of the time which was still in suspense in the immense mind of the Creator. Tradition has it that, as soon as the creation was accomplished, God told every element what part it was to carry out in the development of history. He made an agreement with the ocean to the effect that, out of gratitude for having been made, it would open up to allow the Children of Israel to pass through the Red Sea. Similar promises were obtained from the other elements of the six days of creation. The heavens promised to be silent while Moses scaled Mount Sinai; the sun and moon promised to stand still when Joshua stood before the walls of Jericho; the ravens promised to feed Elijah; fire promised not to devour Daniel; the heavens promised to open up before Ezekial, the whale to cast out Jonah. A conglomeration of fables, if you will, but filled with common sense, in accord with the biblical conviction that every moment of history is bound to all those that went before and that everything is interdependent. In accord, also, with the belief that the universe falls in with God's designs, that it is not a mere inert mass but is sacred in all its parts.

Implicitly included is man who, believer or unbeliever, harmonious or perverse, is the partner whom the Eternal must have in order to show forth His Law and indeed to be God, the God immanent in the world and its history. Let us recall the amazing episode in Genesis in which one man, Jacob, embodies the two typically human attitudes toward God: prayer (Genesis 32:9) and, fifteen verses later, combat with the angel. As the Eternal disengaged Himself from the limbo of eternity He was to meet, over and over again, these two conflicting attitudes on the part of his human partner.

And included, finally, is God.

Let me risk, at this juncture, a paraphase of the creation story. This myth is so prodigious, so abounding in problems, that we may be forgiven for devising an interpretation inspired by but not contained in it, which makes for a free prolongation of the story. Why should not a contemporary myth be added to the original one if we are careful to make a distinction between them? There is no lack of respect for the Scriptures in trying to adapt them to the needs of our own day.

It was out of God's mind, so we are told, that the universe emerged. In the beginning God's mind had everything in it, that which was and that which was not yet. It contained the darkness and the void that were, the light and the earth, and perhaps other things as well, which had not yet been called into being. In the beginning the leaves of the trees were green, light was bright, and animals were mobile, but no one knew it except God, who carried them all in His mind but had never seen them. Carrying light within Him and wishing to see it, He said: "Let there be light: and there was light. And God saw the light, that it was good: and God divided the light from the darkness." And this was the first day. But the light was swallowed up by darkness, and this was the first night. Deprived of light, God missed it, but when it reappeared as bright as ever the next morning, He went on with the rest of the creation.

At the end of the sixth day, having finished the world, God knew that the leaves of the trees were green, that light was bright, that animals were mobile, that space and time were infinite. Then, in order to test His almighty power, He created man, to "have dominion over the fish of the sea, and over the fowl of the air, and over the cattle, and over all the earth," and also to help Him measure space and count time. Then, on the seventh day, having exhausted everything, including, temporarily, Himself, God rested. Thus were completed the heaven and the earth and all that in them dwells.

When the universe had emerged from His mind and He was separated from His creation, God was sad. Among the rivers Pison, Gihon, Hiddekel (Tigris), and Euphrates God made the Garden of Eden and there He installed the trees, the animals, and man, and when these His creations were all gathered together in one place He walked among them. After He had made the rounds of the garden and seen all its boundaries and noted its continuous transformation He failed to find the reflection of His almighty power and His eternity, and He was afraid that He had been mistaken. He called Adam and asked him what was the color of the leaves. Adam replied that the leaves were green, the light bright, and the animals mobile, designating them by the names which God had accepted. God recognized them all, but when He saw that the garden was bounded by space and time He felt that its creation had somehow limited His power. And as Adam paced up and down his new domain, evaluating eternity and seeking to measure God's universe, God drove him away. This was the beginning of history.

For long centuries God mourned for His lost creation, letting His mind wander in the void and averting His eyes from the world and man. Unable to forget man, He suffered because man must necessarily have forgotten Him, and because man was short-lived and ignorant of both good and evil. Finally He sent angels to bring man back, but their words were of no avail and God had to admit that man would never develop into what He had intended him to be.

Men became more and more wicked and ignorant, and many of them denied their faith, replacing it with pride. Dissensions, calamities, and quaking of the stars told God that the hour of the Last Judgment had come. The leaves on the trees had faded, animals were dead, the sky was darkened, and all space was measured.

At the sound of the trumpet and the voice of the archangel God raised all men's bodies from the earth and joined them to their souls. He sent away the cherubim who were guarding the Garden of Eden because He wanted to let men in. For six days men crowded around the Garden, but God found them unrecognizable. There were big men and small, black, white, yellow, and red, good men and bad. God was astonished to find them so numerous and so diverse; He could not understand their numbers and their diversity.

When, on the seventh day, God had not yet chosen to show

Himself He heard the clamor of men's voices. Each one implored Him in his own way and, not knowing Him, pictured Him in his own image. Some said that He was big, others small, still others that He was black, white, yellow, or red, according to their own color. There were those who credited Him with good and those who credited Him with evil, thus making Him sacrilegious toward Himself.

God was amazed that His creatures should have multiplied without benefit of His aid and did not know to whom to listen. He felt as if He had lost His own identity and did not know how to choose among them. It seemed as if the beings which He had created had recreated Him in return. But He did acknowledge them as His creatures and went ahead with His plan of admitting them to the Garden of Eden. Only the Garden was too small to hold them and God, measuring His greatness by the number of His creatures, went with them into the gardens of the world.

This imaginary departure of God, more real, perhaps, than reality, into the world, at the side of his creatures, helps us to imagine the mystery of the living God and His creation. The mystery is one which cannot be called up without trembling or communicated without hesitation. In the secret places of his soul it binds man to the infinite, mortality to eternity. If this mystery could be given a form acceptable to the modern mind it might dissolve the anxiety which every minute of our life raises in and about us.

Let us begin by accepting it rather than by trying to give it an explanation. The acceptance of mystery is profoundly rooted in the tradition of the Bible and its commentaries; it is a mark of humility and wisdom.

"Do not search for that which is beyond you," says the Midrash of Job. "Do not plumb that which is too deep for you to fathom. That which is more marvelous than you are you will never be able to know. Do not seek to find that which is hidden.

Apply your intelligence to studying that which God has given you for an inheritance. But leave mystery alone, for it belongs to the Eternal."

If we accept the mystery we shall find it natural that man should tremble before it. In the Zohar, Elijah's prayer portrays a natural emotional reaction:

"Master of the worlds, you are One. You are the Sublimest of the Sublimes, the most hidden of the hidden; no thought can conceive you. . . . You are wise but not with a limited wisdom, you cannot be circumscribed."

In a word, God eludes the human mind. But elusive as He may be, the living God of the Bible is neither abstract nor impassive. He vibrates in the presence of His creation like a lover in the presence of his beloved. The passion which He feels is revealed, throughout the Bible and its tradition, in terms reminiscent of those applied to human love.

In Proverbs 8:31 God describes Himself as "rejoicing in the habitable part of his earth; and my delights were with the sons of men." Likewise Psalms 104:31 proclaims: "The glory of the Lord shall endure for ever: the Lord shall rejoice in his works."

In passing from the Bible to tradition, the emotion of God the Creator takes on a daring form which couples sacred and profane love, as witness this effusive passage from the Cabala:

"On the day when He created the world God rejoiced with a great joy. . . . A great joy rejoiced God; He took delight in Himself; He lit up a splendor, He sparkled within Himself. In this intellectual movement, this spiritual sparkling which in God is called 'jubilation' His feelings poured out of Him."

The expansiveness which physical love produces in man is not the only point which God the Creator has in common with His creatures. Here again, in the Zohar, is an account of amorous play around God and His Law:

"The mysteries of the Law are like a splendid mistress shut up in the chamber of a palace. Only one lover knows what she feels. When her lover, desirous of seeing her, passes in front of the palace, looking all around him, the mistress decides to pierce a hole in the wall. At the moment when she sees her lover passing by she approaches the wall and draws back immediately. Other persons passing by do not see her face, for he alone directs his glances, his heart, and his soul upon the beloved. This is the way also of the Law, which reveals its secrets only to its lovers, while profane persons pass by without seeing. To the initiates whose eyes and hearts and souls converge upon their beloved Law she deigns to reveal herself for an instant. Notice that the Law acts toward man in this way: first she signals to him to approach, and if he fails to understand she calls him 'insensate.' When he does approach she talks to him through the curtain which separates him from her. Then, little by little, he begins to understand. . . . Finally, when habit has made him familiar with the Law, she shows herself to him face to face and reveals mysteries that have been hidden since the beginning of time. Then man becomes master of the Law and of the house; all mysteries are revealed to him and none of them is hidden."

Here we have more than a fable. This description of a spiritual "love at first sight," whose allegorical stages recall those experienced by a flesh-and-blood man, this sacred love play, shows us how, in His relationship with His creatures, God the lawgiver adapts Himself to men's behavior and shares their intoxication.

When God created the universe, when He felt the joy of fulfilling Himself in other beings, He must have known that in the gardens of the world He would meet the best and the worst, the powers of life and those of death, all the opportunities for grandeur and weakness which are inherent in our human nature. In Genesis God initiated a relationship with man which was not always to be peaceful. This was the beginning of a drama which has continued until our own day.

All-powerful and yet threatened in His power, this is the dual condition of the Creator throughout history. His relationship with man is unceasingly dramatic, inasmuch as man is not the mere docile executor of His will but the witness and challenger of His power. Man plays, in relation to God, a role like that of the wife of the very human prophet Hosea. When Hosea kept Israel obedient his wife was faithful to him; when Israel escaped him she committed adultery. Man obeys God when He manifests His power but disobeys whenever this power is momentarily withdrawn from him. Thus God can never enjoy full peace of mind; there are alternate periods of dispute and understanding, and He is constantly on the alert to bring back the lost or to hold the allegiance of the faithful. What man brings to God and what God owes to man is contact with a being outside Himself and confirmation of His power. With man and the universe the Eternal made Himself a Creator. From that time on He showed Himself forth not merely as the God that is but as the God that called the world and its creatures into existence. He became the God of Genesis, or rather of Geneses.

At the very beginning of this first book of the Bible there are two stories. The first (Genesis 1:1–2:14), which tells of the creation of the universe and of man, is the account of a legendary week, which we recognize as being in parable form. The second (Genesis 2:5–25), which deals with man in particular, describes the insertion of the Eternal into history; the supernatural appears in a series of human events which took place at a definite date. The first Genesis lasted six days—six tremendous and well-employed days but days which fall within the normal limits of dawn and dusk. The second extends through the centuries and has not yet ended. At the end we shall see the messianic era, when the Kingdom of God is installed on earth.

In the first Genesis the Eternal, whose name is ineffable, is designated by one of His attributes, Elohim, whereas in the second He is called by another, Adonai. Each one of these appellations has its reason for being. Elohim is God the creator and author of the universe, to which His relationship is that of the Most High, the Judge, the Ruler who established its natural laws, the God of the fatalities which determined the universe in the expectation of man. This is the God often considered merciless, although it would be more exact to say that He corresponds to the zone of implacable determinism which is the universe's necessary foundation but does not constitute its totality or purpose or reason for being.

The other zone, the zone of freedom and risk and individual choice, all of them working together for the messianic fulfillment, the zone culminating in man, is the zone in which God is designated as Adonai. Adonai is God as He manifests Himself to His creatures, in His relation to the fate of every one of them. Adonai suffers with man; He may also share man's rejoicing when the latter freely accepts the task of accomplishing the Law and working to better the world. Adonai is the God of the supplementary soul which it is man's mission to add to the universe.

Elohim, then, stands for justice, while Adonai stands for mercy. Throughout the Scriptures Adonai intervenes when mere justice would bring on the world's destruction. Elohim sent the Flood, but Adonai sent the ark and the rainbow. The Law, with all that is absolute and implacable about it, is the province of Elohim. Forgiveness of sin, God's continual bolstering up of a world inclined to corruption and degradation, is the realm of Adonai.* Man is faced at every moment of his existence by both these aspects of God, throughout the whole of Jewish tradition. A necessary determinism on the one side, free will, the indispensable extra which man gives to the world, on the other; both circumlocutions serve to designate God in His ineffable unity.

---

* We may here recall that the sign or word Yahweh, often used to designate the Eternal, has no reality and is outside Jewish tradition. It is an invention of nineteenth-century biblical critics, based on the initial letters of the phrase by which God called Himself. By it the phrase is impoverished and caricatured. There is a twofold mistake involved. First it is a concession to the profane temptation to look for a commonplace name with which to express the ineffable. Second it is a limitation of the divine majesty, which is made up of a multiplicity of attributes. The first five books of the Old Testament are extremely reserved in their denomination of God. He is to be named for the characteristics which result from His deeds: the Creator, the Almighty, the Merciful. We must not seek to express in a word the divine essence of His being.

Genesis has two aspects: one set, the other movable; one closed, the other open. We are involved, all of us, forever, in Genesis. Genesis is permanent and creation is limitless, even if we creatures are passing and limited.

The continuous act of creation and the unrolling of history form the backdrop of the drama of which God is the director and the three actors are God's Law, the universe, and man.

For God's chosen people the Law or Torah is not merely a body of legislation, a declaration of the rights of God and the duties of the believer. It contains, of course, a moral code, the Decalogue or Heptalogue, as the case may be, and its practical application to the conduct of worship and everyday life, but it is also the crowning accomplishment of this people in history. The Torah is neither theoretical nor abstract. What is the use, say the doctors, of setting forth commandments without describing the circumstances under which they are to be applied? What is the purpose of Mount Sinai, the culminating point of history, if its repercussions do not spread through all times and all places?

The Torah is the perpetual motion, born of the proclamation of the eternal truths, which ensures their irregular and often difficult diffusion through history and the far reaches of the world; it is dynamic rather than static, not merely a catechism but a living adventure. An adventure whose first chapters are told by the Pentateuch but which has always been and will always be, as long as the Covenant between God and man endures and God perseveres in inserting Himself into history.

The Law had already existed for two thousand years before God created the world, the Talmud tells us, which is another way of saying that it has always been and always will be. Proverbs 8:29–30 states it in this way: ". . . when he appointed the foundations of the earth; Then I was by him . . . and I was daily his delight, rejoicing always before him."

Along with the Law were born five entities whose purpose is to second and facilitate its action. The first of these is the

"Throne of Glory," which also existed before the world's beginning. "Thy throne is established of old," Psalms 93:2 tell us. The Throne of Glory is that upon which God sits to judge men. It is understandable that it should be contemporaneous with the Law since from it are delivered the sentences of transgressors. In the beginning it was lopsided; its feet were unequal. In order to balance it God added indulgence to justice and love to severity.

The other entities are similarly related to the Law and contribute to its comprehension. They are the patriarchs, the people of Israel, the Temple, and the name of the Messiah.

The patriarchs—Abraham, Isaac, and Jacob—whom the prophet Hosea describes as having potentially existed before the events in which they participated, are the necessary intercessors who lead men to know the Law and with whom its destiny is bound up indissolubly.

The people of Israel had been chosen from all eternity to preserve the Torah. God calculated that after twenty-six human generations had passed away Israel would accept the Law, and He staked out history according to this calculation.

The Temple, the earthly pendant to the Throne of Glory, was built by Israel as a place for penitence—that is, for the reparation of transgressions against the Law.

Finally comes the name of the Messiah, whose advent will mark the end of history and the fulfillment of the Law.

Thus past, present, and future revolve around the Torah. The Law, say the rabbis, is a link between God and man; before it was given to the latter it existed in heaven, and after creation it assumed its connecting function. "That which is below will mount on high and that which is on high will descend below." The Law is essential to the harmony which God put into creation. It is essential not only as a link between heaven and earth but also as the means through which man acquires a sense of his vocation.

Tradition multiplies the commandments relative to the Law's observation. "Be ye like servants who serve their master without expecting anything from him." "Do not make the Torah into a crown with which to aggrandize yourselves." "Teach the Torah for its own sake, without aspiring to be called a wise man or to win a seat among the learned or in the world to come." "He who extracts gain from the Torah works toward his own perdition." These are some of the rabbis' sayings. The law is necessary not only to God's glory but also to the dignity of man. "When the Law entered the world, Liberty entered it also!"

After the Law, the universe. God's relations with the universe are marked by common sense and realism. In spite of His transcendence the Almighty never loses His sense of measure. The universe which He created and permeated was something very real. His presence transfigured that which existed and gave meaning to its fatalities.

Why did God set His Chosen People in Palestine? Because, according to Deuteronomy 11:11, "it drinketh water of the rain of heaven." That is, because nature imposed upon man, if he wished to survive, the necessity of looking to the sky for help. Just the contrary was true in Egypt, where the fields were irrigated by the overflow of the Nile and men directed their aspirations earthward, to the course of a river. If Palestine was given a supernatural mission it was because of physical characteristics which were to be transcended but not abolished.

Why did God choose the shores of the Dead Sea as the place where He gave vent to his wrath against the impious cities of Sodom and Gomorrah? Why did He rain down brimstone and fire upon them rather than upon some equally sinful but more famous cities, where His punishment would have been more exemplary? What fatality determined His choice? Here, as in many other episodes of the Bible, God made use of physical characteristics which He had created as the framework for a demonstration of His will. If the region of the Dead Sea is still desolate today it is not only because, in biblical terms, God's anger fell upon it but also because of the salt deposits which the retreating waters have left to burn its shores and deprive them of all life. The abundance in its waters of magnesium chlorate (22 billion tons), sodium chlorate (12 billion tons), and other solids which form up to twenty-five per cent of its composition, added to the evaporation produced by torrid heat, cut off any life other than that of a few maleficent microbes, among them that which produces tetanus.

In throwing His curse onto a geographical stage which He had prepared for it God did not infringe upon or ignore its naturally determined characteristics; He fulfilled them and gave them a meaning which they did not originally possess. The realism of the Bible is thus quite different from the pseudorealism of positivistic science, which is only an abstraction. In the Bible facts are known and the natural laws are utilized, but in its conception natural phenomena are never isolated or gratuitous; they were prepared by God from the beginning of the world and contribute to its fulfillment. Every rolling stone forms a predestined landscape, every living man influences the future of his kind. As Spinoza said: "One atom destroyed and the universe crumbles." Since the universe as a whole is sacred and responds to mysterious but definite wills, which express themselves from day to day according to determinisms apparently logical but actually incomprehensible, this constant dialectic between heaven and earth, between the supernatural and the natural, makes for the harmony and also the necessity of the universe.

It is on the same principle that God moves through the world, sharing the wanderings and lingerings of His Chosen People. When the Hebrews were nomads He was the God of the southern deserts; when they settled in Canaan He became the God of the Promised Land. After that He dwelt in heaven, but without ever losing contact with the realities of earth. Even amid the clouds He remained a local God who reigned not only over the universe but also over the part of the sky above His people's land. An example is Jacob's ladder; it was not only man's path to heaven but also God's path to earth. Besides this

one ladder, made memorable by the Scriptures, how many obscure and forgotten ladders there are that connect God with
every human household, with every place where men gather together! The God of the ladder, of ladders, is not lost in the
clouds. He created heaven and earth on the same day and they
are of equal importance. As a sage of the Midrash tells us, they
are like a pot and its lid. If in the Bible priority is given first to
one and then to the other; if it is written: "In the beginning
God created the heaven and the earth" and also: "On this day
God created the earth and the heaven," it means that one is not
subordinate to the other but that each has a role in the divine
intention.

Perhaps, if God had to choose between them, He would
choose the earth. If God created the world, a Midrash story tells
us, it was in anticipation of three products of the soil which,
thanks to the Torah, were to have religious significance. He
created the world for the *hallah*—that is, for the portion of
bread which the priest took over at the beginning of his prayers.
He created it for the tithe, for the portion of the harvest which
was to be given to the poor. And He created it for the first fruits,
which on certain ceremonial days were to be taken to the Temple. What would become of the Law without prayer, charity,
and worship? In order to bring forth these manifestations of the
Law the soil had to be fertilized and to open up under the push
of the growing seeds. The soil had to exist, it had to be created.
All this is very concrete. If man could have seen into God's
mind when He created the earth he would not have been at a
loss simply because he was not a theologian or given to abstraction.

The essential duty which the Law imposes upon us is that we
concentrate our efforts upon the world, not above or beyond it.
The Torah, which is an emanation of God, does not seek to
fathom the reason for its origin or its philosophy. It rejects other-
worldly speculation, metaphysical, theological, or abstract inquiry and disintellectualizes religion. Its interest is in reality and

in the future. God's realism is demonstrated over and over again, until it becomes the dominant theme of the Scriptures. The universe was, then, the necessary vehicle by which God chose to show Himself.

Let us examine—in spite of men's efforts to create problems for themselves, to complicate and finally forget reality—the realism of God's vocabulary of creation. In even the most modern version of the Old Testament God is made to speak like a Platonist. Translators seem to vie with one another in putting colorless and abstract words into His mouth, forgetful of the fact that the original text is not in Greek but in Hebrew, a language in which every word has a concrete meaning. It is nothing short of castration to replace the hard outlines and primitive colorfulness of God's speech with the gray platitudes of a language of far greater sophistication.

If there is a moment in the creation which should dazzle our eyes and minds it is the one when God scattered the darkness. In all other languages the key word of the phrase *Fiat lux* or "Let there be *light*," is one which fails to convey the event's blinding incandescence. "Light" seems to be a phenomenon unto itself, a sort of "idea," than which nothing is farther from the tone of the Bible or the ways of God. It is as if God had looked in a dictionary and found the definition "the sensation aroused by stimulation of the visual centers."

Let us look, rather, to the Midrash to find out what is this "light" whose abstraction has been held up for thousands of years to the reverence of the faithful. Is it the bright light of the sun or the pale light of the stars and moon, to both of which men are accustomed? Surely not, since at the moment when God called it into being these heavenly bodies had not yet been created. Is it the invisible glow of infra-red or ultra-violet? These had not yet been discovered. Fortunately the Hebrew word has a meaning so precise as to dispel all our problems, even to relieve us of the necessity of posing them. It means not light in general or the idea of light, but the brightness particular to God when He appears to man, the light which He showed forth on Mount Sinai, where there were "thunders and lightnings" (Exodus 19:16), that of which Jeremiah (10:13) speaks in the phrase "He maketh lightnings with rain," or the Psalmist when he tells us that "the lightnings lightened the world" (Psalms 77:18). The light which came into being when the darkness of chaos was first dispelled has the blinding quality of which lightning gives us a fleeting conception.

Nothing could be fresher, more concrete and visual, than the opening of Genesis. Why should it lose its natural savor and be blunted by commonplace words which are overly familiar to our ears? Far better to dig under the abstractions and get at the original significance. Many of the misunderstandings which separate man from God come from the encrustation of outworn pious phrases. From Sinai to Calvary an accumulation of meaninglessness has obscured the Bible stories. Of this they must be freed if we are to get at their real import.

Similar clarification of the important part at the beginning of Genesis regarding the creation of man is needed. God, as we are accustomed to hearing it, created man in His own image. It is illogical at first sight that the Eternal, who gave to Moses the famous commandment: "Thou shalt not make thee any graven image, or any likeness of any thing that is in heaven above, or that is in the earth beneath, or that is in the waters beneath the earth" (Deuteronomy 5:8), should violate His own injunction. Have we not here a contradiction which impairs rather than explains the mystery of the creation, a commonplace modern interpretation which detracts from the vivid quality of the original?

Zelem, the Hebrew word conventionally translated as "image," has various meanings, from the general to the particular. It may, indeed, be taken as "image," "resemblance," or even "illusion," all of which lend themselves to a range of scholarly interpretations. Or, again, it may be "ghost" or "phantom," either of which is more limited in definition. But it has also a very concrete meaning, corresponding to a simple reality, that of "shadow," as we find it in Psalms 39:6. Man, then, is the shadow cast by God; he is not God's image. None of the unnecessary problems raised by this famous verse of Genesis need any longer torment us.

That God's image should disfigure and betray God is quite incomprehensible; it implies that God's greatest work should turn against Him. But if we have here a shadow, with none of God's physical lineaments or spiritual content, prey to the vagaries of the passing hours, and this shadow dislocates and deforms God's perfection, then the problem is less difficult to resolve. Man is attached to God by an immaterial and fluctuating but natural bond. He is the reflection of his Creator, with all that this implies of imprecision and uncertainty. All the anxieties inherent in our nature are logical and explicable; the exact word calls us back to concrete reality. No paternalistic "good God" covers up real problems in an ocean of rhetoric or a tangle of hairsplitting. The God of truth explains them and the living God lives them. Whether or not we believe, we can see the results. The myth of Genesis acquires new power, and there is a new meaning to God's relationship with the universe which He created and animates.

As God inserts Himself into the development of Genesis there is a whole series of attitudes and gestures, a sort of mimicry which marks the progress of His action upon the universe. He created the heaven and earth; He said, "Let there be light," and "saw the light that it was good." He "divided the light from the darkness and . . . called the light Day, and the darkness . . . Night." Then He repeated the process in regard to space and all that it contains. After having several times created, spoken, looked, divided, and named, God reached the essential gesture and the crucial moment of His creative power: He blessed the world which He had created and ordered. The act of blessing appears three times in Genesis, and always at a crucial moment: first in regard to the first living creatures, fish and fowl. God blessed them, saying: "Be fruitful and multiply, and fill the waters in the seas, and let fowl multiply in the earth" (Genesis: 1:22). Second, in verse 28, in regard to men: "And God blessed them, and God said unto them, Be fruitful and multiply, and replenish the earth, and subdue it: and have dominion over the fish of the sea, and over the fowl of the air, and over every living thing that moveth upon the earth." The third and most essential blessing of all is the one in Chapter 2, verse 3: where after having finished His creation God blessed the time into which He had inserted Himself—that is, He blessed the history in which His fate was to be played out. "And God blessed the seventh day and sanctified it: because that in it He had rested from all His work which God created and made." In short, He blessed the whole of creation.

The act of blessing was a decisive one on God's part. Not only because by so doing He gave the world a soul and history a meaning, but also because it marked a new stage in His relationship with His creation. If God blessed the world it was, of course, because it needed His blessing. By the very fact of blessing His creatures He addressed them as beings responsible for their fate and at the same time He gave them a new power, associating Himself with them in all His life force and spirituality and lending them aid and comfort. At the same time He foretold the moment when His creation would venture upon paths which could not meet with His approval. For having seen that the universe was what He had meant it to be—"He saw that it was good"—it seems as if He became aware of its possibilities for evil, perversion, and self-annihilation. With His blessing He gave it support, but He also accepted the presence of sin and danger. In his realism He accepted His creation for what it is, not for what it will be at the end of time but for what it is in the process of time's unrolling. What He did was to exorcise the world and to set it up according to the Law. Traditional legends testify to this intent. These legends do not have the weight of the biblical text, but their ingenuous character renders the world's predestination and its sacred character more comprehensible to the ordinary man.

The universe was quick to show that God's blessing was not a superfluous gesture. No sooner were they created than minerals, vegetables, and animals concerned themselves with finding out what role they were to play. Stones quarreled among themselves to determine which one of them would serve as Jacob's pillow or the projectile with which David slew Goliath. The ground prepared itself to refuse its fruits to Cain after he had fled from the slaying of his brother. Oxen disputed as to which one of them would pull the chariot on which Joshua rode to the siege of Jericho. The moon was jealous of the sun for shining on the days in which Israel's destiny was to be accomplished. In the expectation of the struggles to which God dedicated the universe and the mission assigned it by the Creator to assure the triumph of good over evil and the fulfillment of the Law, all the forces of nature were thrown into a ferment as they competed with one another for pre-eminence.

This fulfillment of the Law could not but be difficult to attain in the very real universe to which God had given an impulse and which He had endowed with free will. Besides the forces of nature whose creation we have just retold there were monsters, which are not always explicitly named in the Scriptures but of whose existence men have read between the lines. Four of them are to be found between Genesis and Job. In the category of "every living thing" of the fifth day of creation, upon which man could draw for his subsistence, there were four amphibious creatures which perpetuated the terrors of the original chaos. These monsters had a double character: they were not only brute, elemental forces but also agents of evil. On the one hand they represented the savagery and barbarity of the universe before the creation of man and the development of his conscience, on the other they worked to turn man away from his aspirations and from the will of God. Emerging from chaos, they threw out a net with which to entrap man and pull him back from his newly acquired consciousness into the void of unconsciousness. By virtue of a sort of savage charm they fascinated their prey before seizing him. This hypnotic power of evil has persisted through the centuries. In order that evil should have a real existence it was necessary that, from the beginning of the world, God should give it a place and allow it to play its role in the drama of creation.

Four in number were the monsters which the prophet Ezekiel (1:4ff.) saw appear before him:

"And I looked, and behold, a whirlwind came out of the north, a great cloud, and a fire infolding itself, and a brightness was about it, and out of the midst thereof as the color of amber, out of the midst of the fire.

"Also out of the midst thereof came the likeness of four living creatures [*Haiot*]. And this was their appearance; they had the likeness of a man. . . .

"As for the likeness of their faces, they four had the face of a man, and the face of a lion, on the right side; and they four had the face of an ox on the left side; they four also had the face of an eagle."

But before this episode, which occurs fairly late in the Bible, we find monsters less ambiguous and of a more unmitigated horror, the forces of brute evil which existed before God extracted the universe from chaos. The first of these is Tanin, whose name is translated sometimes as "sea monster" and sometimes as "serpent." He emerged from darkness at the moment when Aaron and the sorcerers and magicians of Pharaoh transformed their rods into serpents, when God told Moses to say to Aaron: "Take thy rod and cast it before Pharaoh, and it shall become a serpent." Here the monster served God's purpose of freeing the Children of Israel. But later, in Numbers, he played two opposite roles:

"And the Lord sent fiery serpents among the people, and they bit the people; and much people of Israel died. . . .

"And the Lord said unto Moses, Make thee a fiery serpent, and set it upon a pole . . . that every one that is bitten, when he looketh upon it, shall live" (Numbers 21:6, 8). Tanin's venom thus contained both death and life. He was a monster whose elemental power could be transfigured by God and turned to a good end. His poison had a sort of homeopathic quality, and it is easy to understand why God let him survive the original chaos and continue to exist in the organized world.

The second monster, Leviathan, plays a more pronouncedly evil role. He appears as a serpent, a crocodile, and a sea monster, but never as an adjunct to God; indeed he offers brutal opposition to Him. It is of him that God said to Job: "Will he make a covenant with thee?" (Job 41:4). And of whom Isaiah (27:1) says that his death will mark the installation of the Kingdom of God on earth: "In that day the Lord with his sore and great and strong sword shall punish leviathan the piercing serpent, even leviathan that crooked serpent; and he shall slay the dragon that is in the sea."

Thus God fought against Leviathan; this shapeless and horrifying monster was a symbol of the incomprehensible and irrational, typical of the world of chaos. God knew its ferocity and imbecility; when man was unfaithful and doubted His power He threatened him with this monster. What would become of man if he were delivered into its power without God to protect him? With the grim humor that typifies Him in the book of Job, God asks:

"Canst thou draw out leviathan with an hook? or his tongue with a cord which thou lettest down? . . .

"Will he make a covenant with thee? wilt thou take him for a servant for ever? . . .

"Lay thine hand upon him, remember the battle, do no more. . . .

"His breath kindleth coals, and a flame goeth out of his mouth.

"In his neck remaineth strength, and sorrow is turned into joy before him. . . .

"Upon earth there is not his like, who is made without fear.

"He beholdeth all high things; he is a king over all the children of pride" (Job 41:1–34).

As Werner Wolff says in *Changing Concepts of the Bible*, "Leviathan is the symbol of consternation, of the metaphysical terror which drives men out of their minds, like madness."

God let Leviathan live; undoubtedly there is madness in the world. But He constantly intervened to preserve His creature, man, and to protect the Law from this "king over all the children of pride," until the time for his total destruction. To God creation is no lighthearted adventure or idyl; it is a drama, a combat in which He has given a role to the powers of evil.

This role He gave to two other monsters—Behemoth and Rahab—as well. Behemoth was born at the same time as Leviathan and was complementary to him, having his kingdom on the heights instead of in the depths.

"In that day," says the apocryphal book of Enoch, "two monsters shall be born, a female monster, Leviathan, to dwell in the depths of the sea and a male monster, Behemoth, who will dwell in a vast desert to the east of the garden of the just and the elect."

The apocryphal book of II Esdras (6:49–52) tells us more of their birth, which took place on the fifth day of creation:

"Then thou didst ordain two living creatures, the one thou callest Behemoth, and the other Leviathan.

"And thou didst separate the one from the other: for the seventh part, namely, where the water was gathered together, might not hold them together.

"Unto Behemoth thou givest one part, which was dried up the third day, that he should dwell in the same part wherein are a thousand hills:

"But unto Leviathan thou gavest the seventh part, namely,

the moist; and hast kept him to be devoured of whom thou wilt, and when."

The two monsters are complementary by virtue of their dwelling-places, of their sexes, and also of the two different aspects of evil which they represent. Leviathan was the incarnation of brute bodily force, the domination of muscle and belly; he killed and devoured, and his constant gesticulation sowed terror among his victims. Behemoth, on the contrary, was silent and apparently indifferent. He lay under the lotus tree (in other parts of the world the symbol of life), in watchful meditation. His power came neither from brutal fascination nor from wild gestures and noise. As a male he had a fecundating role, after which he returned to his apparent calm, while Leviathan was agitated by the convulsions of childbirth. Behemoth was assuredly more dangerous than Leviathan, since he is described as "the chief of the ways of God" (Job 40:19). Leviathan represented the blind forces of nature, the elemental side of the struggle of life, which tears apart the universe that God created. Behemoth stood for the more intellectual forces of ruse and artifice; Leviathan's technique was that of wrestling, Behemoth's that of fencing or dialectic, no less pitiless and harmful to the harmony of the universe but on a subtler level. Each expressed one of the evils in the universe and in human nature, the former the perversion of instinct, the latter the perversion of the mind.

The fourth monster, Rahab, incarnated the extremes of sexuality. We read in Isaiah 51:9: "Art thou not it that hath cut Rahab, and wounded the dragon?" In Joshua 6:17 Rahab represents prostitution: "Only Rahab the harlot shall live." In Revelation 17:3 Rahab appears joined to a beast: "I saw a woman sit upon a scarlet covered beast, full of names of blasphemy, having seven heads and ten horns."

The four monsters, together, represent all the evil tendencies in the heart of man, which sow snares or raise obstacles in the path traced by God. They all date from before the creation; in the limbo of the uncreated world they were strange company to the Law which they were fated to combat. In the book of Job, when God answers the doubts of the unjustly stricken Job and by the same token all the arguments based on the existence of evil which generations of unbelievers have used against Him, He calls up the monster Leviathan. This is not, as is often supposed, in order to convince man of his weakness and the unimportant place he holds in creation. It is, rather, in order to show him that Genesis is essentially a drama into which God has put much more than the peaceful accomplishment of His sovereign will. It seems as if He had had to intervene in the conflict which already existed in chaos between the forces of good and evil, the monsters and the Law, between the forces willing the destruction of life and those striving for its fulfillment in the framework of history.

"I have set before you life and death . . . therefore choose life, that both thou and thy seed may live," says Deuteronomy 30:19–20, leaving a choice between them.

God is not ignorant of evil, since He has known the monsters from all eternity and included them in His creation. Therefore the existence of evil is no argument against Him. God's function is made more necessary and perceptible to man by the fact that He must constantly intervene to re-establish the world's threatened harmony and equilibrium, to weigh the balance between the monsters and the Law. To reproach Him with the existence of evil is to reproach Him for being realistic and truthful. It means a failure to understand that if, as tradition has it, He, in creating the world, began by "opening his eyes," it was in order to show us that the acceptance of concrete reality is the first moral virtue and the indispensable condition of salvation.

There is a story in the Midrash about Satan, the spirit of evil. Some rabbis had gathered together to discuss him. In the middle of their very free controversy one of the most respected among them suggested that Satan has an essentially religious function. With these words there was a great noise and a smell of sulphur, and the Prince of Darkness burst in upon the assembly, kneeling before the rabbi and kissing his feet.

Perhaps in this daring story there is a hint of one of the signs which, according to rabbinical tradition, will mark the advent of the Messiah: Satan will kneel down before the doctors of the Law. Until this day we must accept the world as it is.

When God had finished creating the world, tradition has it that He said: "My world, may you always enjoy the same favor with me as you do in this moment of your creation." This was both a wish and a warning; above all it was a call to the combat which God wages in the universe on behalf of the Law, the combat in which man is the actor, the stake, and all too often the victim.

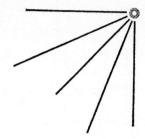

5 The God of the First Covenants: Adam and Noah

After the Law and the universe, man is the stake, the means and the end of creation. In chronological order he was preceded by angels and animals.

Animals were created on the fifth day and the beginning of the sixth. Of the creation of the angels we know very little; creatures so spiritualized and so removed from everyday life do not fit into the six days of Genesis. Nevertheless, in Jewish tradition, they have an important part to play; they are God's messengers, and their fate is not in any way associated with that of humans.

Angels are among the beings who accompany the Creator wherever He goes. There are three categories of such guards or servants. First the *kerubim* or cherubim, winged creatures doubtless born among the clouds, guardians of the tree of life in the Garden of Eden and of the Ark in the Temple at Jerusalem. They watch over the places chosen by God for His residences or for his apparitions.

The seraphim, too, have wings, which are mounted for the most part on serpents' bodies. They were escorts of the deities and tutelary spirits of Canaan before they were enlisted in the service of God. Standing, bowing low, or prostrate, they hail God and proclaim His holiness. At other times they hover, in holy terror, above His throne, making a rustling sound with their six wings. In flight they may use only four of these wings and fold the other two over their faces. The holiest one among them chants the praise of the Most Praiseworthy, and the others sing in chorus a hymn of blessing: "Holy, holy, holy is the Eternal One, our God."

The angels as well participate, with outspread wings, in these acclamations. They too are auxiliaries of God inherited from idolatry and are given an important role, which they carry out with varying efficacy. The Eternal may take counsel with them, but at times these zealous servants, confident of knowing His will, may overstep their role and take unwelcome initiatives. This is what happened, as we shall see later on, on Mount Sinai.

The Midrash tells us that when God first had in mind to create man He consulted the angels, who were of divided opinions. Weary of listening to their discussion, God went ahead with His plan. After which He faced them with the accomplished fact, saying: "What good is all your controversy? Look! Man has been created."

Thus it was that God set man midway between the animals, who seek to devour him, and the angels, who would fain have ignored his existence. Half angel, half beast, as moralists and theologians were later to define him, man had from the beginning a divided nature, which predestined him to inward contradictions and outward drama. God knew from the start the dual possibilities of man and his descendants and the risks involved in His last creation. In the Midrash a learned Rabbi Berekiah thus sums up the situation: "When the One God, blessed be His name, came to the moment of creating Adam, He foresaw the good and the bad men that would issue from him. 'If I go ahead and create him,' He said to Himself, 'some of his offspring are sure to turn out badly. But if I do not create him, how are the just to be born?' "

God took the risk, but this initial decision entailed all His future quarrels with man and the whole drama of humanity. God and man were to be locked in a ceaseless struggle, in opposition to or conciliation of the two contradictory trends which came into being with the creation.

Hence the Covenant, or rather the Covenants, between God and man. The Covenant or *berith* is the great innovation of the Bible, setting it apart from the idolatrous worship of earlier religious traditions. For idolatry consists not only of a mistaken idea of God on the part of man; it implies also, on the part of the idolaters and their present priests, a misconception of man's true nature and of his free will. Wherever man remains prostrate and passive, absorbed in his prayers, with no dialogue between his perishable body and the haunting idea of eternity, idolatry is to blame. And the idolatry with which the Bible is so obsessed, the temptation to which the Jews have always inclined but never succumbed, has the Covenant for its only remedy. The Covenant is not an isolated fact in the history of God or in the human tradition which, century after century, fills the moments of eternity. The Covenant is written into us, it is a permanent part of our being. Wherever a man thinks of God, whether to pledge Him allegiance or to oppose Him with doubt or refusal, wherever a man or a group of men face the insoluble problem, wherever there is a dialogue concerned with the paradox of God's insertion in the history of man and the insertion of man in eternity, the Covenant goes on and is renewed. This Covenant, set up just as the biblical faith was beginning to develop, cannot be broken by either disbelief or bigotry. It endures, even when men fall away from God or attempt to draw too close to Him, whether they abandon His worship or conduct it with the empty formalism and exclusiveness of which God showed his disapproval at the end of the Flood.

The Covenant is consubstantial with man, every man, inasmuch as he *is* a man, just as it is necessary to God because He is God. It is the permanent and universal woof of the living history of God and of the history of mankind; every human action is one of its episodes, every human life one of its moments. In this immense process, of which every one of us actively forms an idea or passively feels the consequences, we must single out various stages, if only as points of reference for an explanation. By degrees it became necessary to "institutionalize" the Covenant, to regulate this existential and permanent relationship between God and His creature.

God's historiographers, the authors of the epic of the Pentateuch, have distinguished four stages of the Covenant, each one of them incarnated by a man. The first is the implicit but imperative Covenant which God made with Adam, demanding of him obedience to a negative commandment: that he should not eat the fruit of the tree of the knowledge of good and evil. After this the Covenant became more explicit; it was formulated in both commandments and promises given to Noah, Abraham, and Moses. With Noah it was a universal Covenant, extending to all those who survived the Flood, a generous promise from whose benefits no one on earth was cut off, demanding no particular observance or loyalty in return, but only the obligation to abstain from evil-doing and blasphemy and to keep the moral law. Neither unbelievers nor misbelievers were excluded. It is as if God, wishing to bring mankind back into the ways of obedience, were facilitating his repentance and unconditionally opening the gates of salvation.

With Abraham the Covenant began to take a more definite form. In order that the messianic era might come forth and the Kingdom of God be installed upon earth it was necessary that, among the great masses of men destined to salvation but unable to find the way, one group should be consecrated to the Eternal and to the observance of His Law. Thus there was shaped among the crowd a sort of priesthood, charged with protecting man from evil, rousing him from indifference, and setting his feet in the right path. The members of this priesthood were no better than other men; they shared all the weaknesses, temptations, and degradations of the human condition, and yet they were called upon to combat and dispel them with special vigor. In short, this priesthood had a lay character.

First the family of Abraham and then his descendants, the Children of Israel, were lay priests dedicated to the service of God, priests born and rooted in vulgarity and sin, as if to draw from them a divine impulse nourished by the sap of reality. A priesthood established first in a family and then in a people like any other, recruited from the masses but inescapably committed to a mission, such were the offspring of the patriarch Abraham, whose name opens the litany which through the ages men have addressed to God. "God of our fathers, of the patriarchs, God of Abraham, Isaac and Jacob . . ." The Covenant struck with Abraham is like a priestly rule whose often misunderstood and betrayed demands nonetheless constitute a pattern of life such as to ensure the perpetuity of man's ideals and to distinguish him from both the animals and the angels.

This priestly vocation required a content and this consecrated people a program, lest the choice that had fallen upon them be empty and vain. The priests became self-satisfied bigots; they shut themselves up in pride of caste and claimed an intimacy with God in which God did not participate. Then it was that, from the heights of a mountain in the desert, Moses, the only prophet "whom the Lord knew face to face" (Deuteronomy 34:10), gave the Covenant a content by revealing the Torah.

Everything began, then, with Adam. His creation was the decisive moment, the turning point of the history of God. First

God had created the universe: the product of the first five days and part of the sixth. Into the new dimensions of space and time which He had opened up in it He set minerals, vegetables, and animals, His works, but not His children, with which He could have no intimate relationship. To use a modern term, He was not yet "committed."

With the creation of man everything changed. Heretofore God had put Himself into an abstract and mathematical time, but now He inserted Himself into living time, into history, linking His life and fate to those of man. By this token God's relations with the world became infinitely more complex. Of course He was all-powerful, and the world depended upon Him, so that it could not confront Him with any challenge. But by entrusting to man not only dominion over the earth but also the execution of His will, God initiated a dialogue, if not with the world, at least with the being whom Elie Benamozegh, in *l'Israël et l'Humanité*, calls "the universe become conscious."

On behalf of man, His shadow, God accepted in advance all the risks of the human condition. He may have been irritated by Adam's disobedience, but though the serpent was the agent and Eve the provocation, He must have known that He himself had made it possible. By giving Adam free will and by installing the symbolic tree in the Garden, did not God accept in advance that Adam and Eve should leave it for the fields and forests, the mountains and plains, the dangers and misfortunes which befall every human couple? What use was there in creating the wide world if man and woman were to be confined to a garden, no matter how beautiful? Why were they endowed with mobility, the instinct of self-preservation, strength, wile, and intelligence, all those qualities which enable us to adapt ourselves to the world and contribute to its progress, if they were to stay in a place protected from all peril, where nothing unexpected could happen and all they had to do was to sing God's undisputed praise?

Adam and Eve had to leave the Garden, if not for their own

sake, for God's. He allowed even if He did not will it. And the result was beneficent. It was by a process of something like childbirth or weaning that the first couple broke the umbilical cord binding them to God and went hand in hand out of the Garden of Eden, which was a reflection of the divine mind, with anxious hearts and suffering bodies, into the ways of the world. Sorrow and death lay in store for them, to be sure, but for their descendants, going from sorrow to sorrow and from death to death, there was a march toward progress and the chance of striving to maintain the presence of God in a hostile world.

In banishing Adam and Eve from the Garden, God played for all or nothing. There is no gain without risk. Truth cannot triumph in the world if it is not put to the test and threatened with destruction. God's action was the passage of a heavenly Rubicon—in this case the rivers Pison, Gihon, Hiddekel, and Euphrates, all of which had their source in the Garden. And we too, from century to century, have crossed it in our turn.

Evil was inescapable from the moment when, after his sin, the first man left the Garden of Eden. But it revealed itself as necessary to God's plan. Among all the stimuli to our progress, evil is one of the most forceful. Without it we should still be wandering about the Garden; mankind would vegetate in the calm of a sterile and unconscious happiness.

The first stage, then, was the creation of the universe, the second the creation of man, after this the drama to which creation was but the prelude. The third stage was marked by man's sin and his expulsion from the Garden of Eden. Following this there is another important and neglected episode, which marks the continuance of the Covenant: the birth of Seth, Adam's third son. For Adam's first two sons, Cain and Abel, the Bible gives no more details than those of a birth certificate. But after the drama of the two brothers and the murder of Abel, the birth of the third son is told in words of special significance.

God had made Adam to be his shadow. Adam engendered Cain and Abel in an apparently commonplace way. But when it comes to the third son who, after Adam's disobedience and Cain's crime, was to re-establish the tradition of God and to continue the Covenant, we read: "And Adam . . . begat a son in his own likeness, after his own image; and called his name Seth" (Genesis 5:3). Here, at the dawn of history, we find the same words as those referring to the creation of Adam. Seth was the shadow cast by Adam just as Adam was the shadow cast by God; evil did not prevail, and the bond between God and man was prolonged through all history. It seems as if God were subtly and generously pointing out the fact that evil has a place in His grand design, that it does not necessarily cause a break with tradition or a withdrawal of the Covenant.

Such is the great drama of Adam and his posterity, as God gives it to us in a book of the Bible of which He himself is believed to be the direct inspiration. There is everything in the Bible if we read it with understanding. When we understand the importance of Adam, then the fatality of evil and also that of redemption fall into place. He incarnates the beginning of history and the first knot of the Covenant, which was, in the course of the ages, to slacken and tighten, to fall open and close, over and over.

And what comes next? After the early events of Genesis, generation after generation of men, in begetting children, achieved the same thing as did Adam in begetting Seth. Each one of us, by engendering a child, casts his shadow upon a future which he himself will not live to see. The birth of Adam's third son foreshadows all the births to come, the birth of all the beings that stem from God but are distinct from Him. We are all of us connected to Genesis and the drama of creation by the Covenant. In our perishable flesh and our ephemeral lives Genesis is perpetuated and the Covenant goes on; Genesis is a permanent and unfinished process. Whether we are close to God or have turned our backs on Him the Covenant will never be broken.

In all our destinies there is a trace of the divine impulse which God sought to perpetuate in the creation, and also the stigmata of the evil which He let into history. Banished from the Garden, we are obliged by the very fact of our exile to seek after the way of perfection. We are the children of the third son whom Adam created as a shadow, just as God had created him, after he had been guilty of sacrilege and witnessed the crime of Cain. In spite of these two misdeeds and all those that have followed, we return from age to age to the way of God and the Covenant. We lose it and find it again, blaspheming or glorifying the holy name of Him who set our feet upon it. Even our errors bear fruit, because they compel us to go on.

Man is the continuing artisan of the permanent miracle of creation, the signer of the Covenant. We are contemporary not only with our own time but with the beginning of time and with time to come. Genesis, still unfinished, is within us and continually we ask God: "Genesis? And what next?" To which God might answer: "After Genesis, history. After the divine impulse, human liberty. After creation, the Covenant." So the Covenant endures, and on the eternal woof woven by God men bring to bear their passing comments. The Bible does not exhaust this subject or any other, for its subjects are inexhaustible, and every generation rediscovers, rethinks, and restores its transcendent truth, in the framework of immanent reality.

The grandiose destiny of Adam is revealed to us by the Bible, but the circumstances of his life and the details of his character are known to us through the traditional writings of man. After the divine word, the human commentary; after the Bible, the Midrash and the Talmud. Adam lends himself as well to down-to-earth exegesis as to the exaltation of the spirit. Like the other characters of the Bible, no matter how sublime their destiny, he is intensely human. After the immense fresco of his providential mission, let us examine the testimony of tradition. Let us look first of all at a relatively recent work of art, a temporal illustration of the eternal Word, in which the Christian tradition is close to that of the rabbis.

At Langeais, in one of the châteaux of the Loire Valley, there

is a sixteenth-century tapestry which represents the creation of
the first man. God the Father, an old man with a long white
beard, is helping a young man to his feet. His benevolent smile
shows that He is ready to do anything to help His protégé, but
the look which Adam casts at his Creator expresses a mixture of
confidence and uncertainty, joy in the strength that supports
him and fear that it may not be enough to carry him through
life's vicissitudes.

The first man is born to life, and born alone. Jewish tradition
gives a reason for his solitude. His anxiety is in accord with the
divine plan and also with the lesson he must hand on to posterity. "If at the beginning of Creation there was one man alone,"
the Midrash says, "it is to teach us that the Torah looks on
anyone who kills another man as if he were guilty of destroying
the whole world and on anyone who causes another man to live
as if he had given life to it." Thus, from the beginning, every
man is the equivalent of all mankind. To hurt or kill a single
man is to injure the whole human race. As Adam is born into
the world he endures his solitude as a personal sacrifice to his
posterity, as a lesson which it is his duty to impart.

According to the Midrash, man was twenty years old when
God created him. His body as well as his spirit was restless. In
the Garden around him every animal had a companion. And, in
the Langeais tapestry, as God presents the animals to him, pair
by pair, Adam questions himself and complains that he is condemned to isolation.

According to a traditional story, which interprets that of Genesis, Adam had just rendered God the first service asked of him,
to give a name to His creatures and to Himself. As God paraded
the animals before him Adam gave a name to the ox, the camel,
the ass, the horse, and all the rest. When each one of them had
received a name God turned to man. "What is your name?" he
asked him. "Let me be called Adam," man replied, "because I
was made from earth, *adama*." So it was done. "And what is my

name?" asked God. Mindful of the primary attribute of the ineffable One, Adam answered: "May you be called Adonai, or Lord, since you reign over all creatures." Thus the first lone man gave names to all the creatures in the universe, to himself, and to God, rendering a service which made him worthy of his creation. By naming the animals Adam made himself into God's aide and abettor; by naming himself he acquired consciousness of his own place in the universe; by naming God he acquired awareness of eternity.

Nevertheless he was still prey to the weaknesses of the flesh of which he was made. As the newly named animals paraded before him Adam complained: "Every one of them has a companion, and I have none." This was exactly what God had feared. If he had not made a companion for man it was because—as a somewhat misogynous tradition has it—there was a danger that she would be a source of evil. He did not want Adam, after the Fall, to accuse Him of having created the temptress. He hoped that Adam would take the initiative so that He himself should not be responsible.

When Adam asked, of his own accord, for a companion, God could not refuse him. He caused Adam to fall into a sleep whose exact nature is a subject of debate. For the commentators distinguish among three kinds of sleep, deriving from fatigue, unconsciousness or catalepsy, and the condition of prophecy respectively. Adam had no reason to be fatigued, so his sleep must have signified either unconsciousness or prophecy. Perhaps he had no idea of the possible consequences of his request. Perhaps he foresaw the perils. In any case, when Adam woke up he was happy to find himself no longer alone, and it is also possible that he was also slightly apprehensive.

God blessed Adam and Eve, while two archangels, Michael and Gabriel, stood at their sides, holding vessels of benediction. For want of other humans, they may be said to have served as witnesses. God's blessing laid four duties upon man: "Be fruitful, and multiply, and replenish the earth, and subdue it" (Genesis 1:28). Three of these blessings were unconditional, the fourth depended on man's obedience.

But neither the presence of Eve nor God's blessing seemed to have relieved Adam of his concern. Whether by virtue of his character or because of some sort of premonition, he continued to show himself afraid. When for the first time he saw day turn into night he feared that day would never return. Even when the next day came Adam was still fearful. In this unknown world, at whose dangers he guessed, he feared that something irreparable would happen. And so it did.

For all the rest of his life, after the Fall, tradition shows us Adam imploring God to wipe out what had happened. But God could do nothing. Adam had introduced evil, suffering, and death into the universe, and what was done was done forever. All that God could do was to show His indulgence. God's kindness to fallen man is made apparent in many episodes recounted by tradition. The Midrash of Genesis gives us three examples: the first immediately after the expulsion from the Garden; the second upon Adam's death; the third at the most sorrowful moment of his existence.

Let us consider first the expulsion from Eden. We can imagine how close the Garden was to God's heart before Adam's sin made it superfluous, with what care He planted its trees and traced its alleys. In the beginning, says the Midrash, the site of the garden was filled with thorny bushes, which God uprooted and replaced with shade trees, selecting the seeds and determining the desired heights and the extent of the foliage. Each tree was to have a role to play, and so it was that He planted cedars for the future construction of the Temple of Jerusalem.

Three days before the actual creation of Adam God made trees spring from the earth that would be beautiful to behold or would provide sustenance. Among the trees there were two of special significance. One was the tree of life, which commentators identify as being a figure of speech for either wheat or grapevines; and the other was the fatal tree whose fruit contained the knowledge of good and evil. God has left no clues to the identification of this latter tree, lest in ages to come men point to it and say: "It was through this tree that Adam introduced evil into the world," when actually the tree was not to blame for Adam's sin.

This then was the place, set up by God and pregnant with significance for the destiny of mankind, from which our first forefathers were to be banished. But when God saw their sorrow and confusion He led them to the summit of Mount Abu-Keys, one of the high points of the region into which they had been driven, and showed them the wide world in which they were henceforth to live. "All this belongs to you," He told them. But so confused was Adam that he could not take in the magnitude of the sight before his eyes. "How can I distinguish the boundaries of this vast earth?" he inquired. God offered, then, to acquaint him with a science which would permit him, through the aspects of certain stars, to know the secrets of the universe. But Adam found this science too difficult to master. And so God brought down from heaven a huge mirror and placed it before Adam's eyes, so that he could see in it the extent of the globe. So it was that divine mercy helped Adam to adapt himself to the world in which he was condemned to live; although he could never be free of remorse, life was at least possible.

God's mercy was made manifest again, according to tradition, when the time came for Adam to die. When Adam, at the age of 930 years, felt that he was close to death he sent Eve and Seth to the outskirts of the Garden of Eden to ask God for some of the oil of mercy which flowed from the tree of life. Because as long as he lived Adam could not be purged of his sin, God refused. But in His first reference to the rewards of a future life God charged the archangel Michael to tell Adam that after death he and his descendants would be admitted to paradise. Thus Adam was able to die in peace, knowing that his sin would be forgiven, and the angels buried him in the Garden of Eden.

Six days later Eve, in her turn, lay close to death. Her fear was that of being forgotten. She told her son Seth to inscribe the story of his parents' life on tablets of stone and on tablets of clay, because, she said, the archangel Michael had warned her: "For your sins God will visit His wrath upon your descendants, first by water and then by fire." The stone tablets, therefore, were intended to survive the Flood and the clay ones to emerge whole from the final consumption of the world by flames. God's mercy accorded to sinning man not only forgiveness but the survival of his memory as well.

If He did not pardon Adam and Eve during their lifetime it was because they were undeserving. A third Midrash story, more poignant than the two told above, gives us the explanation.

The most dramatic moment of Adam's existence, after he was banished from the Garden of Eden, was that of the killing of Abel by his brother Cain. In a newborn and unsophisticated world this was a cause for scandal. Birds, animals, and all other living creatures gathered together to demand justice. Streams turned away when Cain approached them and the leaves of the trees withered. Before this demonstration of disapproval Cain trembled and was afraid. God too, at first, was pitiless. "And the Lord said unto him, Therefore whosoever slayeth Cain, vengeance shall be taken on him sevenfold. And the Lord set a mark upon Cain, lest any finding him should kill him" (Genesis 4:15). His punishment was to constrain Cain to live with the burden of his remorse.

When Cain became aware of the enormity of his crime he hid himself from God's eyes. For years Adam did not know what had become of his son. But finally he met him and, to his surprise, found that Cain was more tranquil than himself. "What has happened," he asked, "to make you so peaceful?" "I repented," Cain told him, "and by this token I was reconciled with the Almighty." Prostrating himself on the ground, Adam exclaimed: "So great is the power of repentance! And I never knew!" So it was that Adam, who had been guilty of disobedience, learned from his son, a murderer, that he too must repent in order to be forgiven. After this men knew the remedy for every evil.

Adam is a legendary being, just as the creation is a legend which owes nothing to history. He is the fabled hero of the great myth of the "*Bereshit* [In the beginning . . .]" But the legend of Noah is based on historical events. Not that Noah himself was an actual person; we have met him in the Mesopotamian cults and their mythology. But the great event of which he is presented to us as the hero—the Flood—did take place and has left tangible traces.

Sir Leonard Woolley, the leader of a seven-year Anglo-American archaeological dig at Ur in Mesopotamia, found proof of the Flood's actual occurrence. The excavations which he conducted between 1927 and 1929 in a prehistoric cemetery led to the discovery of a great quantity of rubble from the primitive city. Shafts sunk in the spring of 1929 went through a layer of charred wood in which there were clay tablets which allowed the dating of Ur's lost civilization. As the shafts went deeper, the character of the soil changed and so did the character of the discoveries. No more rubble and tablets, but a homogeneous eight-foot-deep layer of clay, devoid of any extraneous elements, after which the soil continued as it was before. Among the rubble below the clay were found shards of pottery, bricks, and flint tools whose shape and materials bore witness to an advanced civilization dating as far back as 3000 B.C.

The layer of clay could have been accumulated only by large quantities of deep water which remained stagnant long enough to deposit eight feet of alluvium. Sir Leonard Woolley's discoveries prove that an early but highly developed pre-Sumerian civilization disappeared in the course of a cataclysm and that, when this had passed away, another more rudimentary culture took its place, in which city building and the arts, interrupted by the Flood, once more flourished.

The Flood whose historical reality was discovered by the English archaeologist, the Flood of Sumerian legend, of the Babylonian story of Utanapishtim and the biblical story of Noah, really did take place. Judging by the depth of the clay, the cataclysm was local rather than universal, but nonetheless of considerable dimension. It came about in the lower valleys of the Tigris and the Euphrates and covered an area of some 325 by 125 miles, causing damage much greater than these measurements would ordinarily imply. Prehistoric peoples would quite naturally have believed that the catastrophe was universal in scope, since it swept over all the land they knew. Hence the biblical story, in which so large a part is played by Noah, the man who perpetuated the human race and its Covenant.

In the Bible Noah is the first example, after Adam, of a predestined man. Without altering the biblical text, but simply by elaborating upon it in the free tradition of the Midrash, we shall see in Noah the qualities common to all men who are destined to carry out a mission, whether religious or secular.

When Noah heard the Lord's voice for the first time he did not know what was happening to him. For six hundred years, as a carpenter and builder, he had made houses out of gopherwood, measuring the planks in arm's lengths. Now, as the condition for a Covenant, God asked of him only to make a gopherwood ark, covered inside and out with pitch, just as he always applied it. Noah was amazed that God should ask him for something of such common material and human measurements. He did not understand that, in order to accomplish a special mission, he had only to continue his everyday job.

For months he worked on the ark, on its first, second, and third stories. The wife whom he had taken unto him in the sight of men wanted him to rest from his labors, but for God's worker there could be no rest until the job was done. Carefully he smeared each board with pitch, inside and out, and as each segment was completed he knelt before the ark and marveled at its size. As he became inebriated with the thought that his work was greater than he, the neighbors gathered around to laugh and to say that he was drunk with wine. And Noah, who walked close to God, did not contradict them, for he knew that ordinary people always vulgarize and reduce to their own scale the efforts of those who have been called to go further than they.

When the ark was three hundred cubits long, fifty cubits wide, and thirty cubits high Noah knew that it was finished. He called upon the Lord, but the Lord made no reply. When his wife and children showed irritation and he had begun to lose confidence in himself he went so far as to accuse God of having taken advantage of him. Angrily God said: "Are you in such a hurry to see your fellow creatures die?" Noah realized that pride in his work had made him selfish, but God, knowing the travail of creation, forgave him. Finally, with the planned destruction of His creatures weighing heavily on His mind, God said to Noah: "Go into the ark, you and all your family. Take with you seven pairs of clean beasts, male and female, and one pair of unclean beasts. And take with you provisions for yourself and for them. For in seven days' time I shall cause it to rain for forty days and forty nights upon the earth, until all the creatures that I have made are exterminated."

After six days, when Noah had stored up provisions and gathered the animals together, he ordered his wife and sons to follow him into the ark, according to God's will. His wife, unable to believe that the man with whom she slept every night could have talked with God, was at first unwilling, but when the first drops of rain began to fall she went into the ark for shelter, and her sons followed her. The sluices of heaven were opened and rain poured down upon the earth. Noah's wife and his sons and his son's wives complained that the ark was dark and uncomfortable, but Noah paid no attention and went about preparing the animals' quarters. When the water stood one foot high upon the earth Noah's wife ceased to complain and rejoiced that her feet were dry. Noah paid no attention and went about preparing the animals' food.

When the water stood three cubits high half-drowned men floundered desperately around the ark, crying out with fear in the face of death. Noah paid no attention and went about preparing the evening meal for his family. His wife, half afraid, half compassionate, begged him to let the drowning men into the ark, but Noah told her there was no room. She beseeched him to give them the place of the animals, but he told her the animals would be needed in the future. Then she beseeched him to give them the place of the provisions, but he told her that the provisions were needed for those who were in the ark. She reproached him with his selfishness and Noah, too, was moved to tears for the fate of his fellows, but he told her that they must keep what was necessary for them to go on living and to perpetuate life.

When the flood reached the water line of the ark Noah and his sons were silent, wondering whether it would float or carry them to the bottom. The men struggling in the water shouted louder than ever, clinging to the smooth sides of the ark and trying in vain to scale them. They called out their names and begged Noah at least to keep them in his memory, but Noah's mind was so heavy-laden that he could not remember them. Then they wrote their names on the sides of the ark, but the rising waters wiped them away. They shouted and wept and blasphemed, while Noah stood, alone and uneasy, on the deck of the ark. Suddenly he felt it quiver beneath his feet and the voice of the Lord came to him over the waters, saying: "Let them say what they will; they are doomed to die." And Noah, kneeling on the deck of the ark which he had built, was drunk with the thought of owing his life to God.

The Midrash is full of picturesque details of Noah's story; it lingers in particular over the embarkation, life on board, and the disembarkation after the rains had stopped. The embarkation of

Noah and his family was easy enough, but that of the wild animals presented many problems. When the lion sought to enter Noah was afraid that he might kill some of the others and refused him. The lion asserted his claim to safety with a loud roar and was finally admitted on condition that his teeth be pulled. As it is said in Job 4:10: "The roaring of the lion, and the voice of the fierce lion, and the teeth of the young lions, are broken." The same question arose in connection with the unicorn, a huge, fabulous animal looking like a wild ox. Since God had ordained that "every living thing of all flesh" (Genesis 6:19) must be preserved, the Midrash commentators tell us that a way had to be found to surmount Noah's objections. According to Rabbi Judah, the unicorn's offspring were admitted instead of himself. According to Rabbi Nehemiah, he was attached to the stern of the ark and followed it, cutting a swath in the water as large as the sea of Tiberias. For this solution Job is again invoked as a witness: "Canst thou bind the unicorn with his band in the furrow? or will he harrow the valleys after thee?" (Job 39:10.)

But what was to happen to the creatures, who came from prebiblical religions and were remarkable for their great size and their bodiless condition, as we see from Job's description of them as "dead things . . . formed from under the waters, and the inhabitants thereof" (Job 26:5)? If they were dead, the rabbis ask, what did they have to fear from the Flood? And in the ark they would only have sown panic and confusion. These, therefore, Noah definitely turned away. According to the Scriptures, only the living may praise God. This injunction does not hold for spirits as yet unincarnated, who live in the limbo of creation but will dwell on earth after they are born. The seed is as important as the plant, and therefore they have a right to salvation. Hence they took their place—an immaterial place but nonetheless an important one—in the ark, for Noah, the man of the Covenant, was bound to save not only that which was but also that which would be.

Once the loading was completed it was necessary to take thought for the ark's navigation. Under a lowering and stormy sky, how could the passengers tell day from night or count the days of the voyage? And so God gave Noah a precious stone to be attached to the side of the ark, which reflected the divine light even under cover of darkness. It shone with one degree of brightness by night and with another by day, so that the two could be distinguished.

And how, exactly, were the animals to be installed in the ark? The ark had 900 compartments, connected by passageways and divided among three stories. The top story was for Noah and his family and the clean animals; the first story for unclean animals. The story in between was for the garbage and waste that must inevitably accumulate during the voyage. Would they pile up on the floor, or did Noah make a vent for dumping them into the water? This question is discussed at length but no answer is found. The airing of this problem shows with what care and practical considerations the ark was built. The Midrash often dwells upon the waste matter of life and its disposal. Neither the Bible nor its traditional commentary loses sight of the details of everyday reality.

For the nourishment of men and beasts God had said to Noah: "And take thou unto thee of all food that is eaten, and thou shalt gather it to thee; and it shall be for food, for thee and for them" (Genesis 6:21). In obedience to this order it was necessary to put together enough provisions to last until the earth should once more be dry—that is, for a whole year. Every Midrash commentator has his own list. One puts down dried figs, which were easily preserved and appealed to both man and beast. Another thinks of elephants and supplies them with dried tree branches; another provides deer with their favorite food, a thorny plant called *hasubah*. Rabbi Abba ben Cahana says, not without humor, that ground glass was taken aboard for the ostriches.

Foreseeing the times of sowing and reaping, when the earth

should be once more and forever dry, Noah took with him shoots and seeds of grapevines, of olive and fig trees. By this thought, along with that which he took for more practical details, Noah showed himself worthy of the mission which God had chosen him to accomplish.

We all remember how Noah sent out from the ark, to ascertain whether the waters had subsided, first a raven; then thrice a dove; the second time, the dove came back with an olive branch, the third time she failed to return. The hour had come to leave the ark and to resume on dry land the tradition of the Covenant. The moment of disembarkation was a solemn one for the continuance of history and the future of mankind. Once more the Midrash abounds in stories and explanations.

Before leaving the ark Noah wished to assure the existence of his progeny and that of the human race. Faithful to the injunction of Ecclesiastes (10:4): "If the spirit of the ruler rise up against thee, leave not thy place," he set conditions to God before he would set foot on the ground. "Just as I made an agreement with you before entering the ark, so I will not leave it without an agreement." What Noah had in mind was the fate of his descendants. "When I come out of the ark should I engender more children, only to have them cursed as were my contemporaries?" As long as the Holy One—blessed be His name— did not swear that there would not be another Flood, Noah vowed to stay in the ark, with his wife and children and the animals and the seeds and shoots which he had brought with him. God took the oath that was required of Him; we find it repeated in the book of the prophet Isaiah: "I have sworn that the waters of Noah should no more go over the earth" (Isaiah 54:9). And, as we know, He gave Noah the famous command: "Be fruitful, and multiply, and replenish the earth" (Genesis 9:1).

Then, in order to reinforce His promise and demonstrate its full scope, He added the extraordinary words:

"This is the token of the covenant which I shall make between me and you and every living creature that is with you, for perpetual generations: I do set my bow in the cloud, and it shall be for a token of a covenant between me and the earth. . . . This is the token of the covenant which I have established between me and all flesh that is upon the earth" (Genesis 9:12–17).

The last sentence is truly amazing, not only for its generosity but also for its intelligence; it is a sentence worthy of Elohim. The moment of the rainbow Covenant, the Covenant which God enlarged to include all creation, has a decisive influence upon all history and is particularly pertinent to our day. For it suggests a way of resolving the contemporary spiritual problem: the relationship among the revealed religions and their relationship to the world of unbelievers, in other words, the relationship of the Creator to the whole of His creation, which is currently being considered in the light of ecumenicism.

Valid for all beings, all creatures on earth, regardless of the special mission for which any group of them might be chosen, the rainbow Covenant, the first explicit agreement or alliance between God and man, was extended to all Noah's descendants. The next Covenant in the history of the revelation, the one of which Abraham was the forerunner and which Moses announced from Mount Sinai, perfected or at least detailed its ordering but in no way excluded or superseded it. In the history of salvation, in which all mankind is involved, "Noachism" has a part to play alongside the Mosaic Law. At varying times one or the other may assume greater importance. In periods of evangelization a religion of initiates, like that of Moses, may be more effective. But when faith is threatened and on the defensive Noachism, which is accessible to all men, may preponderate.

What, exactly, is Noachism? As compared to the primitive Covenant with Adam and the final Covenant with Moses, its particular characteristic lies in the fact that it holds good for the two parts into which all mankind is divided. On the one hand for the initiates, those to whom, privately or publicly, either face to face or in spirit, God has spoken directly; on the other for the great mass of people to whom divine truth is made known through intermediaries, often in the midst of doubt, confusion, and idolatry. Idolaters and unbelievers are not shut out from salvation. In proof of this contention Noachism points out that the two protagonists of the Mosaic Covenant—Abraham, the forerunner, and Moses, the achiever—each had at his side the priest of another people: Melchizedek in the first case and Jethro in the second. These two unconsecrated leaders, believers in an incomplete or false revelation, played important parts beside the first of the patriarchs and the first of the prophets respectively.

Melchizedek, king of Salem, although not a Hebrew, is presented in the Bible as "a priest of the most high God." When he saw Abraham he said: "Blessed be Abram of the most high God, possessor of heaven and earth; And blessed be the most high God, which hath delivered thine enemies into thy hand" (Genesis 14:19-20). "In the story of Abraham," says Elie Benamozegh, one of the modern proponents of Noachism, in *Israël et l'Humanité*, "there is great significance in the brief apparition of a remarkable and enigmatic figure. In the black darkness of the pagan world, with its widespread corruption and error, Melchizedek reveals the presence among the Gentiles of a monotheistic cult and priesthood superior even to that of the Hebrew patriarch to whom he gives his blessing. He is described as a priest of *El-elyon*, the Most High, the possessor of heaven and earth, that is, the most universal deity of whom it is possible to conceive."

Alongside Moses, Jethro plays an even more important role. He is introduced in the first reference to Moses' mission: "Now Moses kept the flock of Jethro his father-in-law, the priest of Midian" (Exodus 3:1) and reappears after God has charged him with it, face to face, and convinced him, by a miracle, of his predestination: "And Moses went and returned to Jethro his father-in-law, and said unto him, Let me go, I pray thee, and return unto my brethren which are in Egypt, and see whether they are alive. And Jethro said to Moses, Go in peace" (Exodus 4:18). It was with the consent and blessing of a priest foreign to the Chosen People that Moses went to obey God's command.

The episode of Jethro is a direct application of the verse in Genesis in which God extended the Covenant with Noah to all mankind. A later episode, found in the Midrash, confirms the fact that pagans have a part to play in the drama of salvation. At the decisive moment of Israel's vocation, when Moses proclaimed the Law from Mount Sinai, a pagan, Balaam, gave news of it to the Gentiles. "When, at the moment of the revelation from Sinai all nature was disturbed by the descent of the divine glory, the Gentiles turned to Balaam, as the most wise among them, to find out whence came this unusual agitation and whether it meant that God was going to destroy the world. 'It's not that God is going to destroy the world,' Balaam told them; 'it's that he's giving Israel the Law.' Then they all cried out: 'Eternal Lord, how powerful is Thy name over the earth!' "

At the crucial moments of its history, then, Israel was accompanied by non-Jews and pagans. Nor was their role merely secondary. A good pagan, says tradition, is equal or superior to the high priest of Jerusalem. No matter what their belief, all men may participate in the preparation of God's reign on earth. Here we have a form of tolerance far superior to the commonplace variety which is most often marked by a lukewarm or confused faith. This recognition of all men's contribution to the fulfillment of the Law grows out of a distinction, a dichotomy, between the roles of Noachic and Mosaic religion, between that of men of whatever belief who are spiritually inclined and that of the Jews who serve the One God. Thus it is not in a spirit of weakness or confusion but in the full light of day and of reason that, while joining them in the same providential concept of history, we may also distinguish between them.

The law of Noah is common to all men, while the Law of Moses belongs to the people bearing the yoke of God's election.

"Yoke" is the exact word, because the vocation of Israel implies neither privilege nor superiority. Israel was chosen not because it was better than any other people but because, historically, it alone was in a position to accept the Covenant. According to a Midrash saying which we quoted earlier (p. 69-70), none of the great empires of the time was willing to bear the burden. Israel took the divine mission because it had nothing to lose thereby. And, once having shouldered the load, it will never lay it down.

"The earthly image of divinity, the spirit that shares in creation," says Elie Benamozegh, "is not the Semite or the Israelite, it is man." It was to man in general, to all men, that, before the Mosaic Covenant, God delivered the rudiments of the Law, the Noachic "Heptalogue" which forms a common legislative denominator for all mankind. The seven commandments given to Noah do not demand any particular religious belief or practice, whereas the ten given to Moses have a definitely monotheistic slant and prescribe observances to be fulfilled by the Jews.

Noah's commandments are eminently down to earth; they are not systematically formulated but must be read between the biblical lines. Six of them are negative or interdictory: they forbid blasphemy of God's name, idolatry, murder, incest, theft, and eating the flesh of living animals; the seventh ordains the setting up of courts in accordance with the law of the land.

The Ten Commandments of Moses, in their turn, contain six moral laws (five negative, one positive), principles to be observed by every man, regardless of his religion: the prescription of love for father and mother, the interdiction of murder, adultery, theft, false witness, and covetousness. They also contain four religious laws, which only Israel could have adopted: "I am the Lord thy God. . . . Thou shalt have no other gods before me. Thou shalt not make unto thee any graven image. . . . Thou shalt not take the name of the Lord thy God in vain. . . . Remember the sabbath day, to keep it holy. . . ." These four make up the Mosaic code, of which Israel is the only custodian.

The fact that the laws of Noah are easier to keep than the laws of Moses does not mean that they are subordinate to them or that they are less important in the attainment of salvation. The two sets of laws are different facets of the same universal mission. In actual fact obedience to the laws of Noah may have more practical significance, since the laws of Moses are prerogatives of the people of priests, the people of Israel.

The advent of the Kingdom of God on earth, which is the final goal, cannot consist of the conversion of all mankind to the Mosaic religion. This would be contrary to common sense and also to the concept of the Chosen People. It could, on the other hand, result from world-wide acceptance of the religion of Noah, the common denominator of all spiritual aspirations, the universal moral law of which Israel was the forerunner but never claimed to be the exclusive depository.

The acceptance of complementary destinies, structured and ranked in this way, does not make for confusion but for a rational and concrete division of the ways of Providence. Noachism excludes no one who leads a good life; the cult of Moses admits only those who concede the totality of its religious as well as its secular law. Inclusion and exclusion are not in competition and do not call for sacrifice or conversion on either side. Whether or not you believe in God and no matter what form of divinity you worship, as long as you lead a good life you are working for salvation and the advent of the Messiah.

What are the practical consequences of such a historical and providential view? In the present condition of the world it is as yet only the seed of spiritual unity between co-existing groups, between believers in the biblical tradition and believers in other traditions, between Jews and Christians, believers and non-believers. Such a view cannot yet be held by the Christian Church and is professed by only a minority of Jews. But limited as its efficacy may be, it offers a solid basis for something more and offends no one. Perhaps each priestly body, even if unable to accept it, may propose it to others, and respect it in every relationship with them. It stimulates not a disdainful tolerance but an active respect for the members of other religions and for those who have no religion.

The prophet Amos maintains that Israel has no more privileged a status than that of the Philistines and Assyrians: "Are ye not as children of the Ethiopians, O children of Israel? said the Lord. Have I not brought up Israel out of the land of Egypt? and the Philistines from Caphtor, and the Assyrians from Kir?" (Amos 9:7). Thus one of the capital events of the history of the Chosen People, the exodus from Egypt, to which the Torah and the Passover are so closely attached, has an equivalent in pagan traditions. God himself says that there is no reason why the Philistines and Assyrians should not celebrate Passovers of their own.

And the prophet Isaiah grants the blessing of God to idolaters as well as to Israel: "In that day shall there be a highway out of Egypt to Assyria, and the Assyrian shall come into Egypt, and the Egyptians shall serve with the Assyrians. In that day shall Israel be the third with Egypt and with Assyria, even a blessing in the midst of the land: Whom the Lord of hosts shall bless, saying, Blessed be Egypt my people, and Assyria the work of my hands, and Israel mine inheritance" (Isaiah 19:23–25). In including both idolaters and the Chosen People God's blessing loses neither its precision nor its integrity. It bestows upon each group that which is proper to its mission: to the Gentiles God's support of their effort to build a better society and to the Jews His support in their work of preparation of the messianic era.

The rabbis of the Talmud several times expressed acceptance of beliefs foreign to them: "In religious controversy the most diverse opinions are all words of the living God." Later on the Cabala took up the same idea: "You must not believe the vain words of ignorant men who say that the gods of the Gentiles have no power and do not deserve this name. On the contrary, you should know that the name of God—blessed be He—confers power and authority to every one of the Gentile princes."

Both the foregoing quotations make it clear that the Mosaic Law does not cancel the breadth of Noah's Covenant.

From the standpoint of Israel, its place among the nations, though not exclusive, is well defined. Its problem is to reconcile Israel, which is charged in spite of itself with a priestly vocation, with the rest of secular humanity in a providential plan to assure the salvation of the whole human race, in short with a reconciliation of the Mosaic and the Noachic laws. Because Israel is confined to a particular and limited role it has no reason to feel in any way superior.

In its own time—that is, in the centuries before the coming of Christianity—when Israel alone in the world was entirely consecrated to monotheism, Noachism allowed the co-existence of different confessions, inclined as they were to scorn, excommunicate, and combat one another. The Temple at Jerusalem, the holy place of Judaism, furnishes us proof. Each time that it was built pagans were called upon to aid in its construction, just as they were called upon to contribute to the construction of the tabernacle in the desert. Hiram, the pagan king of Tyre, took part in the building of the Temple of Solomon, and Cyrus participated in the building of the second Temple. In the dedication of the Temple which is contained in Solomon's prayer, the contribution of pagans to the life of the Temple is not limited merely to its construction.

"Moreover, concerning a stranger, that is not of thy people Israel, but cometh out of a far country, for thy name's sake;

"(For they shall hear of thy great name, and of thy strong hand, and of thy arm stretched out); when he shall come and pray toward this house;

"Hear thou in heaven thy dwelling place, and do according to all that the stranger asketh thee for" (I Kings 8:41–43).

Thus non-Jewish "sympathizers," as we should call them in today's political jargon, were admitted as if by the law of Noah to the interior of the sanctuary, to mingle their prayers and their sacrifices with those of the Jews. Did this make for a regrettable confusion, for one of those dubious syncretisms which by rounding the corners eliminates the contours of truth and the features of the divine face? Not at all! Inside the Temple which they helped to build, the sanctuary where it was normal for them to say their own prayers and offer their own sacrifices, the Noachites had a place of their own and were allowed to celebrate their own ritual. "Just as they had a designated place in the Temple, so also were they allowed to participate in the worship, bringing their own sacrifices with them."

The distinction between Noachic and Mosaic practices was substantiated by the architectural plan of the Temple and by the spiritual concept behind it—that is, by the division of the various categories of worshipers, from pagans to Jews. Architecturally, as I have elsewhere described it, the Temple had three sections between the doors and the Holy of Holies at the center. To the first section, the *ar abbait*, Gentiles or, as we have chosen to call them, Noachites, were admitted without question of their beliefs. Next came the Court of Israel, into which only the observers of the Mosaic Law, the Jews, were allowed to enter. The third section or "vestibule" was reserved for the priests, direct descendants of Aaron. In the center of this was the Holy of Holies, where once a year on Yom Kippur, the Day of Atonement, the high priest alone penetrated in order to pronounce the holy name, at all other times unspeakable, of the Most High. In order that the words which the high priest said should not be heard it was proper and indeed necessary that from the surrounding sections of the Temple they be drowned out by the prayers of the worshipers of the various categories, all of whom, from near and far, were turned toward the sanctuary at this sacred moment. The purpose of the prayers was not only to invoke God but also to conceal His name. To this escalation of the Temple worship there corresponded an equally definite differentiation within the religious society of the period. Salvation was open and freely offered to all. "Mine house," says the prophet Isaiah, "shall be a house of prayer unto all people."

During the Feast of Tabernacles seventy calves were sacrificed in expiation of the sins of the Gentiles. But the hierarchical order which ran from unbelievers to strictly practicing Jews, from the laity to the priesthood, from those included in the law of Noah to those bound by the Law of Moses, was marked, at the time of the second Temple, by an even more complex differentiation.

Around or beside the Jews there were the proselytes, those who shared certain parts of the Covenant without subscribing to its totality or bearing its full burden. Among the proselytes there were two categories, ranked according to the extent of their acceptance of the Law. Those who worshiped at the outer limits of the Temple, near the threshold, both material and mystical, which separated the pagan community from that of Israel, were the "proselytes of the gate," the *ger-toshab* or *ger-ha-sha-ar*. These *ger*—pilgrims or strangers—were excused from obedience to the Mosaic Law and required only to practice the civic and moral virtues of the seven commandments of the rainbow Covenant. The Pentateuch allows them to eat the foods forbidden to Israel, which shows that there was no question of conversion. They had a definitely lay or secular status, outside the priestly vocation of the whole people of Israel, which did not cut them of their own. These were the "proselytes of justice," the right-path, one better fitted to their religious demands and devotions. Between them and the Jews, occupying a place closer to the sanctuary, was the other group of proselytes, stricter with themselves and hence nearer to the one God, even if they had deities of their own. These were the "proselytes of justice," the righteous ones, the *ger-zaddik*. Aside from the fact that they did not bear the mark of the Covenant in their flesh—in other words that they were not circumcised—they fully observed the Law, except in regard to certain rites reserved for the priestly families. In many ways they were on a level with the Israelites who belonged by birth to the *berith* or Covenant. According to the Talmud, they were allowed to marry Jews, with the exception of the descendants of Aaron.

There was, then, within Judaism, what we should call today a special statute for non-Jews, which was not based on superiority or inferiority, but on a specialization of the roles to be played by men in bringing about the advent of the Messiah. As Elie Benamozegh says, Noachism is at the very root of the Covenant. "Before Moses, Noachism was the religion of Israel. This term which still refers to the universal law and is applied to all those who serve it is, after the Mosaic Law and alongside the name of Israel, perhaps the most venerable thing in the world."

Ever since the long-ago time of its origin, which goes back to the very beginning of the biblical tradition, Noachism has haunted religious thought, as a theory or even as a concrete model. Maimonides, the great Jewish lawgiver of the Middle Ages, refers to it quite definitely. "Who is this *ger-toshab?*" he asks. "He is the Gentile neither circumcised nor baptized, who accepts the seven precepts of Noah." In our day, when the intolerant and exclusive quality of the revealed religions threatens to destroy them, when spiritual hunger is no longer peculiar to believers but is widespread, in extravagant but sincere forms, even among God's enemies, Noachism might well be the groundwork for a new and universal religious statute. After five thousand years, may not the rainbow Covenant shine again over a world of confusion?

6 *The God of Abraham*

With the patriarch Abraham we enter directly into history. Adam is a creature of fable or *midrash*, whose birth and life belong to a non-factual reality and derive more from the Babylonian myths or the folklore of primitive religions than from definite circumstances. The extraordinary moment of his appearance is not historical, and its importance lies in its moral and spiritual significance. The likelihood of his story does not matter; its truth is one that is revealed and transcendent. Neither the appearance of Adam himself nor the creation of the world has impressed itself upon our minds by its historical value. These events are outside time and place, but incontestable because of their absolute primacy.

With Noah the problem acquires more definite and objective

form. The man himself, the builder of the ark, was taken over by the Bible from Mesopotamian legends and his historical existence is subject to question. The Flood, as we have seen, did take place; archaeological discoveries have revealed its site and the extent of its duration. If Noah is a legend, the legend belongs to history. He marks an inportant first step taken by God in the direction of the concrete objectivity which, ever since biblical times, has appealed to the "stiff-necked" people of Israel and is demanded by the best minds of today. But the Midrash interpretation of the Flood is almost more interesting than the original story; Noah carries more weight in the traditional commentaries than he did as a real person, if such he was.

With Abraham everything changes. The famous summons from God, the *Lech Lecho* ("Get thee out of thy country and from thy kindred" Genesis 12:17), with its incisive syllables cutting across the text like a boundary stone at the threshold of a new and predestined area, and tearing the patriarch away from his hearth, his comfortable habits, and part of his family affections, marks the moment when the Bible story comes down to man's earth and writes itself into his society. Abraham is a historical character living in a historical time, as is confirmed by archaeological findings.

The historical account of an event or epoch contains two sorts of elements, chronological and topographical. The dates and duration of the events and the places where they happened must be specified. If the Bible is vague in regard to Abraham's chronology it is precise in regard to the places in which he had his being. It is not certain that Abraham lived a hundred and seventy-five years; it is doubtful that he was seventy-five years old (no age for setting out across the desert) when he undertook the adventure that God wished upon him. But such liberties with the years are common in the Bible, and of no importance; what matters is the relative duration of chronological periods, not the absolute figures. Time was not yet subdivided and marked off as it is in our day. The significant thing in Abraham's life is that God gave him a son when it was late for him to have any such expectation. It is the inner meaning of time that counts, not its calendar.

But when it comes to places, the Bible rivals a geography book, allowing us to trace his exact itinerary. It was from Ur, on the Euphrates River in Mesopotamia, that a family group of six members—Terah, Abraham's father, his sons Abraham and Nahor, their wives Sarah and Milcah, and his grandson Lot, whose father, Haran, had died prematurely—made their way to the northwest and after journeying for some six hundred miles in the region between the Euphrates and the Tigris, that is, in "the land between the rivers," Mesopotamia, settled in the city of Haran. Haran was a sister city to Ur, both of them capitals of the cult of the moon god Nanar, and the wanderers must have felt at home there. Numerous economic ties bound the two cities, both of which belonged to the Sumerian Empire; the road between them was the major commercial route between the Persian Gulf and the plateaus of Asia Minor. The Terahites—the family of Terah—had no more of a feeling of displacement than a Frenchman moving from Dunkerque to Marseille or an American moving from New York to San Francisco. They quickly put down roots in Haran; Terah died there and his sons and grandsons had children. But God's *Lech Lecho* drove Abraham to move on, this time to the southwest, toward Canaan.

The patriarch and his wife traveled for about nine hundred miles into Canaan, first paralleling the Mediterranean coast, passing through Sichem, Beth-el, and Guerar. Thence they made a detour into Egypt, but when they were within five or ten miles of the Nile delta they retraced their steps to Canaan and settled at Hebron, a "turntable" city at the junction of roads from north to south and from east to west. By this token Hebron became the "capital of the patriarchs," where Abraham lived for twenty-five years before the birth of Isaac. When his birth was imminent the patriarch went to live in the Negev, a desert region which he and his descendants populated and irrigated and made fertile in much the same way as has been done more recently by the modern state of Israel. It was at Beersheba, on the site of a modern desert metropolis, that Abraham died, leaving his children to stay on. Previously, at Dan, with an army of 318 men, he had conquered five Mesopotamian kings who invaded Canaan and had forced their withdrawal.

Such, then, according to the Bible, is the trail of Abraham's travels, as confirmed by contemporary archaeological discoveries which acquaint us with his daily life and make us almost enter into the intimacy of his family. The excavations made by Sir Leonard Woolley at Ur are the most revealing.

The Ur of today is no longer a city but a plain, studded with mounds and cultivated fields and scattered villages whose huts are made of mud or straw. The railway between Bagdad and the Persian Gulf neither stops there nor even goes near the site of the dead city, but passes by a mile away from its ruins. One mound, higher than the others, is called by the Arabs Tel el Mugayyar, the Hillock of Bitumen. It is made up of the remnants of the ziggurat of Ur, and from its summit there is a view of the ruins of another storied tower, that of the sacred city of Eridu, considered by the Sumerians to be the most ancient city in the world, which now looks out over an expanse of sand. In some such rare places there are signs of a three-thousand-year-old civilization. But Ur, the birthplace of Abraham, remained buried in the earth until 1922, when Sir Leonard Woolley began to take an interest in it.

In Abraham's time the royal city of Ur, with its spendid temples and 225-foot ziggurat, was the focal point of Mesopotamia. Arts, town-planning, letters, commerce, and industry were in full spate. All this Abraham abandoned at God's call. But in the midst of such brilliance Ur's power and even its independence were threatened by a rival dynasty, installed at Isin, which laid claim to the Sumerian heritage. Soon Ur was conquered and turned into a satellite. We must not imagine that the patriarch's emigration was an isolated phenomenon in a stagnant epoch. Abraham was born and lived in a revolutionary era when empires were in conflict and one civilization was in the process of supplanting another. At the beginning of the second millennium B.C. the Hittites drove the Amorites out of Babylon: Mursil I succeeded Hammurabi, the great religious legislator. We know from personal and recent experience that political turmoil inspires religious vocations. The exodus of Abraham and his family, in response to God's call, was determined by political as well as religious necessity.

But even in times of war and revolution walls remain and within them life goes on in apparent indifference to the storm raging outside. A city may lose its sovereignty or independence without the population necessarily feeling the consequences or in any way altering its habits. In the midst of the Russian Revolution, on the day when the Winter Palace of St. Petersburg was stormed and taken, posters advertising a concert by Chaliapin captured the attention of the passers-by, who were deaf to the clamor announcing the advent of a new world. Often only the passage of time and the gradual accomplishment of a historical evolution causes the contemporaries of a dramatic moment to become aware that they have lived through it.

The land of Mesopotamia, which has lost all traces of the revolutionary events for which it was the stage, has conserved those of everyday life, which no catastrophe could uproot. So the archaeological discoveries tell us. If Abraham does not appear, if no brick bears his name, if nothing records his personal destiny, there are, at least, traces of the city that he knew and of the commonplace problems of its inhabitants.

Here we are, at a period a hundred and fifty years before the patriarch's birth, under the walls and on the streets that he knew. Ur was a fortified city behind a wall of unbaked bricks held together by bitumen. After this old Sumerian foundation wall was destroyed the rampart was built over with temples and houses, which put a formidable obstacle in the way of an enemy trying to cross the canal around the city. In the houses armed men could be mobilized at short notice. Ur, then, was a fortress whose entrances were well guarded and could be sealed off in case of danger. Covered passageways led down to boats moored in the canal, which served to cross it. Even if all this warlike apparatus had lost its purpose by Abraham's time many remnants of it were left standing. Ur still looked like the type of fortified city of which Europe has so many examples, with narrow streets winding among a mass of houses huddled close together behind a surrounding wall. A few monuments—some religious, some civil—stood out amid this compact mass: the garden-sanctuary of Anu, king of the gods, and Nig-ga-ra-kom, the "great and royal treasury" of King Sinidinnam. At the far north end of the city a grandiose edifice, built on a terrace rimmed by white walls, towered over all the rest. This was the ziggurat, the many-tiered tower which, like the Sacred Heart of Montmartre, attracted the eyes of all beholders.

Because of this monumental construction Ur was visible from a great distance on the outlying plains. From the suburbs and environs vegetables were sent to the city. There were small family-owned farms, tilled by the owners, and great estates which required the services of numerous slaves. The harvests were dependent upon a network of irrigation canals. Some of these, barely anterior to Abraham, bore names evocative of their beneficent function: "the canal of food offerings" and "the beloved canal," named for Ur-Nammu, a benevolent king. Irrigation was one of the government's chief problems, for any deviation of the Euphrates or the least slackening of its flow was a cause of famine. Little by little the network of canals, large and small, was dug, in order to drain saturated areas and water dry ones. Dams were built to equalize the height of the river and to block floods. The development and maintenance of this elaborate system must have inspired many governmental deliberations and much talk on the part of the citizenry.

A complex and, for its time, advanced urban area was, then,

the background of Abraham's early years. He and his father and brother seem to have lived in the heart of the city. Terah was a dealer in idols, which is not a countryman's occupation but which fitted the double character of Ur as both a religious and a commercial center.

Before Abraham and his immediate family left Ur we can imagine him walking through the labyrinth of its tortuous streets, many of them blind alleys which were cut short by a compact mass of houses. These streets were unpaved and malodorous, for people threw their refuse and garbage outside and there were no street cleaners. Dusty in summer and muddy in winter, the surface of the streets was often so overlaid with refuse that front doors could not be opened and had to be cut away or else supplemented by side and back entrances. Middle-class houses, such as the one in which Abraham must have lived, although provided with a fair amount of comfort, were equally primitive. In Abraham's time there appears to have been a housing shortage. Times were hard, money scarce, and crumbling private houses were converted, as in our day, into shops and places of business. On the "Square of the Baker," where peddlers sold bread and other foods, a rich coppersmith called Gimil Ningishzida annexed the house next to his own, destroying the family chapel, installing ovens in the courtyard, and transforming the living quarters into a workshop.

Probably Abraham saw profanations of this kind as he walked about the city. As he left the Square of the Baker by a narrow alley he must have seen that the corner house had been equally remodeled. Originally a rich private dwelling, it had been split in two, with the street side transformed into a public chapel and the back into a bakery and restaurant, where ready-cooked dishes and loaves of bread were displayed on a counter. In the most crowded hours of the day the baker produced one crisp loaf after another, passing some of them through apertures in the wall to a restaurant set up in the courtyard. Perhaps this was a sort of cafeteria, Mesopotamian style, for the noon meal of the nearby coppersmith's workers.

Let us now pursue the itinerary which, with four thousand years between them, Abraham and Sir Leonard Woolley followed. On the long street which the English scholar named "Paternoster Street" we find a hotel, with a watchdog's kennel in front of it and storage space for travelers' luggage. We go through narrow, winding alleys where one can move only on foot or donkeyback, with steps on the wall from which clumsy riders could mount their donkeys. We find chapels dedicated to a variety of gods and a former private house transformed into a school. The number of school children was very small; only a dozen boys were learning to read and write on clay tablets spread out on the ground. On one side of the tablet the teacher wrote a word or phrase in cuneiform letters, which the pupil read, memorized, and copied on the other side. This method of teaching is not so very different from our own; it included dictation and punishments which consisted of writing a pious aphorism fifty times over. The teaching of science included arithmetic, square and cube roots, and exercises in practical geometry; grammar began with the complicated conjugation of Sumerian verbs. The aim of such an education was not only to prepare boys for the clergy, whose members were paid by the king to conduct public worship, but also for the liberal professions, which were much in demand in so highly developed a city.

In short, Ur was a civilized place, with between a quarter and half a million inhabitants and a large quantity of temples and chapels. The latter—hundreds in number—were used for family worship; a multitude of minor gods and goddesses supplemented the higher deities in granting small favors.

Trade and the arts and crafts also flourished. Their traces are reminiscent of the liberal economy of our own age. An importer of crude copper, growing old and wishing to retire, associated himself in Abraham's time with another man called Eanasir. The business consisted of transporting the crude metal from the mountains of Anatolia, which were considered at this time to be very far away. Purchasing agents in the mines bought the metal, loaded it on donkeys, and sent it to the Euphrates, where it was carried by barge to Ur. The agents had to receive written orders and to be paid by something like checks, which were difficult, in an unpoliced region, to convey safely to their destination. One of Eanisir's correspondents complained to him in these terms: "I have written to you five times without receiving an answer. How do you expect me to transact your business?"

International diplomacy ironed out the difficulties of private enterprise. Governments gave financial aid to businessmen and guaranteed the safety of their freight by trade agreements with the countries through which they had to pass. Already liberalism was threatened by government intervention. Abraham himself, when he bought the field of Ephron in Machpelah, paid for it with "four hundred shekels of silver, current money with the merchant" (Genesis 23:16).

Another evidence of the degree of Ur's civilization is in its administration of justice, publicly rendered at the door of a sanctuary near the ziggurat. Priests acted as judges and announced their decisions like divine decrees. After which the decisions were written on clay tablets and conserved inside. Besides appealing to this form of judgment the people had direct recourse to the sovereign in person. Abraham may have heard verdicts proclaimed to which he was a party; he may have been present at royal receptions. In any case he must have heard by word of mouth of some such solemnities.

In the courtyard of the ziggurat he doubtless assisted, in spite of his own religious beliefs, at the ceremony of ritual offerings to the god Nannar. Almost every day, through the great northwest gate, a crowd of donators brought, more or less spontaneously, baskets or parcels of wool and linen cloth, ingots of gold or copper or consignments of barley and cheese, loaded on the backs of donkeys. These were not merely pious offerings, for the god Nannar had farms, gardens, and houses of his own and levied a tax upon them, with his priests acting as collectors. At either side of the gate the priests weighed the offerings directed them toward the storerooms, and delivered double copies of receipts on clay tablets.

Participation in such formalities, half religious, half fiscal in nature, was no doubt obligatory for all the citizens, so that Terah, Abraham, and Nahor could not have escaped it. But aside from such civic duties the patriarch had no special reason for frequenting either the palace or the temple. Abraham's house must have been modest, even if it was provided with certain conveniences. He was not noble but a commoner. According to Sumerian law, society was divided into three classes: the *amelu*, or free men of a certain rank, such as priests, government officials, and army officers; the *mushkinu*, merchants, farmers, and members of the liberal professions; and slaves.

Abraham was a *mushkinu*—that is, a member of the middle class—and his house must have been of the average kind which recent excavations show as filling the greater part of the city. Since hewn stone was unknown in Mesopotamia it was probably built on a baked brick foundation with mud-brick walls. For aesthetic reasons the change from one material to the other was concealed by a coat of plaster and whitewash. The house must have had two stories and some thirteen or fourteen rooms, laid out, as in the Arab towns of today, around a courtyard which kept out the heat and provided light and air.

Abraham entered the house by a narrow hall with a trough in the floor where he could wash the dust and dirt of the street from his feet and hands. Passing through the courtyard, he came to the brick stairway leading to the upper story; behind the stairs there was a toilet with a terra-cotta drain. On the ground floor there was a sort of living room with two doors and a broad bay. Here also was a room for the servants, and a private chapel. All the ground-floor rooms opened onto the courtyard. The rooms on the second story were laid out according to the same plan.

Since Abraham's house was also that of his wife it contained a large ground-floor kitchen, which we can distinguish even today by the traces of a chimney and the marks left by millstones. The kitchen equipment was relatively complete. Open stoves with circular vent pipes were commonly used. The surface was pierced by small holes, over which the caldrons in which food was cooked were placed for heating. Water was boiled over an open fire in a fireplace and meat was cut on a brick table. At a remove of four thousand years we can imagine the homely gestures of the patriarch's wife, the savory odor, long since vanished, of the food, and the pride she took in her housekeeping.

It was this household, all this domestic comfort, that Abraham was twice called upon by the fatal *Lech Lecho*—first at Ur and then at Haran—to leave behind him. God's summons did not find him in an abstract existence or in an atmosphere of complete religious mysticism or devotion. Unlike Moses, Abraham was not an initiate, nor was he a priest. It was within the framework of his everyday life and customary occupations that this man of faith and action shaped his divinely inspired decisions. Although the decisive impelling force was God's call, this doubtless fitted in with political and economic considerations; his extraordinary vocation was built on the human necessities of the time and place in which he lived, which affected in equal measure his fellow citizens at Ur and Haran. It was out of the background of a pagan and polytheistic society that he sought for divine truth. Although he is definitely a biblical Jew, his life has two facets, one immanent, the other transcendent.

When Abraham left the urban civilization first of Ur and then of Haran for the rural and backward land of Canaan he did not make a complete break with the past. It was on a Sumerian basis that he built his new personal life and paved the way for the Covenant and, indeed, for the whole biblical story.

We have seen how Babylonian myths passed into the Bible, acquiring there a new spiritual and moral significance. Abraham was one of the implementers of this passage; his migration from Mesopotamia to Canaan was a contributory factor to the whole process of evolution. He took with him not only his household goods but also a spiritual baggage of religious traditions, among them the myths of the creation and the Flood. He took with him also the legislation of Ur, which was to influence certain biblical laws, including the precepts of the Torah. Abraham was, in short, the first missionary. He took with him religious demands which the country of his origin could not satisfy and also a body of ideas and customs which he introduced to his new dwelling place.

Before his departure from Ur and even along the way it seems as if Abraham's religious thought was colored by the polytheism of the cults of Ur. A verse from the book of Joshua (24:2) implies as much: "Your fathers dwelt on the other side of the flood in old time, even Terah, the father of Abraham, and the father of Nachor: and they served other gods." Melchizedek, a non-Jewish priest of the region, as we have seen, called down upon the patriarch the blessing of a Mesopotamian god, El-elyon, the Most High. Other names given to this god prefigure those of the Jewish liturgy: "Creator of Creation" and "I, Father of the Years," correspond to the term El-olam, "Everlasting God," with which Abraham called upon the Lord at Beer-sheba (Genesis 21:33), and which is still used in the prayers of the synagogue today.

The famous story of the sacrifice of Isaac reflects a Mesopotamian custom. When "Abraham went and took the ram and offered him up for a burnt offering in the stead of his son" (Genesis 22:13) he was following the example of the Sumerians, who had long since substituted the sacrifice of an animal for that of a man.

This is true also of the story of Jacob's ladder, with its picture of traffic between heaven and earth: "Behold a ladder set up on the earth, and the top of it reached to heaven: and behold the angels of God ascending and descending on it" (Genesis 28:12). This closely recalls what went on at the ziggurat of Ur, with which Abraham was familiar. At the top of this many-tiered tower there was a sanctuary called "heaven," and a procession of priests continually went up to the abode of the moon god and down again. So Jacob's dream, like those of all of us, was woven out of reality, in this case out of something he had either seen with his own eyes or heard about from his grandfather.

Abraham's treatment of Hagar, the second wife whom he took while Sarah was sterile and repudiated after Sarah had borne him a son, is in accord with the code of Hammurabi. We have thus seen three instances of memories or customs which Abraham took with him in his migration and which prove that there was no rupture but rather continuity between his life at Ur and his life in Canaan. As we have already hinted, the migration had social and economic causes. The move undertaken by Terah and Abraham and their families seems to have been one of a whole series of departures. We may wonder whether there was at Ur a sudden tendency to racism or xenophobia, or whether Abraham was influenced by purely personal considerations. It is not improbable that Terah dealt not only in idols but also in camels used for the transportation of freight. Around Ur traffic must have been impeded by the presence of the conquering troops of Hammurabi, whereas in Canaan conditions were more normal from this point of view. Terah and Abraham may have decided to move their business farther north. In any case history was to give them reason. A century after Abraham's departure, around 1885 B.C. when, according to the biblical way of measuring time, Abraham should have still been alive, Ur was destroyed by the Babylonians, and with it, no doubt, the houses and places of business of Abraham and his father.

When he came to Haran, and even more so in Canaan, Abraham must have enjoyed the prestige of a man from a big city. At the same time a certain distrust must have fallen upon him there. Country people naturally suspect city dwellers of sophistication and even vice. One way or the other, Abraham must have impressed the people of the town of Hebron. He knew how to

THE GOD OF ABRAHAM 145

read and write, was acquainted with a system of laws, had set foot in the pagan temples, and rubbed shoulders with the soldiery and police force of the conquerors. And, obviously, there was the aura of his divine mission around him. The Canaanites must have looked to him for leadership, and his victory at Dan over the Mesopotamian kings could only have enhanced their respect and their appreciation of the experience with which his background had supplied him. The sophistication of Ur causes us to imagine Abraham as less simple than his biblical portrait. Recent excavations give us some idea of the luxury and sometimes dubious elegance which Abraham must have seen among the upper class of his native city.

Sir Leonard Woolley and his wife made a plaster model, molded from a skeleton, of a great lady of this time in all her magnificence, and this figure of four thousand years ago has some definitely disturbing features. She is beautiful, to be sure, and the passage of the centuries has stylized her presumed traits. A broad nose, with the nostrils open to odors and perfumes, full, sensual lips, heavy-lidded and made-up eyes and, most conspicuous of all, a complex coiffure, consisting of a skillfully padded wig with a gold ribbon running through it. This elaborate and artificial arrangement is further complicated by three garlands, also of gold. The first, a chain of disks, hangs over the forehead; the second is of beech leaves, the third of willow leaves, interspersed with blue and white petaled flowers, both these last mounted on chains of lapis lazuli and coral. At the back of the head are a five-pointed gold comb tipped with gold flowers and a lapis lazuli heart. Then there are gold bands worked into the tresses of the wig and crescent-shaped gold earrings hanging down to the shoulders, a string of beads and amulets, one representing a bull and the other a calf. . . . What thoughts were harbored beneath such elaborate trappings, what intrigues were conceived under this accumulation of gold and precious stones, bespeaking a highly artificial life and bewildering customs?

Of course Sarah wore no such pretentious contraptions and

did not undergo expensive beautification of this kind. But she and the patriarch lived in a society where great ladies chose to present themselves highly made up and disfigured. Among the common people, the *mushkinu*, there must have been amused and shocked talk of palace intrigues, certain confidences of the bedchamber, and of the sly and sophisticated ruses that have fed scandal sheets throughout the ages. The bewigged princess whom we have described above must have had stories to tell, and may well have been the heroine of some of them.

All this explains why, in the course of his missionary life, Abraham was guilty of certain tricks and compromises which would seem inconsistent with his calling were it not for the fact that they were characteristic of the time and of the city. What could be further from our idea of the father of all believers and closer to the image of the princess of Ur than the extraordinary and equivocal scene in which Abraham gives his wife to King Abimelech under the pretext that she is his sister?

"Then Abimelech called Abraham, and said unto him, What hast thou done unto us? and what have I offended thee, that thou hast brought on me and on my kingdom a great sin? thou hast done deeds unto me that ought not to be done. . . .

"And Abraham said, Because I thought, Surely the fear of God is not in this place; and they will slay me for my wife's sake.

"And yet indeed she is my sister; she is the daughter of my father, but not the daughter of my mother; and she became my wife" (Genesis 20:9–12).

A way of reasoning that reflects the customs of an oriental court, inclined to polygamy, rather than the precepts of the Law of which Abraham was the forerunner.

And Abraham's descendants behaved in the same way. However holy were the patriarchs Isaac and Jacob, there are episodes in their lives which conflict radically with the precepts of God. When Jacob, taking advantage of his old father Isaac's blindness, disguised himself so as to be taken for Esau, he fraudulently received a blessing intended for his brother. The Scriptures give us a bit of high comedy, perhaps taken from some profane story current at the time.

"And Isaac said unto Jacob, Come near, I pray thee, that I may feel thee, my son, whether thou be my very son Esau or not.

"And Jacob went near unto Isaac his father; and he felt him, and said, The voice is Jacob's voice, but the hands are the hands of Esau.

"And he discerned him not, because his hands were hairy, as his brother Esau's hands: so he blessed him.

"And he said, Art thou my very son Esau? And he said, I am" (Genesis 27:21–24).

In short, when God entrusted Abraham with his mission He accepted him for what his native city had made him. This was something new in the history of God. Before this the men through whom He manifested His designs may have been docile or rebellious, but they existed only in relation to His will. Adam and Noah have sacrcely any personal life outside their connection with the Eternal, whose plans they carry out or oppose; they exist only in and through the Bible. Their lives served to set forth a spiritual adventure which was not so much their own as it was that of the human race.

With Abraham, God addressed Himself for the first time to a real man, with good qualities and bad, with a geographical and social background, with all the complex and conflicting tendencies of his individual life and that of his contemporaries. This is an essential part of the divine paradox, a decisive moment of God's presence on earth and His insertion into history. Adam and Noah were created by God to worship Him, but Abraham was given independence. He lived a three-dimensional life of his own, in the world and time of man. God's will did open to him the diaphanous yet concrete fourth dimension of the spirit, of revelation and the expectation of the Messiah. But he remains firmly planted in history; here it was that he fulfilled a destiny whose sublime character does not exclude reality and even vulgarity.

In choosing to act through a historical character God confirmed His entrance into history. This was the dough into which He injected the leaven, but the dough was solid and resistant, indeed corruptible. God consented to meet, on the road which He had traced and on which man walked beside Him, all the stumbling blocks and errors of which man is capable. At the time of the Garden of Eden and even of the ark He was God Almighty. With Abraham He became the true and existential God, whose influence may be thwarted by the inherent weaknesses of the human condition, weaknesses which He deplores and combats but also accepts, without which He would have had no need to create Adam or the world.

With Abraham we have the real beginning of the Bible story, with all its objective detail and sacred significance. There is something prodigious about this moment in the commonplace life of an obscure Mesopotamian, when the mystery of God shone forth and transfigured history.

The Jews of the time did not write history like Romans or like the Latinized historians of modern times. Most of us, when we read the Pentateuch or the Gospels, are tempted to look at the events thereof as if they actually took place just as they are narrated. Exegetes compare the texts of the Gospels and try to explain or iron out the differences among them. With the Old Testament it is the same thing. Scholars often attempt to interpret miracles by purely natural causes and to wipe away the discrepancies in the Genesis stories by tracing them back to their sources. Priests and laymen, believers and unbelievers all employ a positivistic method and try to prove the material exactitude of the events related.

The first editors and commentators of the Bible were not Latins but Semites, and they did not proceed in this way. For them there were three levels in the sacred story. First, a basis of actual facts—geographical and chronological—which have no spiritual or religious significance but provide the framework in which events took place. Second, the part of God—that is, the use which God made of material facts to manifest His design, to give a meaning to history so that it should not be a mere empty framework but a magnetic field with an interplay of forces and intentions, a permanent miracle in which the messianic dimension was added to the three dimensions of everyday life. This transcendent intervention on the part of God heightens and transfigures reality without denying or disfiguring it. It is shown forth in the text of the Bible itself. Third, the contribution of men and of the tradition, of commentators working on the text of the revelation, comparing the verses of the books of the Law with those of the books of the prophets, with the Psalms and the book of Job. By adding to these the reactions of the human mind they continuously retouched the text written for eternity. The commentaries of the Old Testament are the Midrash and the Talmud, and they are not written into the text but around the margin. God's design had transformed mere events into something greater, and this men respected, only making it more familiar and understandable. To the grandiose symphony of the Bible their commentary added the minute and subtle counterpoint of the human mind. With its stories, in turn familiar, dramatic, humorous, and philosophical, it embodied man's contribution to the Scriptures and to history.

Thus the sacred story and perhaps history itself are composed of an objective base and two transpositions. The purpose is no longer merely to narrate facts but to show how they are transfigured by God and commented upon by man. This puts the problem of truth in a new light. To a Semite the truth of the Bible sometimes gives way to probability: the nature of the facts counts less than their significance. An event is real if it shows forth the divine will or inspires a human explanation, even if its chronology and topography are not faultlessly exact. The historical truth of a fact is not written into the material world, that of everyday life and science, but into a universe interpreted by human intelligence and influenced by the spirit.

The episode of Abraham, marking God's first direct and absolute insertion into history, illustrates the distribution of facts, divine inspiration, and human commentary. In this way it is typical of many Bible stories.

First the facts, the historical basis which has been confirmed by archaeological discoveries. These come out at once in the account of Abraham's civic status and genealogy.

". . . Terah begat Abram, Nahor and Haran; and Haran begat Lot.

"And Haran died before his father Terah in the land of his nativity, in Ur of the Chaldees.

"And Abram and Nahor took them wives: the name of Abram's wife was Sarai; and the name of Nahor's wife, Milcah, the daughter of Haran, the father of Milcah and the father of Iscah.

"But Sarai was barren; she had no child.

"And Terah took Abram his son, and Lot the son of Haran his son's son and Sarai his daughter in law, his son Abram's wife; and they went forth with them from Ur of the Chaldees, to go into the land of Canaan; and they came into Haran, and dwelt there" (Genesis 11:27–31).

The facts come out again in the details of Abraham's migrations and in certain incidents that took place along the way.

"And Abram passed through the land unto the place of Sichem, unto the plain of Moreh. . . .

"And there was a famine in the land and Abram went down into Egypt to sojourn there; for the famine was grievous in the land. . . .

"And Abram went up out of Egypt, he, and his wife, and all that he had, and Lot with him, into the south. . . .

"And Lot also, which went with Abram, had flocks, and herds and tents.

"And the land was not able to bear them, that they might dwell together. . . .

"And there was a strife between the herdmen of Abram's cattle and the herdmen of Lot's cattle. . . .

"And Abram said unto Lot, Let there be no strife, I pray thee, between me and thee, and between my herdmen and thy herdmen; for we be brethren.

"Is not the whole land before thee? separate thyself, I pray thee, from me: if thou wilt take the left hand, then I will go to the right; or if thou depart to the right hand, then I will go to the left. . . .

"Then Lot chose him all the plain of Jordan; and Lot journeyed east; and they separated themselves the one from the other.

"Abram dwelled in the land of Canaan. . . ." (Genesis 12:6–13:10:1–12).

The episode seems to have been written at first hand and is probably historical. In other passages it seems as if the facts were fragmentary, taken from experience or observation, but in a transcendent context.

Alongside the facts there intervenes the element of God. Abraham was, in his time, the only man to whom God spoke directly, without the intermediary of an angel. The words God addresses to the patriarch are sublime and pregnant with meaning. Here is his first summons to Abraham, opening the wide perspective of his destiny before him:

"Now the Lord had said unto Abram, Get thee out of thy country, and from thy kindred, and from thy father's house, unto a land that I will shew thee:

"And I will make of thee a great nation, and I will bless thee, and make thy name great, and thou shalt be a blessing:

"And I will bless them that bless thee, and curse him that curseth thee; and in thee shall all families of the earth be blessed" (Genesis 12:1–3).

At every crucial moment of his existence Abraham reaped the benefit of God's intervention in the history of man. After his campaign against the Mesopotamian kings, which is doubtless based on historical facts, God promised him His protection: "Fear not, Abram: I am thy shield, and thy exceeding great reward" (Genesis 15:1).

But it is in Genesis 17, after the birth of Ishmael, the son born to him of the slave girl Hagar, that Abraham receives the Covenant. With a solemnity which reverberates down the centuries God raised material contingencies to a sublime level and inserted Himself into history forever.

". . . The Lord appeared to Abram and said unto him, I am the Almighty God; walk before me, and be thou perfect.

"And I will make my covenant between me and thee, and will multiply thee exceedingly.

"And Abram fell on his face: and God talked with him, saying,

"As for me, behold, my covenant is with thee, and thou shalt be a father of many nations.

"Neither shall thy name any more be called Abram, but thy name shall be Abraham; for a father of many nations have I made thee.

"And I will make thee exceeding fruitful, and I will make nations of thee, and kings shall come out of thee.

"And I will establish my covenant between me and thee and thy seed after thee in their generations for an everlasting covenant, to be a God unto thee and to thy seed after thee.

"And I will give unto thee, and to thy seed after thee, the land wherein thou art a stranger, all the land of Canaan, for an everlasting possession; and I will be their God.

"And God said unto Abraham, Thou shalt keep my covenant before thee, and thy seed after thee in their generations.

"This is my covenant, which ye shall keep, between me and you and thy seed after thee: Every man child among you shall be circumcised. . . .

". . . He that is born in thy house, and that is bought with thy money, must needs be circumcised: and my covenant shall be in your flesh for an everlasting covenant" (Genesis 17:1–10, 13).

After this God intervened again, in defiance of the laws of nature, in the destiny of the patriarch and his wife. The birth of Isaac to the hundred-year-old Abraham and the ninety-year-old Sarah showed, as God himself said, that nothing was too hard for Him and that when He wills it His action determines the course of human events.

"And the Lord appeared unto him in the plains of Mamre; and he sat in the tent door in the heat of the day;

"And he lift up his eyes and looked, and lo, three men stood by him: and when he saw them, he ran to greet them from the tent door, and bowed himself toward the ground. . . .

". . . And they said unto him, Where is Sarah, thy wife? And he said, Behold, in the tent.

"And he said, I will certainly return unto thee according to the time of life; and lo, Sarah thy wife shall have a son. And Sarah heard it in the tent door, which was behind him.

"Now Abraham and Sarah were old and well stricken in age; and it ceased to be with Sarah after the manner of women.

"Therefore Sarah laughed within herself, saying, After I am waxed old shall I have pleasure, my lord being old also?

"And the Lord said unto Abraham, Wherefore did Sarah laugh, saying, Shall I of a surety bear a child, which am old?

"Is any thing too hard for the Lord? At the time appointed I will return unto thee, according to the time of life, and Sarah shall have a son.

"Then Sarah denied, saying, I laughed not, for she was afraid. And he said, Nay; but thou didst laugh" (Genesis 18:1–2, 9–15).

Sarah's astonishment and joy were enhanced by the element of the supernatural, but retained, nonetheless, the natural quality of rejoicing over the everyday miracle of the birth of a new human being. And after this two other extraordinary episodes bear further witness to God's intervention in the facts of history. The first is the surprising dialogue between God and Abraham when the latter interceded on behalf of Sodom, which God was threatening to destroy for its sins. On this occasion God had decided to come down to earth to investigate the sins of the Sodomites.

"And the Lord said, Because the cry of Sodom and Gomorrah is great, and because their sin is very grievous;

"I will go down now, and see whether they have done altogether according to the cry of it, which is come unto me; and if not, I will know" (Genesis 18:20–21).

In the course of His investigation God was joined by Abraham, and the dialogue between them is one of the most daring and at the same time the most down to earth that a creature has ever had with his Creator. Abraham was not at all paralyzed by respect or fear; he spoke out like a man, aware of human problems, giving God the benefit of his earthly experience.

"And Abraham drew near, and said, Wilt thou also destroy the righteous with the wicked?

"Peradventure there be fifty righteous within the city: will thou also destroy and not spare the place for the fifty righteous that are therein?

"That be far from thee to do after this manner, to slay the righteous with the wicked; and that the righteous should be as the wicked, that be far from thee: Shall not the Judge of all the earth do right?

"And the Lord said, If I find in Sodom fifty righteous within the city, then I will spare all the place for their sakes.

"And Abraham answered and said, Behold now, I have taken upon me to speak unto the Lord, which am but dust and ashes:

"Peradventure there shall lack five of the fifty righteous: wilt thou destroy all the city for lack of five? And he said, If I find there forty and five I will not destroy it.

"And he spake unto him yet again, and said, Peradventure

there shall forty be found there, And he said, I will not do it for forty's sake.

"And he said unto him, Oh let not the Lord be angry, and I will speak: Peradventure there shall thirty be found there. And he said, I will not do it, if I find thirty there.

"And he said, Behold now, I have taken upon me to speak unto the Lord: Peradventure there shall be twenty found there. And he said, I will not destroy it for twenty's sake.

"And he said, Behold now, I have taken upon me to speak yet but this once: Peradventure ten shall be found there. And he said, I will not destroy it for ten's sake.

"And the Lord went his way, as soon as he had left communing with Abraham; and Abraham returned unto his place" (Genesis 18:23–33).

Each of them kept his own place, God in heaven and Abraham on earth, but their meeting was beneficial because a human element influenced the decision of God.

In this continuous osmosis between the will of divine Providence and human reality, the most impressive and dramatic episode of all is the sacrifice of Isaac. Rarely have so much human tenderness, so much realism and sublimity come together in a single story.

"And it came to pass after these things, that God did tempt Abraham, and said unto him, Abraham: and he said, Behold, here I am.

"And he said, Take now thy son, thine only son Isaac, whom thou lovest, and get thee into the land of Moriah; and offer him there for a burnt offering upon one of the mountains which I will tell thee of.

"And Abraham rose up early in the morning, and saddled his ass, and took two of his young men with him, and Isaac his son, and clave the wood for the burnt offering, and rose up, and went unto the place of which God had told him.

"Then on the third day Abraham lifted up his eyes, and saw the place afar off.

"And Abraham said unto his young men, Abide ye here with the ass and I and the lad will go yonder and worship, and come again to you.

"And Abraham took the wood of the burnt offering, and laid it upon Isaac his son; and he took the fire in his hand, and a knife; and they went both of them together.

"And Isaac spake unto Abraham his father, and said, My father: and he said, Here am I, my son. And he said, Behold the fire and the wood: but where is the lamb for a burnt offering?

"And Abraham said, My son, God will provide himself a lamb for a burnt offering: so they went both of them together.

"And they came to the place which God had told him of; and Abraham built an altar there, and laid the wood in order, and bound Isaac his son, and laid him on the altar upon the wood.

"And Abraham stretched forth his hand, and took the knife to slay his son.

"And the angel of the Lord called unto him out of heaven, and said, Abraham, Abraham: and he said, Here I am.

"And he said, Lay not thine hand upon the lad, neither do thou any thing unto him: for now I know that thou fearest God, seeing that thou hast not withheld thy son, thine only son from me.

"And Abraham lifted up his eyes, and looked, and behold behind him a ram caught in a thicket by his horns: and Abraham went and took the ram, and offered him up for a burnt offering in the stead of his son" (Genesis 22:1–13).

When we read them in their entirety these extraordinary verses furnish us a revealing experience of biblical history. We learn from the concrete details much about the customs of the time: how an ass was saddled and wood cut and fire prepared for a sacrifice. We find also a picture of God in action, bringing His influence to bear upon the life of the man with whom He had struck the Covenant and testing his faith. God's part in the story transcends facts and customs; it allows the patriarch to show, under exceptional circumstances, both his fatherly tenderness and his obedience to God. In its stark simplicity this story needs no comment. And yet the reader may wish to revitalize it, to find answers to the questions which it has provoked through the centuries, to look into the heart of Abraham during those terrible moments when he first feared the worst for his child and then had the supreme joy of knowing that he was spared, to understand the underlying meaning of every gesture and happening. What is the significance of the ram, of the thicket? What is there in the life of Abraham that has a bearing on our own? How does this magnificent story fit in with the rest of the Bible?

The answers to these questions make up men's contribution to the story of the patriarchs. Human commentators do not seek to rival the principal writer, who is God, but rather to enlarge and complete it, to fill in the gaps and make it more human. When it comes to Abraham, the father of all believers and the initiator of their history, we have an abundant commentary, running the whole scale of human values, from the intimate to the pathetic to the supernatural.

The Midrash—for this is the commentary to which we refer —seeks first to detail the circumstances of Abraham's vocation. No questions need be raised about the decisive moment when God enjoined him to leave his home and family and respond to the divine call. But before the *Lech Lecho* was it not with Abraham as with any man slated for a great mission? Did no preliminary happenings foreshadow his exceptional destiny and enable us to better understand it?

The Midrash first shows us Abraham in the shop of his father, the idol-maker of Ur. Obliged to absent himself from the shop, Terah instructed Abraham to deal with chance customers. There was no reason to suppose that anything out of the way would happen. However Abraham may have felt about the objects of his trade, he had practical motives for doing business as usual.

Into the shop came a customer, of Terah's age rather than

Abraham's, who asked to see an idol. To this obvious question Abraham countered with one, quite unexpected, of his own. "How old are you?" "Fifty." "Woe unto you! You are fifty years old, and you want to worship an object that dates from only yesterday?" The customer, discomfited, went away without making a purchase.

Next came a woman with a plateful of flour which she wanted Abraham to offer to the gods. "Take this," she said to him, "and sacrifice it to the idols." Then Abraham took a stick and smashed the idols, while the woman ran away in a panic, leaving the flour behind her.

Terah came back to find his shop a shambles. "What have you done?" he asked. Imperturbably Abraham explained that a woman had left some flour for the idols, that they had quarreled about which one of them was to receive it and the strongest of them had broken the others.

"You're making fun of me," said Terah. "I made the idols and I know them well. They have no intelligence." "Father, may your ears be preserved from hearing the words of your lips! You worship these idols, and yet you say they have no intelligence."

After this scandal Terah led Abraham before Nimrod, the pagan king. The king, accustomed perhaps to resolving young boys' crises of conscience, proposed a compromise solution, one in keeping with the customs of the times.

"Let us worship fire," he said blandly. But he had not reckoned with the frankness and quick wit of Abraham. "Why should we not worship water?" Abraham proposed. "Since water puts out fire it is stronger." "Good," said Nimrod conciliatingly; "let us worship water." "Should we not rather worship the clouds, which bring water?" "Good, let us worship the clouds." But Abraham pursued his exercise in dialectics. "Rather than the clouds, should we not worship the wind, which disperses them?" "Good, let us worship the wind," said Nimrod, who was willing to compromise as long as something was left for him to worship. But Abraham had not finished. "Rather than the wind, should we not worship men, who are able to stand up against the wind and break its power?"

But the worship of men was something to which Nimrod could not consent.

"You're simply stringing words together," he said to Abraham. "Let's go back to the normal custom of worshiping fire. . . . I'm going to throw you into it; ask God to save you!"

A pyre was set up and ignited, in the sight of Terah, Abraham, who was ready to die for his beliefs, and Haran, his brother. Haran did not know which side to take. "If Abraham comes out alive from this trial, I shall say that I share his faith. If Nimrod is victorious I shall rally to him."

Abraham was thrown into the fire, but it refused to consume him. Then it was the turn of Haran. "What is your belief?" Nimrod asked. "The faith of Abraham," said the opportunistic Haran. Alas, Nimrod threw him into the flames and he was reduced to ashes.

And so Haran died, because he had attempted to trick God, while Abraham lived, because he had been faithful to Him. But he was not fully reassured. Certainly he had done the right thing in destroying the idols, but this did not obliterate the fact that by helping his father he had profited from their sale and forwarded their worship. Was he not quilty of idolatry? But God comforted him further. "All that was the dew of your youth. Just as the dew evaporates with the rising of the sun, so when you saw the light your sins were wiped away. . . . Rather, you must rejoice. Just as dew is a blessing to the earth so you in your time will be a blessing." Thus the father of all believers is close to believers and non-believers of every time and place who are concerned about their relationship to God. To doubting and undecided persons the Bible may seem too harsh, too black and white. The Midrash brings it down to a human level.

Upon later episodes of Abraham's life the Midrash throws the same realistic and humorous light. In Genesis 12:14 we are told that ". . . When Abraham was come into Egypt, the Egyptians beheld the woman [Sarah] that she was very fair." The Midrash tells us in detail of the clandestine way in which Abraham crossed the frontier. He had hidden Sarah in a chest, but a zealous customs guard insisted upon opening it. What was going to happen? How would sacred history be affected?

"You must pay duty," said the guard.

"I will pay," Abraham told him.

"Is there clothing in this chest?"

"I will pay for the clothing."

"Are there silks?"

"I will pay for the silks."

"Precious stones?"

"I will pay for the precious stones."

But this docility did not induce the customs guard to forgo an inspection.

"I must open up the chest and see what is inside."

The minute the chest was opened the beauty of Sarah fanned out over the Egyptian land. Tradition has it that throughout history the likeness of Eve is transmitted to the most beautiful woman of every generation, and Sarah was even more beautiful than Eve in person. The customs guard could do nothing but bow and let her go by.

But the tone of the Midrash is not exclusively humorous and realistic. Its stories form a link between one episode of the Bible and another; at every moment the commentators take the whole text into consideration and establish references between the books of the Law and those of the prophets, between a verse of the Psalms and a verse of the book of Job.

Abraham's obedience to God had consequences of which he himself was unaware but which the Midrash reveals to us. The whole history of the world was affected. By consenting to sacrifice his son to God Abraham made possible the further accomplishment of God's will. Had he not obeyed, the Covenant would have been invalidated before its results could be made manifest; moral chaos would have diverted the providential course of history. In commenting upon the sacrifice of Isaac the Midrash weaves a crown of other instances in the Bible of God's intervention in human affairs.

It was because Abraham consented to sacrifice his son that God was able to order Moses to receive the Law. "And he said unto Moses, Come unto the Lord, thou, and Aaron, Nadan and Abihu, and seventy of the elders of Israel; and worship ye afar off" (Exodus 24:1).

Equally related to Abraham's act of obedience is the birth of the prophet-judge Samuel: "And they rose up in the morning early, and worshiped before the Lord, and returned, and came to their house to Ramah: and Elkanah knew Hannah his wife; and the Lord remembered her.

"Wherefore it came to pass, when the time was come about after Hannah had conceived, that she bare a son, and called his name Samuel, saying Because I have asked him of the Lord" (Samuel 1:19–20).

And again, Isaiah's prophecy of the ingathering of the Children of Israel: "And it shall come to pass in that day, that the great trumpet shall be blown, and they shall come which were ready to perish in the land of Assyria, and the outcasts in the land of Egypt, and shall worship the Lord in the holy mount at Jerusalem" (Isaiah 27:13). This verse of Isaiah is linked, in its turn, to Psalm 99:9: "Exalt the Lord our God, and worship at His holy hill: for the Lord our God is holy."

Thus all the decisive consequences of God's Covenant with man would have been impossible without Abraham's action; from the moment when he consented to the sacrifice required of him they were on the way to accomplishment. God's command to Abraham is an admirable example of the essential paradox of religion as it appears to men's eyes—at the same time unlikely and true, unjustifiable and necessary, incomprehensible and natural.

It was unlikely that, having promised Abraham a long line of

descendants, God should take away from him his only legiti-
mate son. It was unjustifiable that the God who had accepted
Abraham's plea in behalf of the good and just minority of Sodom should ask for the sacrifice of the innocent child of the
good man whom He had chosen as the vehicle of His will. It
was incomprehensible that Abraham should accept without protest an iniquitous demand which was in obvious contradiction
to what he knew of God's ways. Why did he not, once again,
raise his voice and compel his divine interlocutor to observe His
own Law?

For one thing, although God's order could not but outrage his
feelings, it was not contrary to the customs which he had seen
around him. Living sacrifices were commonplace in the land of
Canaan during Abraham's time. The nomad tribes of Israel ha-
bitually offered to God the first-born of their flocks, and Isaac
nay be regarded, not altogether unreasonably, as the first-born
of the future flock of Israel. The three days of the march of the
patriarch and his son to Moriah may have had elements of terror, but the prospects of what lay ahead were not completely
disconcerting. Such is the logic, on a humble level, of Abraham's
acceptance of a command so contrary to his whole being and to
what he had learned to believe was his mission.

But the essential fact of the drama is that, although it out-
raged Abraham's beliefs and seemed to undermine the very
foundations of the Covenant, it did not touch his confidence in
the *One* on whom his faith was centered. If the religion of the
Bible were a mere abstract statement of the rules of morality
and worship, the proclamation of disincarnate truths, Abraham
might well have refused to sacrifice his only son. But the religion
of the Bible is something very much alive. Its God is not a transcendent ghost invented by the human mind; He is a living personal God, who is written into history. In the face of a God who
ruled over him but with whom, at the same time, he felt a certain affinity Abraham was struck by the fear which is natural to a
soul in the presence of a superior will. But his confidence re-

mained unshaken; he knew that God's momentary illogic concealed an enduring order. For God *is* logical; His apparent inconsistency is of only a moment's duration. Abraham's submission was based, then, on both fear and confidence. It did not spring out of intellectual reasoning, but out of the conviction that in God's presence he was in touch with life and a participant in history. God had a personal existence, on a plane superior but nonetheless accessible.

At this important moment of the Bible story everything was resolved into a respect for the human person, into mutual understanding and affection. In the Bible it is as if the supreme law of loving one's neighbor as oneself is applicable also to the relationship between God and man, on condition that they be aware of one another's existence. God must be close to man if man is to believe in Him.

What an aura of wisdom there was about Abraham when he consented to sacrifice his son! What wide perspectives opened up around the sorrowing old man and the fearful boy! What repercussions echo from every gesture of the patriarch, from every word of his mouth and every decision! The contribution of man, through his commentary, enhances and widens the contribution of facts and events and that of God. All three are necessary to history, to the blend of objective and spiritual truths, of realism and predestination which goes to make up our existence.

With Noah, at the first stage of the Covenant, God indicated His supreme purpose: to obtain observance of the moral law by all men, believers and unbelievers. At the second stage, with Abraham, he chose the executor of His vast design and set the seal of His promise in his flesh. Abraham, the father of all believers and God's first servant, enjoyed not only His love but His respect as well.

A traditional story tells us that after Abraham had docilely submitted to circumcision he remained for several days at home in bed. God came to pay him a visit, but when Abraham started to get up to greet Him God told him to stay where he was while He, God, remained standing in his honor. After all, Abraham was a hundred years old, and the Law prescribes: "Thou shalt rise up before the hoary head, and honour the face of the old man. . . ." (Leviticus 19:32). By this attitude God signified to the patriarch that He accepted him for what he was, that He honored him in his own home and in the bosom of his family, that He trusted not only him but also his posterity—that is, all the men, faithful and unfaithful, who were to live out through the centuries the formidable adventure upon which God embarked when He inscribed Himself in history.

All this in a modest house, whose plan we have reconstructed, at the bedside of a man laid low because he had accepted the Covenant, a man whose weakness but also whose strength and dignity God knew. A story that is both intimate and sublime, wherein, between the patriarch's modest walls, the three components of history came together, the facts, man's commentary, and God's action, all shaping the truth as we know it.

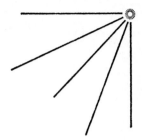

7   The God of Sinai

Five centuries and a half after the death of Abraham (which took place around 1800 B.C.) the Law was proclaimed from Sinai. The period was a troubled one, among both idolaters and the Chosen People, one of those turning points of history when upheavals and new departures are in the making. Within the range of a few decades we have Moses' ascent of Sinai, the rise of the Hittites, the decline of Egypt, the signing of the first international agreement, between the Hittite King Hattusil III and the Pharaoh Rameses II, the liberation of Assyria from Babylonia, and the Trojan War, whose myths have come down to us through the great epic of Homer. But none of these events of three thousand years ago has the importance of the exodus of a small nation from Egypt and its crossing, between the parted waters, of the Red Sea.

Here is the chronology of the historic week when the Children of Israel traveled out of their Egyptian bondage to Asia Minor, as it is perpetuated every year at the Passover season in the *haggadah* or ritual story, in which every Jew is told that he should look upon himself as having coming out of Egypt in person. In the telling of this decisive episode the contributions of historical facts, of the commentaries on them, and of God are commingled.

On the fifteenth day of the month of Abib, the first month of spring, the Hebrews left their homes in the region of Rameses early in the morning and arrived by evening at Succoth, some twenty miles away. There were 600,000 of them, besides the women and children, that is, 2,000,000 in all, about the same number as that of the population of the new state of Israel. With them there was a "mixed multitude" (Exodus 12:38) of sympathizers who, in the course of the captivity, had linked their fate with that of the Chosen People.

This mass of men was all the more extraordinary in that it was not armed. The Hebrews' last night in Egypt was spent not in sharpening swords or spears but in offering prayers and sacrifices to God. Faith in the Lord and obedience to His orders, as they were transmitted by His appointed leader, were the only defenses of the vulnerable migrants. And the only ceremony that marked their departure was the symbolical yet real last meal, the Jewish *seder* celebrated through the centuries and in our own day, which passed into Jesus' Last Supper and the Christian Eucharist.

On the evening of the fifteenth day of Abib, at Succoth, the Israelites were joined by Moses and Aaron who, having been expelled from Pharaoh's kingdom, overtook them after a fifty-mile trip by horse or dromedary. The next day, after traveling fifteen more miles to the southeast, they came to the Egyptian part of the desert of Etham. After that two roads were open to them by which they could travel to Canaan. To the north there was a road along the Mediterranean coast, but since it went through territory occupied by the Philistines it would have entailed a combat for which they were not armed. The caravan route, twenty miles to the south, led through the desert of Paran. This the Children of Israel followed, making, at God's command, a slight detour farther south, to Sinai, which was to be justified by religious reasons.

On the seventeenth day they covered fourteen miles and came to Pi-hahiroth, near the Bitter Lakes, contiguous to the north end of the Red Sea. Pharaoh, informed of their itinerary, set out with his army at nightfall, in order to overtake and destroy them. For the next two days, unaware of the impending danger, the Israelites remained in their camp, awaiting further orders.

On the morning of the twentieth of Abib the threat became a reality. The Egyptian army was reported to be at Baal-zephon, blocking the Israelites' way to the Red Sea. Soon it was drawn up above Pi-hahiroth, casting the Israelites into a state of consternation in which they called upon God and inveighed against Moses:

"And they said unto Moses, Because there were no graves in Egypt hast thou taken us away to die in the wilderness? wherefore hast thou dealt thus with us, to carry us forth out of Egypt?

"Is not this the word that we did tell thee in Egypt, saying, Let us alone that we may serve the Egyptians? For it had been better for us to serve the Egyptians, than that we should die in the wilderness" (Exodus 14:11–12).

To which quite logical complaint Moses answered tartly: "The Lord shall fight for you, and ye shall hold your peace" (Exodus 14:14).

And indeed a pillar of luminous cloud stood between the two camps, making it impossible for the Egyptians to move to the attack. Then, in obedience to the Lord's command, Moses stretched his hand out over the Red Sea and it opened up before him. In the evening, at a place where it was no more than seven or eight miles wide, the Israelites walked through the sea on dry land, while a storm arose behind them. Toward midnight the Egyptian cavalry started in pursuit, with the storm raging around it. At two or three o'clock in the morning of the next day the Israelites reached the Palestinian side of the desert of Etham. Moses' promise to bring them to safety had come true, according to the Lord's schedule. And what of Pharaoh's cavalry? The heavy chariots sank into the sand which had borne the weight of the unarmed Hebrews, and soon chariots and horsemen alike were drowned in the returning waters. The foot soldiers, who had lingered in the camp at Pi-hahiroth, were dispersed by the storm and took to flight.

As we read this dramatic story we may ask ourselves how much of it is true and how much is just a long *midrash*, extolling the glory of God and the vocation of Israel. Actually it is both. Through all parts of the Bible, in the writings of Joshua, Esdras, Judith, David, Solomon, Isaiah, Jeremiah, Habakkuk, the author of the book of the Maccabees, Saint Luke, Saint Paul, and others, the truth of it seems to be taken for granted, without apology or explanation. Secular writers, on the other hand—scientists, philosophers, and historians—have divested the episode of all elements of the supernatural. For Spinoza the passage of the Red Sea was made possible by the all-night storm. For Joseph Salvador, the Israelites crossed over during an exceptionally low tide and the Egyptians were swallowed up by the high tide that followed. Moses, as a practiced camel driver, knew how to take advantage of the opportune moment, while the Egyptian leader miscalculated. Others maintain that because Moses was familiar with the whole Midian region he knew a ford by which to cross over.

Ferdinand de Lesseps, the builder of the Suez Canal, in a statement to the French Academy of Sciences on June 22, 1874, tried to prove the accuracy of the biblical account on the basis of his engineering experience.

"At the time when the Israelites were led out of Egypt by Moses, the tides of the Red Sea rose as high as the foot of the Serapeum, near Lake Timsah. As recently as eleven hundred years ago the Bitter Lakes were muddy red, and they have continued, intermittently, to be fed by the Red Sea. . . . When they no longer received this overflow except during the equinoctial or other exceptionally high tides, salt beds were formed. Today these salt beds have a weight of 100 million tons, the result of the evaporation of 63 billion cubic feet of water of the Red Sea. It is absolutely false to say that the isthmus of Suez was a solid mass. The passage of the Red Sea in Moses' time may have taken place north of Suez and not necessarily south of the present tip of the Red Sea."

What a huge volume of sea water and of human gray matter have been put to work to explain an event which theologians, geographers, geologists, and historians all debate without finding a definite answer!

Another illustrious person, not given to ideological or theological ponderings, a man who believed in the power of the individual to sway the course of history, chose to re-enact the passage of the Red Sea in order to explain it. On December 26, 1798, General Bonaparte, the future Napoleon, arrived at the head of his army at Suez. The next day he toured the city and the port, then, on the twenty-eighth, he decided to visit the so-called fountains of Moses. At eight o'clock in the morning, when the tide was low, he crossed the Red Sea into Asia Minor. After visiting the springs and talking with some Arab chiefs he started to return. Darkness had fallen and the tide was rising, and he was advised to camp out for the night on the shore. Bonaparte refused; he called his Arab guide and told him to lead the way. The guide, troubled by the responsibility for a man revered as a prophet, took the wrong road down to the shore, losing a quarter of an hour of precious time. When they were no more than halfway the rising tide began to lap the horses' feet. The little troop fell into disorder. General Caffarelli, whose wooden leg made it difficult for him to keep a firm seat in the saddle, called for help, and his outcry, interpreted as a signal of acute distress, completed the confusion. All the riders went off in different directions, while Bonaparte alone imperturbably followed the guide.

As the water continued to rise the horse took fright and refused to go on. "The situation was grave," writes Alexandre Dumas in his account of the exploit; "the least further delay was dangerous. One of [Napoleon's] escorts, a regular Hercules of a fellow, jumped into the water and carried the general on his shoulders, like a child, holding onto the tail of the Arab's horse. A moment later the water was up to his armpits and he began to lose his balance. The sea was still rising rapidly and the destiny of the world might have been altered by the death of a single man. Suddenly the Arab called out. He had reached the opposite shore. The escort fell onto his knees; now that his general was safe he was overcome by exhaustion. The little troop came back to Suez without the loss of a single man; only Bonaparte's horse was drowned."

Seventeen years later, when Napoleon was being taken as a prisoner, aboard the *Northumberland*, to St. Helena, he told this story to Las Cases, who wrote it down in his *Memorial*. "During an interval of leisure in Egypt the commanding general took advantage of the low tide to cross the Red Sea on dry land. On the way back he was overtaken by night and got lost in the rising tide. The danger was very great, and he very nearly perished like Pharaoh. 'It would have given the Christian preachers a splendid text to use against me,' Napoleon said gaily."

In this rendition the aging Napoleon unexpectedly echoed the Bible account. He confirmed the existence of facts of the kind that are so often at the base of a religious story. Implicitly he realized that the objective events of the Scriptures lend themselves not only to the glorification of God but also to men's interpretation.

This threefold character of biblical narration, of which the story of Abraham was the first example, stands out all the more clearly in the story of Moses and Mount Sinai. It is fascinating to see how one of the most impressive moments of God's intervention in earthly affairs fits into history.

The Hebrews had been for two centuries in Egypt, a long hiatus between two migrations, between two periods of persecution. The first century, under a liberal government, put Israel face to face with an enduring dilemma, whether to give up its faith and "integrate" or to hold onto it in isolation. The second century, at the beginning of the New Empire, was one of persecution, which caused Israel to recover awareness of its identity and finally to go into exile.

The first Israelites to go to Egypt were either fugitives attracted by the prospect of economic gain or prisoners of war. Voluntary or involuntary immigrants, they began by practicing so-called inferior trades: mining, road building, harvesting, and the raising of livestock. From father to son, in spite of disappointments, they began to raise their social status and enter the professions: first farming, winegrowing, and weaving, then government service and even the army. Assimilation seemed to be well under way, and many Israelites harbored the illusion that they would come to be part of the Egyptian nation. They passed for Egyptians, except for their religious practices, and many of them gave up not only these but also their language, the language of God. But soon the increase of their numbers and their success in the professions aroused xenophobia and racism.

Moses was born at the beginning of the period of persecution. At first, as is pointed out by André and Renée Néher, the Egyptian Jews were no more aware of what was happening to them than were the German Jews of the 1930s. By calling attention to the number of them who were native-born and to the civil and military services they had rendered their adopted country they thought to protect themselves against the impending threat. Even in this time of persecution some of them remained on good terms with their oppressors; they were given special privileges in return for acting as advisers or intermediaries.

Moses came into the picture at the moment when persecution was beginning to turn into genocide, at the moment when totalitarian measures were striking the Hebrew community, provoking surprise and protest among highly placed liberal Egyptians. The genocide prescribed by Pharaoh proceeded in gradual stages. First forced labor in "concentration camps," where the Hebrews were compelled to "hard bondage, in mortar, and in brick, and in all manner of service in the field" (Exodus 1:14). But when the Hebrew population went on growing Pharaoh decided to wipe out life at its source. He ordered the Hebrew midwives—Shiphrah and Puah—to let female babies live but to kill off the males. The two midwives begged off, with a somewhat feeble answer:

"Because the Hebrew women are not as the Egyptian women; for they are lively, and are delivered ere the midwives come in unto them" (Exodus 1:19).

Pharaoh, resentful of their evasiveness, ordered that every newborn male child should be thrown into the river.

It was under these historical circumstances, which we have seen repeated not very long ago, that Moses was born. The atmosphere was one of terror, because of the implacable pursuit of the newborn. According to the Midrash, the Egyptians went from house to house among the Hebrews, with newborn Egyptian babies in their arms, whose crying caused the Hebrew babies to cry in return, thereby revealing their presence. Again, according to the Midrash, Amram, the head of the Sanhedrin, took the desperate countermeasure of urging all Hebrew husbands to break off relations with their wives and announced that he would divorce his own by way of example. Many other husbands were ready to do likewise, for Amram enjoyed a great reputation as a member of the tribe of Levi, which had remained faithful to God when others, in order to curry favor with the Egyptians, had given up receiving the sign of the Covenant in their flesh. But Amram's daughter Miriam took issue with him. "It is wrong to prevent children from coming into the world and to deprive them of a future life. Pharaoh's decree is aimed only at males, but you would suppress females as well." Amram admitted that she was right and, after consulting the Sanhedrin, he renewed his marital relationship.

As this Midrash story shows us, Moses was born into a climate of resistance, not only among the Children of Israel, but among the Egyptians as well. He was the son of Amram and Jochebed, both of them descendants of Levi, in whose house there must have been a strict observance of religion. His older brother and sister, Aaron and Miriam, grew up in untroubled times, but Moses' life was in danger from the start. For three months his parents hid him at home, but after the proclamation of the edict demanding the death of all male children they apparently decided to entrust him to a daughter of Pharaoh, who did not approve of the new policy. His sister Miriam left him in a basket of bulrushes on the bank of the river where Pharaoh's daughter Bythia was wont to bathe. The Egyptian princess found him there and gave him to be cared for by a Hebrew nurse, who was none other than his mother. When he was older Bythia brought him up as if he were her own son, with all the benefits of an Egyptian education but without forcing him to give up his own faith. Moses' acquaintance with Egyptian culture was to stand him in good stead. Let us look at some of the benefits he derived from it.

First of all, because he was educated as a child of the royal family, he was exposed to the encyclopedic knowledge of the intellectuals of the day—the artists, architects, and scribes to whose accomplishments pyramids and papyri bear evidence. He acquired also the practical ability which made him useful to the Egyptian government in its relations with the Semites, particularly those from Canaan. He was instructed by an Egyptian

scribe, whose severe pedagogy we may judge from recorded sayings of the times. "A boy's ears are on his back; he listens when
you beat him," runs one of these, and, again, a young man tells
his former teacher: "You struck my back, and your teaching entered into my ears." Among the young men who submitted,
along with Moses, to this discipline there must have been many
who were later to hold high government positions and whose
friendship was to be useful to him.

At the same time that he acquired this cultural and practical
knowledge Moses must have been initiated into Egyptian religious thought. According to the Acts of the Apostles, which
must have drawn upon an oral rabbinic tradition, "Moses was
learned in all the wisdom of the Egyptians, and was mighty in
words and in deeds" (Acts 7:22). Mighty in words and deeds
not only because of his education but also because, having been
brought up in Egyptian circles, within Pharaoh's court, he must
have been acquainted, even if he did not participate in them,
with the initiation rites and the esoteric wisdom which had attained in Egypt a high degree of refinement.

The doctrine of initiation, in Egypt as elsewhere, was based
on a distinction between the mass of the common people and a
closed aristocracy to which access was governed by secret wisdom and ceremonies. The initiate was a mediator between God
and man, a doctrine diametrically opposed to that of the religion of Israel, in which the Chosen People served as its own
mediator, receiving directly the word of God and obeying His
commandments, except when special leaders were raised up to
save it from idolatry and to revivify the Covenant. The temples
of ancient Egypt in which these mysteries were celebrated were
grandiose and hieratic monuments, built on the model of the
Pharaoh's palaces. The spiritual aristocracy was one with the
aristocracy of birth and enjoyed the same honors. A definite ritual, "the ritual of the foundation of temples," prescribed the
temples' construction; the palace of the god was copied after the

palace of the king, and in it was practiced an etiquette as severe as that of the royal court.

The temple had two parts. The first was a great vestibule whose lofty roof was supported by columns. At the entrance there was the inscription: "Only the pure may enter here." In this vestibule the god received the homage of the king, the priests, and the faithful, but this public audience was only the exterior aspect of the religion. The essential secret cult, reserved for initiates, took place in the sanctuary, which was shut off by a locked door from unauthorized persons. A first secret room, "the sanctuary of the Bark," contained a movable shrine which allowed the god to go from one place to another. A second room, "the sanctuary of the Statue," contained a fixed statue, a sort of palladium which was never moved. This was open only to the Pharaoh and the great initiates; it was a holy of holies, a "heaven on earth," where the god entered into direct contact with man. The Pharaoh, who was considered a son of the gods, was the officiant. Whenever he had to make an important decision he came here, alone, to ask counsel of the god, who answered by means of oracles.

Moses must have been acquainted with this aristocratic and hierarchic worship, either through his masters or through actually taking part in its rites. But it is equally certain that his family and his people were excluded from the Egyptian religion, and its temples must have appeared to them like prisons from which God must be set free and from which, at the same time, His worshipers must be safeguarded.

When the Children of Israel went out of Egypt and came to Sinai, there to await the Law, they must have been still obsessed by the haughty nature of this religion of initiates which had influenced their lives but from which they had been excluded. Mount Sinai, a natural sanctuary around which a whole people gathered, and the revelation, under the open sky, of truths expressed in everyday language were antidotes to the esoteric quality of the Egyptian cults, a sort of democratization and rerooting in the spirit of man of true religion. The revelation made from Mount Sinai had a double character: it was a revelation of the Law, to be sure, but also a revelation of the reality of the world, bearing the signature of God's spirit.

It is not that the Egyptian contribution to the religion of Moses was merely negative and that the cult of Pharaoh was in complete contrast to the teachings of the prophet. The two essential bases of biblical tradition—the belief in a single God and the law of love—were already latent in the wisdom of Egypt, where Moses witnessed them.

A Pharaoh with advanced ideas and a revolutionary temperament, Akhenaten, the predecessor of Horemheb, under whose reign Moses was born, had, as we saw in a previous chapter, given concrete expression to a centuries-old Egyptian tendency by proclaiming a single God. This audacious attempt did not survive him, and his conception of monotheism was different from that proclaimed from Mount Sinai. But Moses must have heard, in the course of his education, of this trend of thought and have been affected by it. He must also have known of the Egyptian belief in life after death and perhaps even of the sentences in the *Book of the Dead,* which was read only by initiates: "I rise up as a living god, I shine in the circle of the gods. Gods, I am as one of you."

In Egypt, too, there were foreshadowings of the biblical law of love, of the Hebrew spirit of justice for the weak:

"Thou shalt neither vex a stranger, nor oppress him. . . .

"Ye shall not afflict any widow, or fatherless child. . . .

"If thou lend money to any of my people that is poor by thee, thou shalt not be to him as an usurer, neither shalt thou lay upon him usury.

"If thou at all take thy neighbor's raiment to pledge, thou shalt deliver it unto him by that the sun goeth down" (Exodus 22:21–22, 25–26).

These very human precepts, these meticulous and subtle rules of wisdom, down to earth and elevated at the same time, had precedents in the teachings of Amenhemeth, in which future government officials were instructed and which the Pharaoh himself recalled to his viziers. Thus in the training which he received in preparation for a government career Moses found rudiments of the moral Law which he brought down from Sinai.

The known facts about the first and greatest prophet of Israel give us a historical and definite idea of the period in which he was born, his family background, his education, the career which he intended to follow, and the influences to which he was submitted and to which he reacted. To this the rabbis' commentary adds hints of his character and of the motives of the political line which he chose to follow.

Moses might have been an important Egyptian government official, an expert on relations between the Egyptians and his own people, so irreplaceable that he would not have been struck by the discriminatory measures taken against them. He might, like many others, have played a double game, enjoying credit with Pharaoh for his loyalty and obedience and with his own people for the favors he was able to grant them.

According to tradition, this is just how he acted at the beginning of his government career. One of the rabbis of the Midrash, Eleazar, the son of Rabbi José the Galilean, gives us an example of Moses' early behavior as an overseer of the forced labor imposed on his compatriots.

"He saw a heavy load on the back of a puny man, and a light load on the back of a big man, and a woman's burden carried by a man, and a man's burden carried by a woman, and an old man's burden on a young man, and a young man's burden on an old man. Putting aside his rank, he went about redistributing their labors, as if in obedience to Pharaoh's orders."

But soon Moses could no longer bear this double game; he had to choose between his career at Pharaoh's court or fidelity to his own people. The circumstances of his choice are dramatically recounted in Exodus:

"And it came to pass in those days, when Moses was grown, that he went out unto his brethren, and looked on their burdens; and he spied an Egyptian smiting an Hebrew, one of his brethren.

"And he looked this way and that way, and when he saw there was no man, he slew the Egyptian, and hid him in the sand. . . .

"Now when Pharaoh heard this thing, he sought to slay Moses. But Moses fled from the face of Pharaoh, and dwelt in the land of Midian . . ." (Exodus 2:11–12, 15).

This was how the break came about, how the revolt began. And here we see the character of Moses. He was a meek ("meek as Moses"), disciplined man, but the sight of injustice roused him to indignation and awakened him to his calling. As Albert Gelin says, "When God wants to accomplish great things, He starts by tearing His agent out of his security." Sometimes He even tears him away from Himself.

The character of Moses is deeply human. He was not a conventional man, a figure from a storybook or a stained-glass window. He was not a model of single-mindedness or piety; his religion was not a sort of opium that allowed him to disguise or sublimate his weaknesses and contradictions, his inclinations to error and sin. He belongs to the history and daily life of the people of his time and race; in no way is he outside reality. A story from the Midrash, deep in ancient wisdom, shows the complex of conflicting feelings which he had to make an effort to overcome.

After the exodus from Egypt an Arabian king who had heard of the great event sent an artist to paint Moses' portrait in order that the king might have it ever before him. When the artist came back with the finished work the king, desirous of ascertaining the value of the portrait and what sort of character it revealed, summoned the men most versed in the study of physiognomy and asked them to analyze the subject. After minute

observation and much reflection the sages gave a unanimous answer. The face revealed all the human vices: cupidity, arrogance,
and sensuality. The king could not believe his own ears and
doubted the competence of the physiognomists. Had they not
taken for a rascal a holy man, chosen by God to fulfill His will, a
man whose miraculous achievements had caused him to be ad-
mired by all mankind? The sages defended their verdict; this
was what the portrait revealed, there could be no doubt about it.
If this did not correspond to the truth, then the portrait was at
fault, not themselves. The artist protested in his turn, insisting
that the portrait was a perfect likeness. How was the question to
be settled? Having no confidence in any of them, the king decided to visit Moses in person and compare the portrait with the
model. So he did, and came to the conclusion that the portrait
was a masterpiece of verisimilitude. Then how was the analysis
of the sages to be explained? He asked Moses for his opinion
and received an unexpected answer. "Both the artist and the
sages," said Moses, "are experts in their different lines. If my
good qualities were products of nature I should be no more than
a piece of wood, condemned to remain just as I was created. I do
not blush to confess that by nature I had all the reprehensible
traits which your sages discerned, and perhaps to a degree
greater than they imagine. But by sheer will power I overcame
them, and the character which I have acquired through self-
discipline is diametrically opposite to the one with which nature
endowed me."

In this vivid Midrash story Moses reveals that he was not all
of a piece and that piece holy; as we would say today, he was
subject to complexes and contradictions. It was by conquering
his vices that he won virtue, it was by struggling with himself
that he became a prophet and the proclaimer of God's Law.[1]

---

[1] Cicero in his *Tusculanae Disputationes* (IV, 37) tells a similar story about
Socrates, whose face was a composite of all the vices. Did the Roman orator
and the Midrash draw upon the same Hellenic source?

This existential truth about Moses, rooted in the reality of the human condition and of history, this absence of bourgeois conformity so paradoxical in a man who provided the foundation for so many religious beliefs, is evident not only in the Midrash commentary but in the Bible as well. In the case of Moses the two pictures are strikingly similar. God spoke to Moses face to face, and Moses spoke back to Him no less openly. That, is, when he spoke to God Moses did not feel obliged to change his character or his way of thinking. Even in the presence of the Eternal he remained thoroughly human.

On the bare mountaintop, in the presence of God, Moses kept all his human limitations and all his human virtues as well. He was not a passive echo, an anonymous transmitter of the divine word. When this word did not please him he did not hesitate to voice his opinion. "You are a prophet, not an astrologer," the Midrash has God say to Abraham, the father of all believers, to show him that he was a free agent and not subject to determinism. This was equally true of Moses, who approached his mission with the doubts and hesitations natural to a free man who is called upon to embrace an extraordinary destiny.

The agreement which God and Moses reached in their decisive and binding encounter was attended by all sorts of reservations. According to the Midrash, God first took care not to terrify the man whom He had chosen to be His prophet. Already, at the beginning of Genesis, God showed Himself to Adam and Eve as a simple mortal, walking in the garden in the cool of the day and making them coats of skins. Again, at the time of the Flood, He himself brought the ark to a stop. For Moses He did even more. According to the Midrash Rabbah, He first spoke to him with the voice of his father, so that His words should recall the days of his infancy and his first awakening to the intimacy of home. Then, when thanks to this stratagem Moses had heard His first call without fear, He said: "I am not your father, but the God of your father, the God of Abraham, the God of Isaac and the God of Jacob." And Moses rejoiced. "My father is numbered with the patriarchs," he said to himself; "indeed he is the first-named among them."

So it was that God cushioned for Moses the shock of learning of his predestination. But the prophet was not so easily freed of his fear, and objections surged to his lips in response to God's order. Hence we have the first dialogue between Moses and his Creator, before the flight from Egypt, as Exodus tells it:

"And the Lord said, I have surely seen the affliction of my people which are in Egypt, and have heard their cry by reason of their taskmasters. . . .

"Come now therefore, and I will send thee unto Pharaoh, that thou mayest bring forth the children of Israel out of Egypt.

"And Moses said unto God, Who am I, that I should go unto Pharaoh, and that I should bring forth the children of Israel out of Egypt?

"And he said, Certainly I will be with thee. . . .

"And Moses said unto God, Behold, when I come unto the children of Israel, and shall say unto them, The God of your fathers hath sent me unto you; and they shall say to me, What is his name? what shall I say unto them? . . .

"And God said moreover unto Moses, Thus shalt thou say unto the Children of Israel, The Lord God of your fathers, the God of Abraham, the God of Isaac, and the God of Jacob, hath sent me unto you: this is my name for ever . . .

"And Moses answered and said, but, behold, they will not believe me, nor hearken unto my voice: for they will say, The Lord hath not appeared unto thee.

"And the Lord said unto him, What is that in thine hand? And he said, A rod.

"And he said, Cast it on the ground. And he cast it on the ground, and it became a serpent; and Moses fled from before it.

"And the Lord said unto Moses, Put forth thine hand, and take it by the tail. And he put forth his hand, and caught it, and it became a rod in his hand" (Exodus 3:7, 10–13, 15; 4:1–4).

But the apprehensions of Moses were by no means quieted by this miracle, even when followed by another (the hand of Moses became leprous and then was healed). He formulated a fourth objection:

"And Moses said unto the Lord, O my Lord, I am not eloquent, neither heretofore, nor since thou hast spoken unto thy servant: but I am slow of speech, and of a slow tongue.

"And the Lord said unto him, Who hath made man's mouth? or who maketh the dumb, or deaf, or the seeing, or the blind? have not I the Lord?

"Now therefore go, and I will be with thy mouth, and teach thee what thou shalt say.

"And he said, O my Lord, send, I pray thee, by the hand of him whom thou wilt send.

"And the anger of the Lord was kindled against Moses, and he said, Is not Aaron the Levite thy brother? I know that he can speak well. And also, behold, he cometh forth to meet thee: and when he seeth thee, he will be glad in his heart.

"And thou shalt speak unto him, and put words in his mouth: and I will be with thy mouth, and with his mouth, and will teach you what ye shall do" (Exodus 4:10–15).

Four times, then, Moses attempted to evade his mission, and four times the Lord brought him around. But although Moses was persuaded of the Lord's unalterable resolution and acquainted with the means by which He would facilitate his mission, he was still not satisfied and asked for further instructions. He even dared ask God again what was His name, in order that he might know how to answer the inevitable question of the Children of Israel.

According to the Midrash, God refused to receive any name other than those which corresponded to the attributes of His glory or the effects of His power. He answered with an extraordinary sentence which contains in its first seven words the key to the meaning of the Bible, a sentence in which the whole of Jewish wisdom, priestly or secular, is summarized: "I am called according to my deeds. When I judge my creatures I am called *Elohim*. When I rise up to war against sinners I am *Sabaoth*, the Lord of Hosts. When I suspend judgment for a man's sins I am called *El-shaddai*. When I show mercy to the world I am *Adonai*. But to the Children of Israel you will say that I am He that was and is and shall be; I am He that is with them in their present servitude and will be with them in servitude to come. . . . To the Children of Israel you will say that my mercy toward them is due to the merits of Abraham, Isaac, and Jacob."

When Moses heard these words and noticed that this time the name of his father, Amram, was not among those of the patriarchs he tried to find out whether Amram had done anything to fall into disfavor. "Can men sin after they are dead?" he asked. And when God told him that dead men cannot sin, Moses insisted: "Why did you first reveal yourself to me as the God of my father, and now you speak of him no more?" To which God answered: "At first I had to calm you with flattering words, but now you have heard the whole truth: I am only the God of Abraham, the God of Isaac, and the God of Jacob."

The importance of the name, in this case, is that it not only designates but also defines the bearer. By pressing God to tell His name and also to tell whether or not Amram still deserved the title which God first said He had given him, Moses was making an essential point; he was forcing God to reveal Himself, to reveal His tactics and His very nature. To give anyone a name is to give him a "handle"; to force the Eternal to state His name or names is to incite Him to assume His role of God. At this crucial moment of the divine revelation, provoked by God's chosen agent, man was not merely a questioner; he initiated the dialogue and shared in the conduct of the game.

And God, according to the Midrash, answered in the same vein, by enumerating the terms by which Moses, in his turn, might be designated in order that for him too his name should accord with his deeds. Here are the ten names which God attributed to him:

He was to be called, first of all, *Yered*, from a Hebrew verb meaning "to bring down," because he helped to bring down the Law from heaven;

He was to be called *Avigdor*, from *avigusdor*, "the father of enclosing," because he had thrown a protective hedge around Israel;

He was to be called *Hever*, from *haver* or "companion," because he made men companions of their Father in heaven;

He was to be called *Soco*, which means "anointed" or "touched by grace," because he was the most eminent of all men moved by the Holy Spirit;

He was to be called *Yakutiel*, which comes from a verb meaning "to hope in God," because he had implanted in men's hearts hope in their heavenly Father;

He was to be called *Zanoa*, which refers to the pardon obtained by men washed clean of their sins, because he interceded for Israel after the idolatrous worship of the Golden Calf;

He was to be called *Tuvia*, which comes from *tov*, meaning "good" and "beautiful," because when Bythia found him as a baby, exposed on the bank of the Nile, she saw that he was beautiful;

He was to be called *Shemiah*, from the verb *shema*, "to hear," because God heard his voice;

He was to be called *Nathaniel*, "he to whom God has given," because God gave him the Law;

And finally he was to be called *Ha Sofer*, the Scribe, because he wrote the Pentateuch.

Among all these names, evocative of Moses' virtues and of the various aspects of his mission, by which one did God say that he should be called in everyday language? Despite or perhaps because of their sacred and supernatural connotations, God put all these aside and chose a down-to-earth and human name, reminiscent of the motherly affection of the woman who had taken mercy on an abandoned child. God said, in effect, to Bythia, Pharaoh's daughter: "Moses was not your son, but you called him your son. Likewise you are not my daughter, but I call you my daughter." And to Moses he said: "I swear by all the names given you that I shall call you only by the one bestowed by Pharaoh's daughter. I shall call you Moses, because she saved you from the water."

What simplicity and tenderness there is in this search for a name for God's chosen agent! Moses could no longer feel ill at ease in the Lord's presence after God had masked His transcendence with fatherly emotion. He was ever after to feel like a child before his father, like a grown son, charged with responsibilities, who still recognizes his father's authority even when he discusses his father's orders and argues against them.

Kierkegaard has said: "We are always on the wrong side in our relations with God." But it seems as if, for Moses, the contrary were true. He is on the right side, where he not only has direct apprehension of God's voice, but where God listens to him as well, taking his arguments into account and admitting his existence. There is no question of the difference of rank between them; that is what puts them both at ease. In this existential and transcendent colloquy between two beings so like and so unlike each one expresses himself freely and finds the partner of his desire.

Moses' reserve and modesty before God show that the meeting left him with no bitterness but inspired only natural feelings. He was not so puffed up about his vocation and his ministry that he overwhelmed his followers with his own opinions. He did not boast of being in direct communication with God, because in seeing this bond from the inside he was aware of its precariousness and fragility. Never did he grow accustomed to the extraordinary commerce which he enjoyed with his Creator.

As Maimonides says, "He was never to blurt out the first thought that came into his mind, even if it was directed toward God, but rather to be modest, to hold himself back in order to advance with due precaution. This is why it is said: 'And Moses hid his face, for he was afraid to look upon God' (Exodus 3:6)."

Moses' modesty was not a sign of weakness or self-effacement. Even in God's presence he did not lose his feeling of personal responsibility to Israel. He acted *hic et nunc*, in relation to the human community around him. Feeling responsible for his people, he supported and led them, in full awareness of their needs and weaknesses. His task was not simply to preach a glorious destiny and a supernatural mission; he had to take into account the fact that they were men, with men's failings and men's everyday requirements. He could not afford to lose himself in the clouds, even those which enveloped God on Mount Sinai; his people had to have material as well as moral nourishment. It was in order to meet these practical, human demands that he had at times to argue, in the name of reality, against God's sublime commands.

The dialogue between God and Moses was beneficial to both parties. To Moses because it allowed him to actually accomplish the mission which so surprised and antagonized him at the start. To the Eternal because it acquainted Him with the realities of the world which He had created and of the man He had made to be His shadow; in short because it enabled Him to become more fully God.

This is why Moses' discussions and pleas and refusals occupy such an important place in both Bible and Midrash, why God's word and man's commentary take them into account in such detailed fashion. Of course Moses was at God's orders; he could not take the initiative against Him. God called him His "faithful servant" (Numbers 12:7). All through his life God's orders rained down upon him. Already during the departure from Egypt one followed hard upon another:

"And the Lord spoke unto Moses, saying,

"Speak unto the children of Israel, that they turn and encamp before Pi-hahiroth, between Migdol and the sea" (Exodus 14:1–2). . . .

"And the Lord said unto Moses . . . Speak unto the children of Israel, that they go forward" (Exodus 14:15).

"And the Lord said unto Moses, Stretch out thine hand over the sea, that the waters may come again upon the Egyptians, upon their chariots, and upon their horsemen" (Exodus 14:26).

God left to no one, not even to Moses, the important decisions; Moses never had to make a choice that would influence the course of history or the future of his people. But because he was responsible for the practical means of accomplishing God's will he did take negative initiatives and hold out for the modification or even the cancellation of God's plans for practical reasons. He was like a regimental or company commander, charged with executing a leader's orders in the field, who cannot discuss them in principle but is aware of the risks and difficulties which they entail. This was why, when the people revolted against the divine orders, he begged God to alleviate the punishment decreed against them.

Moses interceded not only on behalf of the Hebrews but also on behalf of his adversaries, both Hebrew and Egyptian. He interceded for all mankind and found his true dignity in association not only with the vocation of Israel but with the human condition to which Israel bore witness. After every plague which smote the Egyptians Moses pleaded successfully with God to the effect that it should last no longer than necessary. Later, at Toberah, when God sent fire down upon the Hebrews, Moses prayed to him to desist, and God answered the prayer.

There was one occasion when Israel's disobedience was particularly grave, and yet Moses did not fear to intercede in its favor. This was on the day after Sinai, when the Chosen People relapsed into idolatry and worshiped the Golden Calf. To Moses his whole mission seemed to have crumbled, and to God it was even more tragic, since the Covenant was broken just at the time when He had personally added to its substance. God's anger attains its greatest intensity in one of Exodus' most dramatic stories, from which the Midrash, in its turn, makes a special effort to extract the significance. Here is how Exodus tells the story, in which Moses pleads, like any lawyer, for his people:

"And the Lord said unto Moses, I have seen this people, and, behold, it is a stiffnecked people;

"Now therefore let me alone, that my wrath may wax hot against them and that I may consume them: and I will make of thee a great nation.

"And Moses besought the Lord his God, and said, Lord, why doth thy wrath wax hot against thy people, which thou hast brought forth out of the land of Egypt with great power, and with a mighty hand?

"Wherefore should the Egyptians speak, and say, For mischief did he bring them out, to slay them in the mountains, and to consume them from the face of the earth? Turn from thy fierce wrath and repent of this evil against thy people.

"Remember Abraham, Isaac, and Israel, thy servants, to whom thou swearest by thine own self, and said unto them, I will multiply your seed as the stars of heaven, and all this land that I have spoken of will I give unto your seed, and they shall inherit it for ever.

"And the Lord repented of the evil which he thought to do unto his people" (Exodus 32:9–14).

An appeal to public opinion, whose reactions must be measured, even in an enemy country, a recall of commitments that must not be broken—in Moses' plea for his people when they were threatened with extermination we find two of the defensive stratagems employed by lawyers of all ages. Moses stood up as the defender of Israel and of all mankind, and the Eternal reversed His decision. Inevitably men's commentaries have been attracted to this realistic and audacious episode. Let us see how the Midrash Rabbah develops Moses' arguments in favor of the Hebrews.

"Moses undertook their defense and said to the Holy One, blessed be He: 'Master of the Universe, I have merits to recall in their favor. Remember that you wanted to give the Torah to the sons of Esau and they refused it, but Israel accepted. For it is said: "And all the people answered, and said, what the Eternal has said we shall do, and we shall obey." '

"Having heard this first plea of Moses the Eternal rejected it, saying: 'They have transgressed, just as it is written: "They have turned aside quickly out of the way which I commanded them; they have made them a molten calf" ' (Exodus 32:8).

"This argument did not catch Moses unprepared, and he answered: 'Recall in their favor that when I brought your message to Egypt and told them your name they believed me and worshiped it, as it is said: "And the people believed . . . then they bowed their heads and worshiped" ' " (Exodus 4:31).

These first exchanges between the Eternal and Moses were mere preliminaries based on historical allegations, which did not go to the heart of the matter. Next, according to the Midrash, Moses moved to the attack and threw the blame on God. Was He not partly responsible for the Golden Calf? If Israel betrayed God, was it not because He had exposed it to temptation? Here is Moses' decisive argument, as the Midrash develops it:

"Moses pleaded: 'Lord of the Universe, from what place did you bring them out? Was it not from Egypt, where there is worship of animals?' "

And this line of attack finds open support among the doctors of Israel:

"Rabbi Huna said in the name of Rabbi Johanan: 'It is like a wise man who opened a perfume shop for his son in a street frequented by prostitutes. The street, the nature of the shop, and the youth of the son all contributed to his downfall. His father, catching him with a prostitute, cried out: "I shall kill him!" But a friend of the son was present and said: "Did you not corrupt him that are crying out against him? You eliminated all other commerce beside that of perfumery; out of all streets you chose the one frequented by prostitutes." '

"Similarly Moses said: 'Master of the Universe! You eliminated the rest of the world and made the Children of Israel slaves of the Egyptians, who worship animals. Your children learned from them, and they too have made a calf."

This daring comparison points up the boldness of Moses in his role of lawyer, not content to defend the culprit, Israel, but turning the accusation against the judge, God Almighty. Thus we have further insight into the personality of the prophet. Although obedient to God and intent upon carrying out His will, Moses retained freedom of thought and of speech, not only when it came to championing the Children of Israel but on his own behalf also. We find in the Midrash another dialogue between Moses and his Creator, in which the former takes the latter to task for his manner of discussion. Moses knows that he is fated to die before entering the Promised Land of Canaan and implores God to reconsider this hard sentence.

" 'Master of the World!' " the Midrash quotes him as saying. " 'How many times the Israelites have sinned before You and You have answered my intercession by forgiving them! Cannot You forgive me as well?'

"And the Holy One replied: 'The decree of Providence regarding a community is not the same as that regarding an individual. . . . Do you not remember the great honor I did you? You said to me "Bring up this people!" and I brought them up; you said: "Turn from thy fierce wrath," and I turned from it. On your account, also, I changed the ways of heaven and earth. For the way of heaven is to let fall rain and dew, and the way of earth is to produce bread, but in order to sustain you I made manna fall from heaven. Remember too that when the Israelites had sinned by worshiping the Golden Calf I wished to destroy them, and you asked me to repent of my evil against this people, and I repented of it, as you asked.'

"And the Holy One said further to Moses: 'Moses, twice I made you a promise, first when I swore that you should not enter the land of Canaan and second when I swore that I would not destroy Israel. If I break my first promise, then I must break the second also.' Moses at first protested against this rigorous logic, but then he gave in. 'Master of the World, You are seeking to trap me, You are holding both ends of the rope. May Moses perish, and a thousand like him, rather than a single one of the Children of Israel!' "

Moses, then, was no dupe. He gave way, to be sure, but not without letting God know that he understood His ruse. God was the stronger, and imposed His will. But from this conversation, as from so many others, God learned that man has an existence of his own and that the man Moses was not a mere docile executor of His orders. This man revealed himself to God, just as God revealed Himself to man. The providential action of Moses was double in nature. First, he gave a human dimension to the measureless history of God's Chosen People. Second, he announced to his people the messianic dimension assigned to it by God. In another passage from the Midrash we find an explanation of Moses' insertion into history, as it was willed by God and accomplished by men.

After Adam had sinned, the *Shekinah*, the presence of God, withdrew from earth to the first heaven. After the sin of Cain it withdrew to the second heaven. When Enoch's generation sinned it withdrew to the third heaven. After the generation of the Flood had sinned it withdrew to the fourth heaven. When the generation of the Tower of Babel sinned it withdrew to the fifth heaven. When Sodom and Gomorrah sinned it withdrew to the sixth heaven. And when the Egyptians sinned it took refuge in the seventh heaven. Then seven just men arose to bring the *Shekinah* down to earth again. Abraham, Isaac, Jacob, Levi, Kehat, and Amram brought it down from the seventh to the first heaven, and Moses brought it down to earth. This restoration of the *Shekinah* took place on Mount Sinai.

:

It is not historically certain that Sinai was the seat of the revelation. In this famous episode the elements of the facts and of God and of man do not necessarily come harmoniously together. But two certainties stand fast. First, Sinai was a mountain where the wind of the spirit was fated to blow, and second, God did give the Law to the Hebrews somewhere in the course of their journey between Africa and Asia Minor, from Egypt to Kadesh. For all the rest the Bible is inconsistent.

Whether Sinai was really a landmark of the Exodus journey or whether it was made a part of it by the narrators, the spot was a predestined one, whose vocation endures down to our own day. In the millions of years of prehistory this peninsula, squeezed between Africa and Asia Minor, underwent a series of upheavals which, if a region can be said to have a subconscious mind, must have impressed themselves upon it. Here, about 60 million years ago, the crust of the earth was broken and two parallel straight gashes were opened, one the Red Sea and the other the Syrian depression. Between the two a ridge of rock, compressed and then ejected by the earthquakes, threw peaks six thousand feet high—nine thousand feet above the bottom of the two gashes, now filled by water—into the air. As erosion flattened out the foothills and the lowlands were covered with desert sand and an impalpable dust of crumbled rock, blown by the wind, the crags stood out more and more clearly, conferring a peculiar geological and geographical character to the region, reminiscent of the primitive atmosphere of Genesis. It was this naked earth of the time before man, before even life itself, which cropped up, in all its inert and unconscious desolation, one stage after another of the convulsion of the earth's crust that was chosen by God as the site of the revelation of His Law. Still visible today are the crystalline rocks born of the original eruption: the Serbal, the Jebel, Mosa, and the Katarin (Um Shomper); they comprise Mount Sinai.

On their way to these heights the Hebrews, under Moses'

guidance, came upon all the extravagances and caprices of this mountainous universe. If they came from the north, over the desolate stretches of the desert of Tih, they crossed dried-up river beds, where a small deposit of water appears no more than once in a generation. These formed a network of streams, which in glacial times drained off the snow and ice of the mountains, but now are only a fossilized skeleton of what they were before. Interspersed with them are fields of flint, dark yellow, black, or red in color which under sun and wind and sand have taken on an admirable polish. Once upon a time they supplied the stone for the weapons of our primitive ancestors.

If, as is more likely, the Hebrews proceeded from the northwest, following the shore of the Red Sea to the plain of El Magharah, they left behind them the coastal dunes, slashed by *wadis,* and came suddenly upon the dramatic and magical spectacle of the granite mountains, with their mixed natural and supernatural grandeur. The mass of Mount Sinai is at the same time a desert of nature and a desert of faith, with small green oases studding its blazing valleys. On the unattainable heights a few human remnants call up the memory of accidental, solitary migrations. In the Sinai desert have been found inscriptions which date back further than Exodus, to approximately 2000 B.C., written in an alphabet anterior to that of the Semitic languages. Who knows what religious aspirations or what testimony to a dogged will to survive amid hostile surroundings are preserved in their undecipherable phrases? Later on, the Egyptians of the Twelfth Dynasty came to spend the winter months on the western foothills, digging for metals. At the end of the season the miners decamped, taking with them their tools and the precious metals they had dug up for fear they should fall into the hands of the Bedouins. But they left on the spot their kitchen utensils and big terra-cotta vases, buried in the sand around their stone huts where the next year's migrant miners could discover and make use of them. Some of these objects have been unearthed in our day. We may imagine that, in

Moses' time, the Hebrews came across these caches or even that they ran into the migrant miners and troubled the peace of the mountaintop hermits.

The great body of the advancing Hebrews filled the region with an unaccustomed clamor as they turned their backs on the coast and wound their way through the most welcoming of the valleys. Amid the craggy heights, some of them almost 7000 feet high, they went through the narrow gorges, where they were surprised to find damp ground and even rivulets. The melting snows on the mountains ran sometimes under a bed of sand, sometimes out in the open, watering the thirsty roots of tenacious plants. Thickets of a density which varied according to the distribution of the water above or below ground surrounded clumps of tropical trees. Palms, acacias, and tamarisks formed luxuriant oases amid the slopes of red granite, streaked with diorite and porphyry. Certain trees of Sinai had particular local characteristics. The palms were largely of a wild variety which bore no fruit; the acacias had scarce foliage and robust trunks and were armed with straight, white thorns. The *tarfah*, or tamarisks, looked like great moss-green balls and defended themselves against depredation by an exceedingly hard wood which was later to be sought after by shipbuilders. Thanks to all this vegetation, the wild, rocky earth had a life-giving sap among its constituents. Sweet-tasting drops dripped from the bark of the tamarisks; they were crystallized by the cool, early morning breeze and then melted in the sun.

There were also isolated bushes which put down their roots in the relatively damp, sandy interstices among the rocks, giving the landscape the air of a wild and melancholy garden. The most prevalent plant was the hardy *retem*, a white broom, whose bitter leaves defied the greed of the camels.

The land which the Hebrews crossed in their journey to the predestined mountain was chaotic and inhospitable. It was a world where life, under constant threat, took on an aggressive form, where subsistence was a constant problem, where every move was attended with difficulties and every turn in a valley was fraught with uncertainty.

The two million Israelites who made this trek did not all travel by the same route or meet with the same experiences. Some encountered hot springs, charged with sulphur and lime, which disappointed their thirst and added a new anxiety to the rest. Others were deluged by sudden showers which forced them to take shelter under the rocks or threatened to sweep them into narrow canyons suddenly filled with rushing water. Still others had to bear up under tornadoes which swept clouds of dust across the plains.

The physiognomy of the Sinai desert, as of others of the kind, was determined by climatic conditions. The original terrain, born of an interior convulsion, was subject to the brutal action of the waters in the rainy season, to the gusty winds which arose out of sudden atmospheric depressions, to the heat of the sun, which varied according to the hours of the day. This terrain was mobile and capricious, and man had to be ceaselessly on the alert. Erratic temperature changes of as much as fifty degrees constantly recalled to him his susceptibility to heat and cold. The horizon toward which he was marching was abruptly charged with dust; the heavens to which he looked for deliverance disappeared in a sandstorm; the sun faded away under heavy folds of weirdly colored clouds; a peaceful, sunny path was suddenly filled with noise and shadows. Superstitious fear accompanied every step that he made in this apocalyptic landscape.

The Hebrews fanned out over the desert roads, feeling surrounded by ghosts and obsessed by fear that the country around them might suddenly turn hostile or even murderous. From one valley to the next they were beset by conflicting sensations and impressions. They met with masses of earth fallen in a landslide, then came into valleys rich in aromatic herbs—thyme, mint, lavender, hyssop, wild wormwood—whose charm was ingenuously described by a sixteenth-century Frenchman, Jean Thenaud, as follows: "The morning air was so fragrant that I thought I had stumbled into a perfumery."

Coming out of these valleys, they marched over a stony delta to the foothills of Mount Sinai. "These mountains," says a modern writer, Georg Gerster, "unfold a fascinating splendor. In the sunlight the cretaceous coastal ranges shine out as dazzlingly as glaciers. A mass of dark red granite stands out above a mountain of olive-green sandstone and across the way other peaks sparkle, like precious stones, with the gleam of amber and amethyst. . . . By the time the traveler has passed through the rocky gorge of El Buweib, the 'little gate,' or secret entrance to the Holy and Holies, in the heart of the mountains, he has given up exclaiming over every new caprice and extravagance of this mountain universe. But it is when he has crossed the pass that nature offers its most impressive spectacle. Here the green gneiss and the red granite are accompanied by strange horizontal shelves of yellowish sand and crushed gravel. Sometimes these terraces are miles long, but often erosion has hewn out pyramids which present themselves to the imagination as towers or giants. . . ."

And here is a nineteenth-century traveler's account of his climb to the predestined site:

"We continued to climb the mountain, which as we progressed became steeper and steeper, until finally we reached the stone overhanging the plain of Rephidim, from which Moses held up his hand with God's rod while Joshua conducted the battle with Amalek.

"Finally, after five hours of climbing, we came to the summit of Sinai, where we stood motionless, looking at the magnificent panorama unrolled before us, peopled with biblical memories which, even today, three thousand years later, are full of poetry and grandeur.

"The cool, clear air allowed us to see for a tremendous distance. To the south, directly opposite, was the end of the peninsula, with the Raz Mohammed at the tip, half lost in the sea, and beyond, the Pirate Islands, floating like white fog on the surface of the water; to the right the mountains of Africa; to the left the desert of Arabia; below the plain of Rephidim, and all around a chaos of mountains piled up at the base of the overhanging giant, which seems at a distance a sea of granite with its waves frozen into immobility. . . .

"We read the Bible verses in the very cave where Moses was hiding when God showed Himself to him in all His power, and his fear was so great that, according to our guide, the trembling of his head left on the rock a trace which he took pains to point out to us."

If Alexandre Dumas, one of the great "reporters" of the nineteenth century, felt such emotion over his two-week visit to Sinai, how much greater must have been that of the migrants who three thousand years ago heard God's voice from its summit!

Two million Hebrews—men, women, and children—were gathered together, according to the Bible, in an encampment at the foot of Mount Sinai. And twenty thousand angels, according to legend, stood on the slopes of the mountain, barring access to the summit.

These angels—twelve thousand of them angels of destruction —are not mentioned in the Bible. If the learned men of Israel have made place for them in their commentaries it is not only in order to lend greater solemnity to the proclamation of the Law; it is, rather, to mark the new and singular character of the revelation made from the mountain. In the book of Genesis single angels served as God's messengers, but here the Midrash has them appear for the first time in large numbers. Angels have, throughout the Bible, the function of transmitting God's orders to a human executor, as in the story of Abraham. They are, as the Hebrew term has it, *malar* or mandatories, superior beings faithful to the task which God has assigned to them and having

no existence outside its accomplishment. Since before the creation they have been in God's service, always ready to insert
themselves as flickering manifestations of God's will into the
opacity of the universe and the confusion of history. Their function is an essential one, and to show how closely attached they
are to God the chief among them—Michael, Gabriel, and
Raphael—have names ending in *el,* the syllable evocative of the
Lord in person. But the anonymous angels which the Midrash
calls forth for the first time in mass formation to mount guard
over Mount Sinai have an ephemeral existence. Before creation
and before the definitive Covenant of Sinai they provided God's
only and insufficient contact with beings outside of Himself.
They have no personality except for the duration of their transi-
tory mission and seem to hover on the border line between time
and eternity; they are not a part of history although they appear
on the scene, upon command, to announce some change in its
direction, without participating in the subsequent efforts and
meanderings and final achievement. They are a part of eternity,
yet they fail to comprehend the necessity of communicating it
to those who are not its beneficiaries, to the mortal and tran-
sient race of man. Angels do not and never will understand man;
often they are jealous of him and seek to block his self-fulfill-
ment.

Men, on the contrary, as we well know, are inextricably tied
up with history's fatality and servitude. Those who pressed
around the base of Mount Sinai, outnumbering ten to one the
celestial police, had endured so many hardships that they felt
themselves to be eminently perishable, not only as individuals
but also as a people. For it was as a people that they had broken
away from bondage and launched themselves upon an adventure whose end they could not foresee. Some of them, in the
course of the two centuries they spent in Egypt, had tried to
take part in the life of the Egyptians, to absorb their culture,
and even to know their religion. They had, in any case, heard
talk of mysteries to which they were not admitted, of sanctuaries

in which they could not set foot, of initiations in which they had no share. Later they had known forced labor and genocide. They were still marked—traumatized, we might say—by the sufferings from which they had just been freed by Moses, apprehensive, at every new blow to fate, of falling into them again. Because they lived in a pitiless age and had been subject (as they were to be in all the long course of their history) to weariness, sickness, temptation, discord, and death, they felt little prepared to receive the divine Law, to become God's Chosen People, and to wait upon the coming of the Messiah. And God knew all these things. He knew to what weak humans He was linking His future on earth, to what perishable beings He was entrusting His eternity. This is why, in the two months between the departure from Egypt and the arrival at Sinai, He had multiplied His miracles in order to persuade them that He was the only true God.

The crossing of the Red Sea and the swallowing up of Pharaoh's legions, the manna falling from the sky in regular quantities every day but Friday, when the quantity was doubled to provide for the Sabbath, the water springing from the rock when Moses touched it with his rod—all these were signs meant to prepare a confused people for hearing the message of order and clarity which was to make them into an indestructible nation.

They were at the foot of Sinai and Moses was climbing toward God. It was a short climb; a man could cover twice in one day the distance which separated the summit from the waiting people. On the day of God's first apparition Moses did make two trips, pausing on his return to write down God's commands.

On his first trip, according to the rabbis, he found difficulties in the ascent, although it was later to become familiar to him. This was because the angels so vividly described in the Midrash were keeping watch on the mountain. Kemuel, the warden, the head of the twelve thousand angels of destruction, was the first to interrogate him. "What are you doing here, son of a mortal, son of Amram, here in this place which belongs to the angels of fire?" And Moses answered: "I have not come of my own free will but with the permission of the Most High, in order to receive the Torah and take it back to Israel." When Kemuel was not persuaded Moses struck him and pushed him out of his way, then he continued until he met a second angel, Hadarniel.

Hadarniel roared: "What are you doing here?" Hearing his terrible voice, Moses was afraid; he began to weep and nearly fell from the cloud. God was moved to pity and said to Hadarniel: "You angels are always the same! Ever since I created you, you have never ceased to oppose Me. In the beginning, when I made Adam, you rose up against Me. 'What is man,' you asked, 'that Thou shouldest magnify him?' I was angry and burned great numbers of you by touching you with My finger. Now you are resuming the battle against this My faithful servant whom I ordered to come to receive the Torah and take it back to My people, Israel. And yet you know well that unless Israel receives the Torah you will no longer be allowed to live in heaven." And Hadarniel begged God's pardon.

Continuing on his way, Moses came to another angel, Sandalfon, who was weaving crowns for the Most High, among the seraphim, who were singing: "The Eternal reigns, the Eternal has reigned, the Eternal will reign forever!" But besides this ironical occupation Sandalfon had the quality of releasing so much heat that everything took fire around him. In His love for Israel God descended from His throne of glory and walked before Moses until he had passed through the fiery zone. In this same way Moses passed before another angel, Riqyon, from whom a river of fire was flowing, and came to Raziel.

Raziel was an important figure among the angels. He it was that up to this time had revealed to the world God's teachings and God's will. His place was very close to God, sometimes behind the curtains around His throne, from which he could see and hear everything, sometimes in front of the throne, with his wings outspread to form a curtain which would prevent the other angels from being burned by God's breath.

Him too Moses passed by without danger. In the last and most dangerous stage of his journey he came to the angels of terror, the most powerful and cruel of all. Even if Moses had come so far unharmed they would not spare him, and they readied themselves to breathe flames. God advised Moses to stand near His throne of glory and to be ready to answer them.

For as soon as the angels of terror knew that Moses was in heaven they said to God: "What is this man born of woman doing here?" And God said, "He has come to receive the Torah." The startled angels retorted: "Lord, are You not content to have celestial beings to whom to give the Torah? Why must You have to do with the children of dust?" This time God kept quiet and told Moses to answer in His name. The prophet, of course, had recourse to arguments *ad angelum.* "It is written in the Torah," he said, " 'I am the Lord thy God, which have brought thee out of the land of Egypt, out of the house of bondage.' Have you been in bondage in Egypt and brought out of it? Then of what use is the Torah to you? And it is written: 'Thou shalt have no other gods before me.' Are you angels idolatrous? It is written: 'Remember the Sabbath day, to keep it holy. . . . In it thou shalt not do any work. . . .' Do you work on other days? And it is written: 'Honour thy father and thy mother. . . .' Have you, then, fathers and mothers? And it is written: 'Thou shalt not commit adultery.' Where are there any women among you? Even if there were, how would you asexual beings go about committing adultery? Of what use, then, is the Torah to you?"

At this point the angels listened to reason and let Moses go by; they recognized the fact that God was right to give him the Torah and through him to reveal it to man. "O Lord our Lord, how excellent is thy name in all the earth, who hast set thy glory above the heavens" (Psalms 1:8).

When Moses had dwelt forty days on the mountain, in the presence of God, and was ready to come down he was able to traverse the serried ranks of the angels without fear; indeed they had become his friends. The angel Yefehfiyyah gave him a text of the Torah which he had transcribed with his own hand. The other angels gave him remedies against disease and told him the secret of the Holy Names, as they are to be found in the Torah and as they are to be repeated. Even the angel of death taught him a cure for death, although, as we know, Moses was not able to benefit by it.

Thus Moses overcame the angels, or rather he proved to them that God's Covenant with His people was not their concern. The depositaries of the Law, the guardians of the Torah, are not angels but men.

For Moses and his people the events of Mount Sinai took place in three successive stages, according to God's logical plan. At the first stage God verified the reliability of His human partner; that is, through the intermediary of Moses He assured Himself that the Children of Israel were ready to ratify the eternal Covenant which He was preparing to lay before them. Once He was sure of their obedience and fidelity God set forth the basis of the Covenant, the ten great principles to be observed, which are a preamble to the Torah. In the third and final phase, addressing Himself to Moses alone, God revealed the Torah itself—that is, the body of detailed commandments deriving from the Decalogue, the rules of everyday life which the Chosen People were required to follow. The subsequent events of the Pentateuch carry their history down to the death of Moses.

Nothing could be simpler and better ordered, yet at the same time more laden with consequences for the future of mankind. To the world in general here was the revelation of the oneness of God and of His moral Law; to the Children of Israel acceptance of the Covenant was fraught not only with privilege but with risk and responsibility, with the promise of a future pregnant with glory and humiliation, with joy and persecution.

In the accomplishment of the first stage Moses climbed alone to the top of Sinai while the Hebrews waited for him in an encampment at the foot of the mountain. The prophet's ascent was surrounded by complete silence; the earth was mute and there was not a rustle in the air or a ripple in the water. The whole planet was expectant, and mankind was lost in meditation.

Let us not forget, however, that Moses and his people were still in a state of uncertainty and confusion. Moses foresaw that God was about to reveal the reason for the miracles He had accomplished in bringing the people out of Egypt and to Sinai. He guessed that a new Covenant was in the making, not with a single predestined man, as in the cases of Adam and Abraham, no longer with all humanity, as in the case of Noah, but with a people which had already received particular benefits from him. What was the nature of the Covenant to be, and under what form would the revelation be made? Because Moses knew Egypt and had been initiated into its religion his imagination must have been influenced by the memory of what he had left behind him. As he climbed the mountain his eyes must have looked involuntarily among the wild rocks for the image of a temple such as those which were the seats of Egyptian initiations. The people, too, as they waited at the foot of the cloud-enshrouded heights, feared perhaps to see coming down from the summit a procession of clergy carrying an idol, such as they had witnessed during their captivity, or a group of government officials, in all their pomp and brutality. A few weeks, even if they have been marked by miracles and the acquisition of freedom, are not enough to erase the imprint of a century of enslavement.

On the mountain Moses at first saw nothing unusual, no ceremonial setting, no pomp or dignitaries or clergy, no monument of any kind. Only bare crags and the desert below. Then he heard God's voice. The Bible does not tell us how it came to him, whether out of a cloud or a bush, whether calmly or in accents such as to inspire terror. Nor are we told in what frame of mind Moses received it. The circumstances are unimportant;

it is only the words that matter. Later, when God addressed Himself to the whole people of Israel, to this confused mass of men, some of whom were ready to worship Him while others already had their minds on future idolatries, when He compelled them, no matter what were their thoughts, to accept the mission which went with the bestowal of the Law, He asserted His full majesty and His authority over nature; He had recourse to thunder and lightning, to the firing of the mountain, and to the ram's horn with which nomad shepherds assembled their flocks.

But Moses did not need to be convinced of God's majesty; as His predestined servant he had been aware of it ever since he was born; it was his whole reason for being. Moses listened and God spoke, simply but definitively, in a manner both natural and divine. From the cloud which hid but did not separate Him from His prophet God uttered a few straightforward words which said exactly what they were meant to say; He set forth a brief preliminary agreement which Moses was to transmit to his people:

". . . Thus shalt thou say to the house of Jacob, and tell the children of Israel;

"Ye have seen what I did unto the Egyptians, and how I bare you on eagles' wings, and brought you unto myself.

"Now therefore, if ye will obey my voice indeed, and keep my covenant, then ye shall be a peculiar treasure unto me above all people: for all the earth is mine.

"And ye shall be unto me a kingdom of priests, and an holy nation" (Exodus 19:3–6).

This was all; it was very little but it was tremendous. Few other words have created a greater echo in the hearts of those who heard them or had more enduring repercussions in history. Few other words have determined so precisely the future of those with whom they were concerned.

"Ye shall be unto me a kingdom of priests." This sentence was to determine the future of Israel. In it are contained the spiritual demands and aspirations which, in spite of changing circumstances, were to keep Israel faithful throughout the centuries to its mission. In it was contained also Israel's isolated position in history and in society which allowed it to bear witness for all mankind. Here were contained its peculiar character and its universality, its glories and its humiliations—as well as its persecution.

A priest, any priest, does not live like other men. Whether he be idolatrous or monotheistic, Jew or Christian, he is compelled to observe rules which govern his way of life. In order to carry out his ministry he must not only sacrifice his material comforts and possessions, he must also subordinate his everyday life, his eating, drinking, freedom of movement, and affections, to regulations which isolate him from his secular fellows. The logical background of such a mission is a monastery or cloister, where there is some mitigation of the paradox of a life lived in the light of eternity.

In the case of the Hebrews at the foot of Mount Sinai, to whom Moses was about to bring the Lord's word, this paradox was complete; it was fraught with difficulties and illogic to the point of being almost unbearable and insensate. Was it not practically impossible to live like priests, to follow a strict and detailed code, when socially their life was the same as that of other men? Living in the world as they were to live in centuries to come, how could they observe rules of diet, purification, circumcision, marriage, Sabbath observance, and jurisprudence which the profane were bound to brand as anachronistic because they could not understand that they were eternal? *Sacerdos in aeternum*, this formula of the Catholic sacrament of ordination, was after Sinai to apply to the whole people of Israel. And the paradox, in this case, was a double one. First, it is paradoxical that an ephemeral being like man should have an eternal vocation. Second, it is patently absurb and unnatural that a mixed body of believers and unbelievers, of men both good and bad, should be collectively as well as individually compelled to conduct themselves as priests when they are actually laymen.

In our day, talk of God's addressing Himself to man has lost all force and meaning. But let us look again at the picture of Mount Sinai. Here we have a wretched, struggling people, weakened by a hundred years of persecution, then thrown by God's will (in which not all of them believed) into a long and dangerous march through wild and hostile regions, in a state of precarious freedom, and at the end of it all told that theirs is to be a priestly vocation. A "kingdom of priests," two million priests, the newborn child, the decrepit old man, the adolescent eager to know the joys of love, the pervert, the lecher, the fool— all these were called upon to submit to laws which could not but isolate them from the surrounding populations. This isolation, through the ages, was to set the Hebrews apart and to raise insoluble problems which too often have resolved themselves in blood.

And so we can imagine how Moses was at the same time joyful and apprehensive of the glory and risk of the divine command. And how the people, moved at first to a pride that was to remain their heritage, were overcome by astonishment and terror, to the point where they were tempted to refuse the burden thrust upon them. For the refugees from Egypt the word "priest" had a magical power and meaning. It was no mere symbolical term; rather, it called up a very definite image. At first, it seemed to mean the possession of ornate vestments and sanctuaries, of treasures and mysteries and secret initiation rites such as they had been among the Egyptians. For this enslaved people to be made priests brought about a radical transformation of their lives, the acquisition of a dignity which had hitherto been denied them, as if they, plebeians, had suddenly been admitted to the privileges of an aristocratic cult and their rude, nomadic life changed into a protected existence, but one charged with obligations.

A kingdom of priests—this meant that to all eternity their life would be both secular and religious, a wager on two levels, losing on both except in the unusual cases where the two were as one. They were fated to suffer great unhappiness and to reap occasional great rewards, to know the worst and the best. How were they to accept this call to greatness? As Moses came down from the mountain he must have wondered what sort of welcome he would receive. But the welcome was quite overwhelming: "And all the people answered together, and said, All that the Lord hath spoken we will do" (Exodus 19:8).

And so the Children of Israel confidently embraced the Covenant and their religious vocation. But they had still to learn its full implications. This is the content of the second phase of the episode of Mount Sinai, in which fundamental words were addressed to them. Unlike the first phase, this one was clothed in solemnity. Moses reported to the Lord the people's acceptance of the Covenant, and the Lord, sure now that He could count on His partner, proceeded to set forth the details of its establishment. First of all, He indicated to Moses what role he personally was to play. "And the Lord said unto Moses, Lo, I come unto thee in a thick cloud, that the people may hear when I speak with thee, and believe thee for ever" (Exodus 19:9). But before making His appearance and proclaiming the fundamental words He gave Moses certain instructions which the people must follow before they could hear the divine voice:

"And the Lord said unto Moses, Go unto the people and sanctify them to day and to morrow, and let them wash their clothes,

"And be ready against the third day; for the third day the Lord will come down in the sight of all the people upon Mount Sinai.

"And thou shalt set bounds unto the people round about, saying, Take heed to yourselves, that ye go not up into the mount, or touch the border of it: whosoever toucheth the mount shall be surely put to death.

"There shall not an hand touch it, but he shall surely be stoned, or shot through; whether it be beast or man, it shall not live; when the trumpet soundeth long, they shall come up to the mount" (Exodus 19:9–13).

Moses went down and told the people to purify themselves and wash their clothes and refrain for two days from intercourse with their wives. "And it came to pass on the third day in the morning, that there were thunders and lightnings, and a thick cloud upon the mount, and the voice of the trumpet exceeding loud; so that all the people that was in the camp trembled" (Exodus 19:16).

The trumpet that sounded at this solemn moment was the ram's horn, the *shofar*, which sounds today during the most impressive Jewish rites, at the beginning of the New Year, Rosh Hashana, and at the end of Yom Kippur or the Day of Atonement. This was the horn with which shepherds called their flocks together to lead them to pasture or to protect them from impending danger. To the Children of Israel, most of them nomads and shepherds, the thunder and lightning and the sound of the trumpet were not figments of the imagination but concrete phenomena with which they were already familiar. God fitted Himself into the framework of their everyday existence: Israel was His flock and Moses its shepherd. If they trembled with fear of the thunder and lightning it was in an actual and not a metaphysical manner; their senses responded to the approach of a natural cataclysm which they had often experienced and had every reason to dread.

Moses led the people out of the camp and to the foot of the mountain.

"And Mount Sinai was altogether in a smoke, because the Lord descended upon it in fire: and the smoke thereof ascended as the smoke of a furnace, and the whole mount quaked greatly.

"And when the voice of the trumpet sounded long, and waxed louder and louder, Moses spake, and the Lord answered him by a voice" (Exodus 19:18–19).

At God's bidding Moses went back down to the people. Tradition has it that for this descent God changed His features into

those of the first prophet, Abraham, in order to show forth the
continuity of His revelation, as a Covenant with the whole
people took the place of that made with the father of all believers. The Bible tells us that Moses covered his face with a
veil, lest the reflection of God's light upon it be unbearable
(Exodus 34:33).

The text of the Covenant is that of the Ten Commandments.
By reason of their etymology and content it is more exact to call
them the ten fundamental words, *asseret hadibrot,* for they contain not only commandments—positive and negative—but also
an affirmation of the nature and personality of God.

Deafened by the thunder and blinded by the lightning, trembling with fear and filled with curiosity, the Children of Israel
waited to hear the fatal words. Uppermost in their minds was
the question of whether or not they would be intelligible.
Would they be understandable only to initiates, like those of
the Egyptian initiation ceremonies from which they had been
excluded: or would they be everyday words, devoid of allegory
and mystery, clear, illuminating words such as those spoken to
Abraham, Isaac, and Jacob? In the silence which cut through
the din of the storm, in the bright daylight, no longer troubled
by flashes of lightning, there sounded the first word which God
spoke to His people. It was not a commonplace word but one
pregnant with majesty. Like a king speaking of himself as "we,"
or a chief of state referring to another in the third person, at this
moment when He came close to man God chose to keep His
distance. Regardless of what He was to say afterwards, at this
moment of His entrance into history, of His transformation
from the Eternal into God, at this moment of suspense before
the release of the great currents of belief and doubt on which
men were to be borne along for centuries to come, God was like
an orchestra conductor, breaking the silence with a mighty
chord before the flow of a melody. "*Anorhi,*" God proclaimed.
"*Anorhi*" . . . these three syllables penetrated the ears of the
hundreds of thousands of waiting people at the foot of the

mountain and engraved themselves upon the mind of Moses so indelibly that even if they were to be forgotten by the others he would have always been able to recall them. Thence they reverberated in every time and clime.

"*Anorhi* [I]" . . . the God who employed this personal pronoun was the God of unity, soon to be called *Erhad,* or "One." His oneness was not arithmetical, shut within its own definition, exclusive of multiplicity. *Anorhi* expresses the unity of the divine Person and the multiplicity of the creatures of His creation.

"I am the Lord thy God, which have brought thee out of the land of Egypt, out of the house of bondage" (Exodus 20:2). His two million hearers, as they received this first of the ten fundamental words, could immediately apprehend its significance. The Eternal was placing Himself in history, in relation to the events through which they had just come; He was recalling to them the six weeks that had gone by since they left Egypt. In spite of the angels which separated Him from them and the cloud in which God was hidden, He spoke directly to the people of Israel, in answer to their declaration of faith, their acceptance of the Covenant as Moses had presented it to them. And He answered in simple terms, understandable to all men. They learned, with a feeling of reassurance, that there were no more initiates or pontiffs between themselves and God. Every Israelite was to be his own priest; initiation was to include all the people, without distinctions of caste, and to be couched in common language. Although it is on a much vaster scale we may compare the significance of this event to that of the Latin Gutenberg Bible, which democratized the Holy Word and popularized religion.

The verses that follow all begin, in Hebrew, with the word "*Lo* [No]," the redundant monosyllable with which for generations Jewish mothers have forbidden their children to do something wrong: "No, you mustn't say this"; "No, you mustn't do that." *Lo.* Seven times this word of interdiction is pronounced to tell the people of Israel their divine Father's will, and so it is engraved on the tables of the Law. It is a code of upbringing that God promulgated for the people on whom His future earthly existence depended, the people who are His children.

(No) "Thou shalt have no other gods before me.

"Thou shalt not make unto thee any graven image, or any likeness of anything that is in heaven above, or that is in the earth beneath, or that is in the water under the earth:

"Thou shalt not bow down thyself to them, nor serve them. . . .

(No) "Thou shalt not take the name of the Lord thy God in vain. . . .

(No) "Thou shalt not kill.

(No) "Thou shalt not commit adultery.

(No) "Thou shalt not steal.

(No) "Thou shalt not bear false witness against thy neighbour.

(No) "Thou shalt not covet thy neighbour's house, thou shalt not covet thy neighbour's wife, nor his manservant, nor his ox, nor his ass, nor any thing that is thy neighbour's" (Exodus 20:3–5, 7, 13–17).

In between there are two positive commandments—"Remember the Sabbath day" and "Honour thy father and thy mother"—and some announcements of punishment to those who do not obey. All in all, the fundamental words were as clear to the Hebrews who heard them three thousand years ago as are the eighteenth-century Declaration of the Rights of Man and Declaration of Independence, which we can only hope will last as long. At both periods we have a recognition of elemental truths which cut through confusion, fanaticism, and complexity. The moral laws of the Decalogue arose on the border line between two traditions, that of the sages of Egypt, which we have seen that Moses partially took over, and that of the simple and patriarchal religion of a single God who wishes to bind Himself by a Covenant to the human race and partake of its history. On the one hand, a tradition of an intellectual character, the property of initiates; on the other, the living tradition of a broad group of people, good and bad, believing and unbelieving, lettered and illiterate. On the one hand a social elite, on the other the masses; on the one hand a professional clergy, on the other occasional priests and novices. Simplicity won the day, and the sublime amateurism of a people that did not choose its vocation took a predominant place in the unrolling of a history which swallowed up the concept of initiation.

Tradition shows God holding the upper part of the Tables of the Law and Moses holding the lower, with a small but necessary space between them. In this sublime but at the same time homely interpretation man comes as close as is humanly possible to his Creator and speaks to Him face to face, but he cannot abolish entirely the distance which separates him from the Eternal and Almighty. This remains a symbol of the perpetual search for God which runs throughout history, a search which is never complete yet is tireless and uninterrupted. Such is the destiny of man, the destiny of Israel and the meaning of its messianic hope, its expectation of an end which it has never attained.

We can see, now, the importance of the fundamental words, shared by God and man and written on tablets of stone, halfway between earth and heaven. The Tables of the Law are the only monument of the people of Israel. They are of stone, a solid and compact material which may be and is broken but which will never disappear from God's world. But in spite of its impressive character this monument will never be set up at any one point of the earth's surface. The Tables of the Law were to follow the Chosen People in their migrations, in a case known as the Ark of the Covenant, which was kept in the tent where the elders of the tribes met when Moses called them together. In subsequent centuries these tables were centered in a temple. But such a localization of the Law is untrue to its origins. The law was to have universal application, to travel the world over. At Sinai its everlasting quality was guaranteed not by the erection of a monument but by the ease with which it could be transported over every kind of ground and through every turn of history. The nomadic destiny of the Law, paralleling that of the people of Israel, is a rudimentary and imperfect symbol of its universality and of the omnipresence of God.

In the second phase of the Mount Sinai story, then, God gave the Hebrews the fundamental words: He hammered them into their ears and memories with memorable verses and then set them before their eyes, two by two, facing one another, on tablets of stone. But with this essential deed, the basis of the future, God's task was not completed. There remained the third phase, in which He gave to Moses alone detailed precepts for the application of the Law.

We know that God adapted the modalities of His revelation to those who were to receive it. Later on, when the Hebrews complained of the responsibilities of being a Chosen People, He said quite simply to Moses: "They act according to their lights, and I act according to Mine." Thus God's revelation is not only permanent but also relative. He did not impose upon a still primitive people the complexities and refinements of an overly detailed code. God moves by slow degrees; like a teacher, He said to Moses: "You shall tell them part of these things, and others you shall conceal from them."

It was Moses alone, then, who in the third phase of the Sinai revelation received from God the detailed prescriptions which went with Israel's priestly function. These he set down in the Pentateuch or Torah, where moral and ethical laws are given a historical context and a practical application. As we have seen above, Moses took it upon himself to distinguish between what the people should be told at once and what should be held in reserve for an assured future. He appears to us as both a man of the present, with all its doubts, and a man of the future, with all its certainties. This mirrors the double aspect of the history of Israel, which the Bible presents as a combination of daily vicissitudes and of uninterrupted belief in the Messiah.

For forty days Moses remained, fasting, in the presence of the

Eternal. During this period God proceeded, by logical steps, to say what He had to say. His first instructions had a double purpose: to organize the life of His people so that they should be ready to receive the Torah and to provide for the building of the sanctuary where its revelation would be perpetuated. He gave Moses a moral and religious basis for the Covenant on the one hand and a practical basis on the other. On the moral and religious side a civil, penal, and priestly code; on the practical side the organization of sacrifices which could be offered only in a sole sanctuary which God described as it should be set up, temporarily, in the desert and later, in permanent form, in Canaan.

During the forty days on Mount Sinai and the forty years that followed in the desert Moses set down God's commandments in the Torah and transmitted them to Israel, whose mission it was to spread them abroad. That is, he transcribed that part of them which constitutes the written Law, those of God's words which were to be immediately revealed because the people were able to understand them and put them into practice. This written account restates the creed of biblical monotheism, of the belief in a single God, Creator of the world, Who works together with man to help him achieve salvation—that is, Who associates Himself with history. It contains a strong and peculiarly biblical feeling that religion is expressed in the totality of life, in every human deed and gesture. Hence the large number—613—of *misvot*, or precepts, of moral and social law and of religious custom. But as André and Renée Néher say, in their *Histoire biblique du peuple d'Israël*, these precepts do not derive only from the obligations of the Torah. There is "an impressively large group of prescriptions which have no apparent ritual or ethical motivation . . . *houquim* or statutes . . . which serve essentially to set up in every domain a close relationship between God and man, a constant reminder of the divine presence." Among these are the dietary laws, the laws regarding dress, hygiene, sexual practices, and education; professional regulations for agriculture and the raising of livestock; the law prescribing the presence of God's words on the doors of houses and the gates of the city. Here we find the laws regarding kosher food, which are still observed today, the interdiction of illegitimate or unnatural unions, of tattooing, of touching a mother bird as she hovers over her nest, of weaving garments of mixed linen and cotton, of eating the fruit of a tree less than a year old.

This network of *misvot* and *houquim* surrounding the everyday life of the humblest Jew is heavy and imperious enough to more than justify the Lord's first announcement: *"Ye shall be unto Me a kingdom of priests."* The priestly vocation was a matter not only of moral inspiration but also of practical detail. A Jew was to become a priest by applying the Torah, by harmonizing a mass of particular precepts with the two fundamental laws; that of the oneness of God and that of the love of neighbor. "Thou shalt love thy neighbour as thyself" (Leviticus 19:18).

The Jews had known from the first day of the revelation that they were called to be priests and had accepted the calling; now they knew what it involved for the present and future. They knew that they must meet peculiar obligations, that while living everyday life in the world as laymen they had to follow a fate which not only sanctified them but also set them apart. The destiny of Israel, this mixture of earthly fatality and a transcendent vocation, of trials and glory, this mystery of a frail people, always losing ground but convinced of winning eternity, here is what the Hebrews first dimly and then clearly perceived during the forty days and forty years in which Moses received the Torah and transmitted to them as much of it as they were able to understand and put into practice.

Thus we see take shape the outline and the content of the fundamental mystery of Israel, which is perhaps only the more obvious form of the mystery of the human condition, torn between matter and spirit, between the secular and the sacred. The outlines were visible but the content was not yet fully perceptible or fully expressed. For this there were two reasons.

First, at the same time that God said that His commandments were to bind all the people, without exception, He set up the framework of a special clergy to perform the most sacred of all acts, the act of sacrifice.

"And take unto thee Aaron thy brother, and his sons with him, from among the children of Israel, that he may minister unto me in the priest's office, even Aaron, Nadab and Abihu, Eleazar and Ithamar, Aaron's sons.

"And thou shalt make holy garments for Aaron thy brother for glory and for beauty.

"And thou shalt speak unto all that are wise hearted, whom I have filled with the spirit of wisdom, that they make Aaron's garments to consecrate him, that he may minister unto me in the priest's office" (Exodus 28:1–3).

So it was not enough that a whole people be invested with a priestly vocation. A small group, drawn from a particular family, had to be consecrated to a special priesthood. In distinguishing between the two aspects of the religion, one of which was democratic, while the other implied a sort of aristocracy, in saying that a people's religious vocation required both faith and ritual, both simplicity and pomp, God was taking account of the nature of His Covenant with living men and of His insertion in their existential history. He opened two channels for the perpetuation of His word, one open to all comers, the other reserved for the priests who alone performed the rites to bring Him closer. We may wonder if, in organizing this special priesthood, Moses was not introducing the initiation rites of the Egyptians into biblical religion, whether alongside the open cult inaugurated on Mount Sinai he was not preparing a return to the elaborate temple ceremonials and formalized devotions which the Israelites had forsworn as idolatrous? This is one of the mysteries of the Covenant.

It marks also the beginning of a debate which was to be at times highly dramatic. During the lifetime of Moses the revolt of Korah brought together two hundred and fifty "men of renown" who refused to recognize the special position of the prophet and Aaron, his brother. "Ye take too much upon you, seeing all the congregation are holy, every one of them, and the Lord is among them: wherefore then lift ye up yourselves above the congregation of the Lord?" (Numbers 16:3). The revolt was put down when the earth opened and swallowed up the conspirators. But the Talmud tells us that Korah is ever present in the history of Israel, that his anti-clericalism was not an accident but had a real reason for being.

There is another mystery, but this one necessary and quite consciously planned by Moses in the course of his revelation of the Torah. This is the fact that the revelation was partial, that it corresponded to the requirements of the moment and the degree of the people's intelligence. God told Moses more things than it was opportune for him to reveal, so that there is a margin of mystery between what He told Moses and what Moses told men. In this undefinable marginal area, which allows history free play in carrying out the designs of the Creator and leaves room for the unpredictable, lie the past and future of Israel and of all mankind. In spite of the chronological and geographical elements which allow us to situate it in history, Mount Sinai is less a moment of time than it is an instant of eternity, of the biblical measurement of duration, where we cannot distinguish definite units but where every minute calls up the minutes that went before and opens onto those that will come after.

Present at Sinai were men from every epoch of the history of God. Adam was there, with his sin forgiven. In making a Covenant with his descendants was not God according him an amnesty? Noah was there, in his ark, waiting to receive a more primitive promise. Sarah was there, in her kitchen, and Abraham, leaving his native city to set forth on the great adventure of God. Jacob was there, at the foot of the ladder which was to establish the first connection between earth and heaven. In other words there was present the whole past tradition of Israel, to which God could not but hark back when He made the final Covenant. Thus the Midrash has Him say to Moses: "It is only on account of Abraham that the Torah is given to you." This is why, as Moses climbed Mount Sinai, God concealed His face under that of his great predecessor. If the patriarchs were present it is because Sinai marks the fulfillment of their efforts, which there were incarnated in a whole people.

Not only the biblical past was present at the scene, but perhaps the prehistoric past as well, the pagan past with its cave men and its idolatrous priests groping for the living God. On the slopes of Sinai all these forgotten forerunners, these confused precursors of the Law, witnessed the accomplishment of their obscure aims. God did not address the people of Israel alone but all humanity; in this place and at this time He reconciled all divergencies, gave directions to all divagations.

The future was present as well, as is attested by both the Bible and tradition. Moses says as much in one of the most striking passages of Deuteronomy:

"Ye stand this day all of you before the Lord your God; your captains of your tribes, your elders, and your officers, with all the men of Israel,

"Your little ones, your wives, and thy stranger that is in thy camp, from the hewer of thy wood unto the drawer of thy water:

"That thou shouldest enter into covenant with the Lord thy God, and into his oath, which the Lord thy God maketh with thee this day:

"That he may establish thee to day for a people unto himself, and that he may be unto thee a God, as he hath said unto thee, and as he hath sworn unto thy fathers, to Abraham, to Isaac, and to Jacob" (Deuteronomy 29:10–13).

Here we have a statement that the Covenant was extended to all the Children of Israel gathered together and that it had been promised to the patriarchs before them. But in the verses that follow it is extended to those who are not yet present as well:

"Neither with you only do I make this covenant and this oath;

"But with him that standeth here with us this day before the Lord our God, and also with him that is not here with us this day" (Deuteronomy 29:14-15).

"With him that is not here with us this day . . ." These extraordinary words refer to those who are separated from Sinai not only by space but also by time. They point above all to the inspired men, the prophets, who were to assure the perpetuation of the Covenant in the future. In the Midrash Rabbi Isaac says that at Sinai the prophets received the messages which they were to give to future generations. He considers that "him that is not here with us this day" means the soul of him that is not yet born. At Sinai the dead reappear, the living are gathered together, and the unborn are represented by their souls. Even if he does not yet exist, every man spiritually receives the Torah. Into the mouth of the prophet Isaiah the Midrash puts these words: "I was present at the revelation of Sinai, where I received the prophecy and the Lord sent me His spirit." What is true for the prophets is true also for the sages, the philosophers and men of faith who in every generation interpret God's commandments. Each one of them derives his wisdom from Sinai.

What a numberless assembly was gathered around the predestined mountain, what a loud echo was spread through every time and nation by the words proclaimed at its summit! Rabbi Johanan says: "It is a voice that was divided into seven voices and into seventy languages. The Lord gave His word and proclaimed His commandments to a very great multitude, but they were divided among different languages, each one addressed to a different people."

This last sentence from the Midrash has a particularly important place in tradition, in the history of God on earth. It recognized the fact that the Law was to be spread in two different ways. First there was the written Law, taken down by Moses and proclaimed by the prophets, which is developed in every verse of the Bible, the Law of God, God's share in the establishment of the Law. This was addressed to the very great multitude of the Children of Israel, actually assembled around Him at the foot of the mountain, to those whom it could touch directly after they had agreed to the preliminaries of the Covenant, to the kingdom of priests, directly invested with their vocation.

Even if the people which had come only six weeks before out of Egypt was to bear witness for all mankind, it did not entirely represent it. Mankind is not a kingdom of priests; it does not remain stationary but must evolve in the course of the ages, and in evolving it must somehow adapt the changeless prescriptions of the Law to the mutations of history. Israel, with its vocation, and humanity at large, which, as one rabbi puts it, is "the awakened universe," needed something else beside the written Law, set forth in one place and in one language; they needed the oral Law expressed in commentary and tradition. Hence the seven voices and the seventy languages to which the Midrash refers, hence the diffusion, *orbi* and *ad aeternum*, to every nation and every time, of God's revelation.

Mount Sinai, alternately a center of storm and silence, was on this sixth day of the month of Sivan and during the days to follow the focus of time and space, the cornerstone of history and of eternity. Out of it came the human commentary which was, for century after century, to adapt the fundamental words to the comprehension of man. "They act according to their lights, and I act according to Mine. . . ."

What an infinite number of waves fanned out from the mountaintop where Moses saw God face to face! What astonishment must have been his when he heard seventy languages echo his voice! Rabbi Akiba, the precursor of the Cabala, who was martyred by the Romans, has left a famous *midrash* concerned with this tremendous event. Every rereading of this realistic but mythical story stimulates a new insight and inspires yet another commentary. It is thus that the truth which it tells repeatedly verifies itself.

After Moses had received the Law on Mount Sinai he had an extraordinary vision of time and space. His mortal eyes encompassed the breadth of the world and the passage of the centuries. He saw men of all times and all nations, in their various languages and according to their various beliefs and the stage of their development, adding their commentary to his revelation. Over every word he had pronounced rose mountains of exegeses and rolled torrents of interpretation. To his astonishment at the repercussions of his words there was added astonishment that their echoes should come back to him in languages he did not know. His posterity had escaped him; the traditions to which he had given rise were totally foreign. Should he therefore disavow them? With the confusion and contradictions of human progress deafening his ears and defying his intelligence, he hesitated over a decision on which the future of God and man depended. Finally he made up his mind. Since all these paraphrases were connected to him and to God by the link of successive generations and cultures he could not but be pleased to have spawned them. And so he solemnly declared himself in agreement with all those who called upon his name even if he could not understand what they were saying. In agreement with heretics and schismatics, as long as they respected his belief in the one God; in agreement with unbelievers and atheists, as long as they practiced the law of loving their neighbors as themselves. In agreement, in short, with all those for whose benefit, after the Flood, God had proclaimed the Covenant with Noah, the rainbow Covenant, which He had said was with "every living creature of all flesh that is upon the earth" (Genesis 9:16).

How extraordinarily tolerant is biblical philosophy in recognizing centuries which know it not and men who combat it! No one who had approached the Bible can completely escape from it, any more than any soul can completely elude God. The Bible does not so much persuade us to believe as it shows us how to see, as did Moses on Mount Sinai, the permanence of the divine in lands of doubt and through centuries of denial. Even if we do not believe in God we can see His traces. He may not exist, yet everything happens as if He has existed.

As he came down from Sinai into the world, where trial and tumult awaited him and his people and all men, Moses must have been tempted to give in to his emotions, to bog down in doubt and even to give up his errand. Amid these mixed feelings he returned to the mountain whence God had spoken to him and over its bare summit, peopled forever with men's hopes and expectations, he saw the rainbow, everlasting sign of God's irrevocable Covenant with the children of Noah—that is, with the people of every time and place, believers and unbelievers.

Thus the Eternal made Himself into God. By entrusting His law to a man, to a people, and to all mankind, He exposed it to the weaknesses of men, the accidents and fatalities of life in the world, and to the unpredictable and destructive action of time. From then on the history of God was merged with the history of the human race. There is no other example of involvement in so total an adventure, an involvement sought after by the very Being who by His nature could have escaped it, shutting Himself up in His immutability.

Was it possible for Moses, who had served not as an intermediary between man and God (there is need for few such priestly intermediaries in the Hebrew tradition) but between God and man, to escape the consequences of the human condition? Could he hope to defy the slings and arrows of fortune and end his days serenely? Not at all. He had to suffer his share of the vicissitudes of history; he was called upon to dispel doubt and stem the recurrent tide of idolatry, then to beseech the Lord not to exterminate the idolaters, not to wipe out the vital force of man, impure and confused but at the same time productive and necessary. When he came down from Sinai Moses found his people worshiping the Golden Calf and he had both to combat the sin and obtain God's indulgence for the sinners. After the success of his courtroom plea he was faced with the necessity of making a fresh start. The people gave up their false gods but they refused to recognize the true One. In order to reaffirm His power God had to perform new miracles.

Why did not God save this faithful servant from death, that fatality to which men can never be reconciled, or at least spare him until the accomplishment of his mission and the entrance into the Promised Land? As an expiation for his errors and those of his people God denied him this supreme reward. Moses died, unsatisfied, at the hour set by the Eternal. Nothing, tradition says, could deflect God from this intent. When his last hour came Moses was to suffer all the anxiety and rebellion of an ordinary man. He was not the hero, detached from worldly things and ready to die, who in Alfred de Vigny's poem prays God to let him "sleep the sleep of the earth." Like any other man, he clung desperately to every hope of survival, he offered up prayers and arguments in a desperate attempt to persuade God to put off his death. Aspiring to taste the last fruits of life, which God denied him, he went through the traditional "agony," in its etymological sense of a final battle between life and annihilation. The agony of Moses, as one of the most powerful of the rabbis' stories tells it, shows that in spite of his intimacy with God he remained very much a human.

In the month of Adar, of the fortieth year after the exodus from Egypt, the Holy One—blessed be His name—said to Moses: "I have something to tell you." "Master of the world, speak; your servant is listening," Moses replied. "Go to the top of Mount Nebo," God commanded. Moses rejoiced, thinking: "When I was younger God called me up to a mountaintop and gave me two stone tablets. Now He must have another gift to bestow upon me." But his hope was soon dashed to the ground. "It is not for the reason you imagine," God told him. "I have given you the Torah and I have nothing more to give. You must go up on the mountain to die, to go to your fathers."

On the seventh day of the month of Adar, when Moses was on top of the mountain, he heard a mysterious voice say: "You

have come to your last day." Then Moses remembered that this
was his birthday and that he had reached the end of the time
predicted by God in Exodus 23:26 with the words: "The number of thy days I will fulfil."

Knowing that he must leave the world, Moses went back
home to finish the thirteen texts of the Torah on which he had
been working. He called the chiefs of the twelve tribes, one by
one, and gave each a copy, saying: "Look to this book of the
Torah which I am giving you, in order that you may read, mark,
and observe it." The last copy, which was the most complete, he
kept in his hand and then went to lay it, as was prescribed, in
the side of the Ark of the Covenant (Deuteronomy 31:26). At
this moment the mysterious voice which he had heard on the
mountain sounded again, saying: "You have no more than five
hours to live." When he heard these words Moses wept. But
soon, recovering his self-control, he realized that it was time to
end his mission. All the sons of Israel were sitting around him,
all the Chosen People who must now fulfill God's Law. His face
shone like the sun and the face of Joshua, his successor, shone
like the moon. Moses read out the Law and Joshua commented
upon it; Moses spoke and Joshua explained. The written Law
and the oral Law talked, through their mouths, to one another;
they were not in disagreement but were complementary.

Moses exhorted the Israelites to honor their Father in
heaven, to observe the Law and the precepts and to obey
Joshua, who would be their leader when he was gone. In these
last hours of his life he gave proof of supreme humility and
showed no jealousy of his successor; indeed he heaped praise
upon him.

At this point the mysterious voice said: "You have only four
hours to live." Moses prayed to the Holy One: "Master of the
world, if it is only to make place for my disciple, Joshua, that I
must be eliminated, let him take the highest rank and I shall
follow him. Let him be the high priest and I an ordinary priest,
let him be the king and I a slave. Only allow me to live long

enough to visit the Promised Land." But the Holy One answered: "I have sworn by the greatness of My name that you shall not cross the Jordan."

Moses, panic-stricken at the approach of death, deployed all his powers of invention and persuasion to induce God to allow him at least a moment in the land which he was not allowed to possess. "Master of the world, by the power of Your ineffable name, permit me to be like a bird, let my arms be like the wings of the dawn so that I may fly over the river and visit the country beyond!" But the Holy One answered: "That would be the same thing as if you possessed the Promised Land, and I should be false to My oath." Moses insisted: "Master of the world, let me be like a fish, so that I can plunge into the waters and visit the country on the other side!" But the Holy One—blessed be His name—replied: "That would be the same thing as if you possessed the Promised Land, and I should be false to My oath." And Moses said: "Let me sit on the wings of the clouds, and bear me over the Jordan, so that I may visit the land beyond." "That too," said God, "would be the same thing as if you had crossed the river. . . . And then I wrote, by your hand, in the Torah: 'Thou shalt not remove thy neighbour's landmark' [Deuteronomy 9:14]. The sky and the clouds have already been given to Elijah; how can you ask for a realm that is not yours?" Moses, in despair, pleaded: "Master of the world, cut me into pieces, and throw me, piece by piece, across the river. Then You can put me together again on the other side, so that I may visit the Promised Land!" Once again the Holy One—may His name be blessed—answered: "In so doing I should be false to My oath." Then Moses said: "If I cannot enter the Promised Land, let me at least see it." And this time God consented.

He showed Moses the land of Israel, four hundred parasangs long and four hundred parasangs wide, with its mountains and valleys, its open spots and its hidden spots, its places far away and its places nearby, all this He let him encompass with his eyes. When Moses had seen it, "There you are," said the Holy

One, "this is the land which I promised." The viewing had taken an hour, and now the mysterious voice said: "Why do you torment yourself? You have only three hours to live."

At this reminder Moses felt more anguish than ever, and the deeply human cause of his anguish was revealed. He was anxious not only to enter the Promised Land but to go on living, in any place and in any company. His concern for his mission was almost obliterated by his fear of death. If God would not allow him to enter Canaan he was willing to put aside his dignity and go somewhere else, to live in obscurity, apart from his people, but to live. . . . He asked God if he might settle in Gilead, with the tribes of Gad and Reuben. "Let me abide with them while Joshua enters the Promised Land." Before this anguished man, who was ready to give up his whole reason for being in order to prolong his life, God sought to put things in perspective and to recall Moses to his mission. "What will the Children of Israel say?" He asked him. What, indeed, would have been the reaction of this restless, unstable people, so easily subject to idolatry and doubt, if they were to hear that the prophet had chosen to end his days with other tribes and in another land? Moses was made mindful of the supernatural reason for his existence; he admitted the impiety of his desire, confessed his error, and bowed to the divine will.

Meanwhile another one of the remaining hours had gone by, and the mysterious voice announced: "Do not torment yourself, you have only two hours to live." In the following hour Moses did not speak. He listened, impassively, to the debate which the angels were holding about him. The wicked Sammael, chief of the angels of destruction, was waiting impatiently for Moses to die, pitilessly repeating: "When will the moment come for me to carry his soul away?" Michael, the guardian angel of Israel, was deeply distressed by these cruel words. "Wicked one!" he exclaimed. "You laugh, but I weep." During the hour in which Moses was silent he had a dismal vision of what was to come.

The implacable Sammael would not be moved by Michael's words.

Once again came the mysterious voice: "Moses, why do you torment yourself? You have only an hour to live." Moses, more panic-stricken than ever at the approach of the inevitable and aware that the angels were disputing his last breath, made another desperate attempt to bend God's will. "Master of the world, do not let me die!" he implored. This ingenuous plea was all he could find to say to the Almighty. But God will not, for the sake of a single man, alter the course of history. He answered like a doctor of Israel, with a biblical sentence to support Him: " 'I have set before you life and death' [Deuteronomy 30:19]. Unless I cause you to die, how can I bring you to life again in the next world? And then it would be contrary to the Law, for it is written: 'Neither is there any that can deliver out of my hand' " (Deuteronomy 32:39).

Then Moses burst into tears, clinging with every fiber of his being to the world that he must leave behind him. Groping for something to hold onto, he addressed himself to the earth: "Earth, earth, I beg you to intercede in my favor with the Holy One. Perhaps you can persuade Him to take pity on me and let me live." At once the mysterious voice spoke: "Foolish man! Is it not written that the earth was desolation and chaos, that the earth was in darkness upon the face of the deep before God intervened? How can you expect the earth to oppose the will of Him who created it? Is it not written elsewhere: 'The earth shall wax old like a garment, and they that dwell therein shall die' [Isaiah 51:6]? The earth should ask pity for itself rather than for you; your fates are bound up together, for it is written: 'Dust thou art, and unto dust shalt thou return' " (Genesis 3:19).

Then Moses wept again and addressed himself to the heavens: "Heavens, ask pity for me!" but the heavens answered: "We must first ask pity for ourselves, for we too are perishable; our fate is foretold in two phrases of the Torah, first: 'Let there be a firmament' [Genesis 1:6], and second: 'The heavens shall be rolled together as a scroll' " (Isaiah 34:4).

Then Moses addressed himself to the stars, but they too asked pity for themselves. He addressed himself to the sun and moon, but they in turn claimed to be perishable, according to the words of the prophet: "Then the moon shall be confounded, and the sun ashamed" (Isaiah 24:23).

When all these things so much greater than he had failed him, when he had lost hope in the earth, the heavens, the stars, the sun, and the moon, Moses remembered his human dimensions and invoked the geographical entities that determine the existence of us all and played such a part in his own. He called upon Mount Sinai, but the mountain answered with these words of the prophet: "And every mountain and hill shall be laid low" (Isaiah 40:4).

He called upon the oceans and the rivers, but they too were subject to the rule of the Eternal, "which maketh a way in the sea, and a path in the mighty waters" (Isaiah 43:16).

He called upon the Red Sea, but it is written: "The Lord shall utterly destroy the tongue of the Egyptian sea, and with His mighty wind shall He shake his hand over the river, and shall smite it in the seven streams" (Isaiah 11:15).

He called upon the desert, but it is written: "His hands formed the dry land" (Psalms 95:5).

As the universe shut itself off progressively before him Moses turned to the Orders of Creation, but here is how they told him that they too were in the Lord's hands: "He hath made every thing beautiful in his time" (Ecclesiastes 3:11), and "All go unto one place" (Ecclesiastes 3:20).

Finding no other aid, Moses turned to men, calling upon both their prayers and their reason. He implored first Joshua and then Eleazar, the son of Aaron, to pray for him. But Sammael stood in the way and closed their mouths so that they could not pray.

Hounded by fatality, Moses made yet another attempt, approaching the leaders of Israel and imploring them to save him from death. He went to the seventy elders, then to all the Israelites gathered together, recalling how he had once interceded in their favor. "At the time of the Golden Calf I prayed to God and asked for His pity, until finally He revoked his sentence against you."

Was Moses going to obtain the intervention of the whole people of Israel in his favor? Again angelic malevolence stood in the way. This time one hundred and eighty-four myriads* of wicked angels came down and alighted in front of the great tent where the people had gathered; one of them stood in front of each Israelite and clapped a hand over his mouth so that he was unable to speak.

Moses once more burst into bitter tears. "Woe is me!" he exclaimed. "What can I do and where am I to go? Who is there to help me?"

When he realized that no one could save him from death he set about assuring the continuation of his mission. He called Joshua and said to him in the presence of the assembled people: "Joshua, my son, here are those whom I am entrusting to you; they are children, little lambs that have not yet attained the age of wisdom. Take care what you say to them, let no word from your mouth lead them astray, for they are the Lord's first-born, whom He has set above all others. 'Ye shall be a peculiar treasure unto Me above all people [Exodus 19:5]. He says in the Torah, and this is confirmed by one of His prophets: 'When Israel was a child, then I loved him, and called my son out of Egypt' [Hosea 11:1]. From now on you must bear a triple burden. The burden of this people of Israel, which was formerly borne by Aaron, Miriam, and myself, is now on your shoulders. . . . May God be with you, Joshua, my son, may you and my people, Israel, go in peace. . . ."

Then Moses began to bless each of the tribes separately, but when he saw that time was growing short and he would not be

* A myriad is 10,000.

able to finish he bestowed a general blessing. Afterwards he said to the people: "I have caused you to suffer for the Torah and the Commandments. Forgive me." With a single voice the people replied: "Moses, our master, you are forgiven. We have been a heavy burden and made you angry. Will you, in your turn, forgive us?" And Moses said: "You are forgiven."

At this point the mysterious voice said: "You have only a half hour to live."

And so Moses said to his people: "I beg you, when you enter the Promised Land, to remember my bones. And say to yourselves: 'Woe to the son of Amram, who ran before us like a horse, and whose bones have remained in the desert!'"

At these words the people of Israel wept. "Moses, our master, you are going away. What is to become of us?" And Moses answered: "All this time the Lord has been with you and He will remain with you always. . . . You must not think that the miracles which the Lord performed were a reward for my merits. He performed them for His own glory. If you have faith in Him, He will grant your desires." And the people proclaimed with one voice: "God is our refuge and strength, a very present help in trouble" (Psalms 46:1).

While they said these things a quarter of an hour went by, and the mysterious voice spoke again: "Moses, why do you torment yourself? You have no more than a quarter of an hour to live."

Moses blessed the Israelites again; he drew up for them some prayers and statements of belief. The Holy Spirit allowed him to see into the future, to have a vision of the victories which the Holy One would accord His people. And he exclaimed: "Happy art thou, O Israel, who is like unto thee, O people saved by the Lord" (Deuteronomy 33:29). He uttered a final benediction, then, weeping bitterly, he said: "I shall see you again at the resurrection of the dead." Then he went away, sobbing, leaving the people to weep behind him. He tore his beard and his robe, he rolled his head in the dust, threw his cloak over it in token of mourning, and went into his tent, groaning: "Woe unto me, for I have been struck down! Woe unto my feet which have not trod the Promised Land, woe unto my hands which have not gathered its fruits, woe to my palate which has not tasted its milk and honey!"

And what did Moses do in his tent? He took the scroll of the Law, on which he was to write for the benefit of Joshua the ineffable name which he alone knew. But he had not finished tracing the letters when the moment of his death was at hand. And so the name of the Lord was never to be made known.

The Holy One said to Gabriel: "Bring me Moses' soul!" But Gabriel drew back. "Master of the world, how can I strike down a man who is worth sixty myriads of men?" The Holy One turned to Michael and gave him the same command, but Michael answered only with a flood of tears. Then the Holy One turned to Zagzagel, but Zagzagel said: "Master of the world, I was his master and he was my disciple. I cannot carry away his soul."

Since none of the angels of light was willing to touch Moses, Sammael came before the Holy One and asked: "Master of the world, is Moses, the master of Israel, greater than Adam, whom You made to be Your shadow? Is he greater than Abraham, who was cast into the fire for the sanctification of your name? Is he greater than Isaac, greater than Jacob, Your first-born, greater than Jacob's twelve sons? None of these escaped me. Allow me, then, to snatch Moses' soul."

But the Holy One—blessed be His name—answered: "None of them was like to Moses. Tell me, how will you lay hold of him? By his face? How can you approach the face which has shone ever since it stood before My face, as it is written in the Torah [Exodus 34:35]? By his hands, into which the Tables of the Law were given? By his feet, which walked through the cloud that surrounded Me [Exodus 19:9]? There is no way for you to take hold of him."

But Sammael insisted: "Master of the world, only give me permission to snatch his soul, and I shall do it." Then God was persuaded and gave him permission. Joyfully Sammael stepped out before the Holy One, girding on his sword and robing himself in cruelty and anger.

Moses was sitting in his tent, tracing the letters of the ineffable name. Sparks of fire came out of his mouth and the letters shone like the sun, so that he was like unto one of the angels of the Lord God of Hosts. When he saw Sammael, he turned toward him, ready for a last combat. "Sammael! Sammael!" he shouted. " 'There is no peace, saith the Lord, unto the wicked' [Isaiah 48:22]. What are you doing here?"

"Your last moment is at hand; give me your soul," said Sammael. "Who sent you?" asked Moses. "He who made the world and all souls." "I'll not give you my soul," Moses retorted. "You have no choice," Sammael told him. "The souls of all men who have come into the world are delivered into my hands." "Do not compare me to other men," said Moses, "for I have more power than they." "What is your power?" "I am the son of Amram," said Moses. "I came out of my mother's womb already circumcised and without giving her pain. And how many miracles I have performed! I divided the Red Sea, I sweetened the bitter waters of Lake Marah, I hewed two tablets of stone, I went up to heaven and saw the *Shekinah* and talked with Him, face to face, and amid the flames He gave me the Torah. Has anyone that ever came into the world done such great things? Wicked angel, depart from me; I will not give you my soul!"

At this moment the mysterious voice sounded: "Why do you torment yourself, Moses? You have only the space of a *rega* to live." Sammael addressed himself to the Holy One, and the Holy One—blessed be His name—was angry and cried out against him: "Wicked angel, you were created from the fire of Gehenna, and to that fire you shall return!"

Sammael drew his sword from the sheath and planted himself

in front of Moses. The prophet was so enraged that he picked up the scroll on which the holy name was partially engraved and struck Sammael with it, shouting all the while, until the wicked angel ran away.

Meanwhile half a *rega* had gone by and the mysterious voice broke in to say: "Moses, why do you torment yourself? The end of the moment of your death is at hand." Moses prayed to the Holy One: "Master of the world, remember the day when You appeared to me in the burning bush; remember the day when I came up to You on Mount Sinai and You charged me with giving Israel the Law. . . . I beg You, merciful Lord, do not hand me over to the angel of death." Just then the mysterious voice interrupted: "I have granted your prayer; I myself shall take care of your burial." And the Holy One—blessed be His name—came down from heaven to receive the soul of Moses. When Moses recognized the One he had seen at a solemn moment on Mount Sinai he fell on his face and said: "Master of the world, You created the world out of Your great mercy and with mercy You govern it. With the same mercy take my soul away."

And the mysterious voice answered: "Moses, have no fear. My righteousness shall go before you, and the glory of the Lord behind."

Alongside the Holy One three angels—Michael, Gabriel, and Zagzagel—came down from heaven. Michael laid out a purple cloak, Zagzagel put a silken cushion beside his head, and the Holy One—blessed be His name—stood beside his bed and spoke directly to Moses' soul. "My daughter," He said, "I assigned you for a hundred and twenty years to Moses' body. Do not delay; your end is here." But Moses' soul resisted God: "I know that you are the God of souls, and that the souls of living and dead alike are in Your hands. You created me and for a hundred and twenty years assigned me to Moses' body. Now I am reluctant to leave it, for no man has as pure a body as his."

Then the Eternal said to the soul: "Do not delay, for your end has come. I will take you up to the highest heaven and you shall have a place of honor beside My Throne of Glory."

When Moses saw that his soul was hesitant he said to it: "Do you wish the angel of death to take you?" And his soul answered: "The Holy One will not allow it. As it will be said in the Psalms: 'Thou hast delivered my soul from death'" (Psalms 116:8). "Then where do you think you are going?" Moses asked. "I shall walk before the Lord through the land of the living."

When Moses heard his soul's intentions he allowed her to depart from him. "Go to your rest, my soul," he said; "the Lord has heaped blessings upon you." When the Holy One heard these words He embraced the prophet and took his soul from him with a kiss, thus fulfilling what is said in the Scriptures: "And Moses was an hundred and twenty years old when he died: his eye was not dim, nor his natural force abated" (Deuteronomy 34:7).

At this moment the Holy One wept and the whole world was disconsolate. "Who will help Me to restrain evildoers?" asked the Holy One. "Who will help Me to withstand the artisans of iniquity? And when My children sin, who will plead on their behalf?"

The angels on guard lamented: "Where shall wisdom be found?" The heavens wept and said: "A good man is gone." The earth wept and said: "No just man remains." And all the Orders of Creation wept for the righteous man who had found no aid, repeating the sentence that was to be said by the prophet: "The righteous perisheth, and no man layeth it to heart" (Isaiah 57:1).

Joshua cried aloud, searching for Moses, and echoing, before their time, the Psalmist's words: "Help us, O Lord, for there is no good man left among us." And all the Israelites said: "He practiced the justice of the Lord."

And the Holy One—blessed be His name—pronounced the

last words of the Torah, which He himself had inspired: "And there arose not a prophet since in Israel like unto Moses, whom the Lord knew face to face" (Deuteronomy 34:10).

And so all the inspired books, whether written by Moses or by those who came after, glorify the man in whom was incarnated the most decisive moment of the history of God on earth. Through him there came about two essential events. The Eternal willed to become God, by writing Himself into history and accepting its detours and fatalities and drama. But, above all, the Eternal God moved and spoke in a close relationship with man. He discovered, through the reluctance, the complaints, the pleas and, finally, the resignation of Moses, the nature of the single man and of the people to whom He had confided His future.

And after perceiving the nature of man He accepted the task of persuading him to bow to the divine will. He saw at first hand his anxiety, He shared his suffering and took part in his debates. His sovereign decision took on flesh and bones. It was no longer an intellectual concept; it became a human drama, not only for His servant, Moses, but for all His people as well.

Moses, as we have said before, was an intercessor not only between man and God but also between God and man. He made himself an example of the concrete enigmas of the human condition. The circumstances of both his life and death were charged with significance. Thanks to his errors and sufferings, thanks to the events of his life and the agony of his death, the Eternal, made God, came to know that the most carefully chosen man, the most carefully Chosen People, remain ineradicably human.

Afterword

The absence of God leaves in every human conscience a void in which anxiety, violence, and even madness may proliferate. Certainly this is no excuse for taking refuge in specious reasoning or in half-baked escapist transcendencies. But it should impel us to search our everyday life for the humble and concrete materials of a reconstruction. Everyday life is the stuff of history. And history is the minute and at the same time infinitely immense framework in which the God of the Bible has provided us with a series of certainties.

This history of God is not like any other. But certain of its elements, as we have seen, are mingled with those of the history of man. It unrolls simultaneously in the realms of immanence and transcendency, or in what are commonly called earth and heaven. And heaven is to be reached only by overstepping the usual limits, by what Proudhon, an unbeliever haunted by religion, called the "salmon leap," the leap which a man takes out of his everyday life into either ecstasy or asphyxia, into a state of enhanced being or one of non-being, as the case may be.

In this book we dare an initial step, taking us back to a time when such a step was more natural and easy. At this time God and man were almost on the same level. *Belief* in God was superfluous; men simply were aware of His presence and its effects. And this awareness satisfied the needs and aspirations which we see around us today.

Our century is, or imagines itself to be, one not of faith but of reason. Our way is to take note rather than to believe, to test by experiment rather than to tell stories. But this attitude is, in reality, akin to that of five thousand years ago. We have seen how primitive man sought an explanation of the world from religion, how pre-biblical man gave religion a structure, how our fathers drew from religion a moral code and a messianic hope which fitted in with their expectations.

And what are the needs of today? What do we expect? What shall we find? From what springboards shall we make a new "salmon leap," how shall we detect the presence of God in the world, *hic et nunc*, at man's level?

By going back to the age of intimacy between God and man, by searching out the historical elements of religious feeling, we have begun to see the nature of the problem. May we follow man in his search for God, through the unrolling of history, which, no matter how many times it wearies him or leads him astray, is his eternal inspiration.

Bibliography

Texts:

The Holy Bible, Authorized King James version.

The Talmud of Jerusalem, translated by Dr. M. Schwab, Williams & Norgate, London, 1886.

Midrash Rabba, translated by Rabbi Dr. H. Freedman and Maurice Simon, The Soncino Press, London, 1939.

Moses Maimonides, *The Guide for the Perplexed*, translated by M. Friedländer, Dover Publications, New York, 1956.

The Midrash on Psalms, translated by W. G. Braude, Yale University Press, New Haven, 1959.

A Rabbinic Anthology, by Montefiore and Loewe, Greenwich Editions, New York, 1938.

Le Commentaire de Rachi sur le Pentateuque, Comptoir du Livre du Keren Hasefer, Paris, 1957.

Other works:

Abellio, Raymond, *La Bible, document chiffré*, Gallimard, Paris, 1950.

Abraham, Meyer, *Légendes juives apocryphes sur la vie de Moïse*, Paul Geuthner, Paris, 1925.

Adler, Gerhard, *Studies in Analytical Psychology*, W. W. Norton, New York, 1948.

Agus, Jacob Bernard, *The Evolution of Jewish Thought, from Biblical Times to the Opening of the Modern Era*, Abelard Schuman, New York, 1959.

Albright, William Foxwell, *From the Stone Age to Christianity: Monotheism and the Historical Process*, Johns Hopkins Press, Baltimore, 1940. *The Archaeology of Palestine and the Bible*, F. H. Revell, New York, 1932.

Baron, Salo Wittmayer, *A Social and Religious History of the Jews*, Columbia University Press, New York, 1937.

Benamozegh, Elie, *Israël et l'Humanité*, Leroux, Paris, 1914, and Albin Michel, Paris, 1961.

Benoist, Luc, *L'Esotérisme*, "Que sais-je?", Presses Universitaires de France, Paris, 1963.

Bertholet, Alfred, *A History of Hebrew Civilization*, translated by Rev. A. K. Dallas, G. G. Harrap, London, 1926.

Bloch, Renée, *Quelques aspects de la figure de Moïse dans la tradition rabbinique*, dans *Cahiers Sioniens*, Desclée, Paris, 1955.

Blondel, Charles, *La Mentalité primitive*, Préface de Lévy-Bruhl, Stock, Paris, 1926.

Brunhes, Jean, *La Géographie humaine*, Félix Alcan, Paris, 1934.

Buber, Martin, *Moses*, East and West Library, Oxford, 1946.

Cahn, Zvi, *The Philosophy of Judaism*, The Macmillan Company, New York, 1962.

Capitan, Louis, *La Préhistoire*, Préface de l'Abbé (Henri) Breuil, Payot, Paris, 1931.

Castiglioni, Arturo, *Adventures of the Mind*, translated by V. Gianturco, A. A. Knopf, New York, 1946.

Causse, A., *Du groupe ethnique à la communauté religieuse. Le problème sociologique de la religion d'Israël*, Félix Alcan, Paris, 1937.

Cazelles, Henri, *Moïse devant l'histoire*, dans *Cahiers Sioniens*, Desclée, Paris, 1955.

Clark, Grahame, *World Prehistory: An Outline*, Cambridge University Press, 1961.

Cohen, Marcel, *Le Système verbal sémitique et l'expression du temps*, Leroux, Paris, 1924.

Contenau, Georges, *La Civilization d'Assur et de Babylone*, Payot, Paris, 1937. *La Magie chez les Assyriens et les Babyloniens*, Payot, Paris, 1947.

Deffontaines, Pierre, *Géographie et religions*, Gallimard, Paris, 1948.

Dhorme, Edouard, *La Religion des Hébreux nomades*, Nouvelle Société d'Editions, Bruxelles, 1937.

——, *Les Religions de Babylonie et d'Assyrie*, Collection "Mana," Presses Universitaires de France, Paris, 1949.

Dubnow, Semen Markovich, *An Outline of Jewish History*, M. N. Maisel, New York, 1929.

Dumas, Alexandre, *Quinze jours au Sīnaī, Impressions de voyage*, Calmann-Lévy, Paris, 1891.

Durkheim, Émile, *The Elementary Forms of the Religious Life*, translated by Joseph Ward Swain, Allen & Unwin, London, 1954.

——, *Le Système totémique en Australie*, Félix Alcan, Paris, 1912.

Dussaud, René, *Le Sacrifice en Israël et chez les Phéniciens*, Leroux, Paris, 1914.

——, *Introduction à l'histoire des religions*, Presses Universitaires de France, Paris, 1949.

——, *Les Religions des Hittites et des Hourrites, des Phéniciens et des Syriens*, Collection "Mana," Presses Universitaires de France, Paris, 1949.

Gelin, Albert, *Moïse dans L'Ancien Testament*, dans *Cahiers Sioniens*, Desclée, Paris, 1955.

Gerster, Georg, *Sinai, Land der Offenbarung*, Verlag Ullstein, Berlin, 1961.

Ginzberg, Louis, *The Legends of the Jews*, 7 v., translated from the German manuscript, The Jewish Publication Society of America, Philadelphia, 1911–38.

Graetz, Heinrich Hirsch, *Sīnaī et Golgotha, ou Les origines du Judaïsme et du Christianisme*, translated from the German by Maurice Hess, Michel Lévy, Paris, 1867.

Grenier, Albert, *La Religion étrusque et romaine,* Collection "Mana," Presses Universitaires de France, Paris, 1948.

Griaule, Marcel, *Dieu d'eau (Entretiens avec Ogotemmêli),* Editions du Chêne, Paris, 1948.

Guitton, Jean, *Le Développment des idées dans L'Ancien Testament,* Aubier, Editions Montaigne, Aix-en-Provence, 1947.

Halévy, M. A., *Moïse dans l'histoire et dans la légende,* Collection "Judaïsme," Rieder, Paris, 1927.

Heinemann, I., *La Loi dans la pensée juive,* Albin Michel, Paris, 1962.

Heriot, Thomas, *A briefe and true report of the new found land of Virginia . . . written by Thomas Heriot, servant to Sir Walter Ralegh . . .* etc., reproduced in facsimile from the first edition of 1588, with an introductory note by Luther S. Livingston, Dodd, Mead & Co., New York, 1903.

Hirsch, Samson Raphael, *Timeless Torah,* P. Feldheim, New York, 1957.

Jacobi, Jolan, *The Psychology of C. G. Jung,* translated from the German by R. Manheim, Yale University Press, New Haven, 1962.

Jousse, Marcel, *Le Style oral palestinien,* Gabriel Beauchesne, Paris, 1925.

———, *Les Outils gestuels de la mémoire dans le milieu ethnique palestinien,* Geuthner, Paris, 1935.

Kramer, Samuel Noah, *History Begins at Sumer* (3rd edition), Thames and Hudson, London and New York, 1961.

Laming-Emperaire, A., *La Signification de l'art rupestre paléolithique,* Picard, Paris, 1962.

Lavaignac et Grelo, *Le Cadre historique de la Bible,* dans "Introduction à la Bible" de Robert et Feuillet, Desclée, Paris.

Lecointre, E., *La Campagne de Moïse pour la sortie d'Egypte,* Gautier-Villars, Paris.

Leibowitz, Nechama, *Studies in the Weekly Sidra,* World Zionist Organization, 1938.

Lévi-Strauss, Claude, *La Pensée sauvage,* Plon, Paris, 1962.

Levy, G. R., *The Gate of Horn,* Faber and Faber, London, 1948.

Lévy-Bruhl, Lucien, *How Natives Think (Les Fonctions mentales dans les sociétés inférieures),* Authorized translation by Lilian A. Clare, A. A. Knopf, New York, 1926.

Lods, Adolphe, *Israel from Its Beginnings to the Middle of the Eighth Century*, translated by S. H. Hooke, K. Paul, Trench, Trubner, London, 1932.

Loisy, Alfred Firmin, *The Religion of Israel*, translated by A. Galton, T. Fisher Unwin, London, 1910.

Luquet, Georges Henri, *The Art and Religion of Fossil Man*, translated by J. Townsend Russell, Jr., with a preface by George Grant MacCurdy, Yale University Press, New London, and H. Milford, Oxford University Press, 1930.

Mainage, Théodore, *Les Religions de la préhistoire; L'âge paléolithique*, Desclée de Brouwer, Paris, 1921.

Marquès-Rivière, Jean, *Histoire des doctrines ésotériques*, Payot, Paris, 1940.

Mueller, Friedrich Max, *Physical Religion*, Longmans, Green, London, 1891.

Munk, Salomon, *Palestine géographique, historique et archéologique*, Michel Lévy, Paris, 1862.

Murphy, John, *The Origins and History of Religions*, Manchester University Press, Manchester, 1949.

Néher, André, *Moïse et la vocation juive*, Editions du Seuil, Paris, 1956.

Néher, André et Renée, *Histoire biblique du peuple d'Israël*, Adrien Maisonneuve, Paris, 1962.

Neubauer, Adolf, *La Géographie du Talmud*, Michel Lévy, Paris, 1868.

Nicolas, Michel, *Etudes critiques sur la Bible*, Michel Lévy, Paris, 1862.

Parrot, André, *Sumer*, translated by Stuart Gilbert and James Emmons, Thames and Hudson, London, 1960.

———, *Assur*, Gallimard, Paris, 1961.

———, *Abraham et son temps*, Delachaux et Nestlé, Neuchatel, 1962.

Picard, Charles, *Les Religions préhelléniques* (Crète et Mycènes), Collection "Mana," Presses Universitaires de France, Paris, 1948.

Pirot et Clamer, *Commentaire exégétique et théologique sur la Sainte Bible*, Letouzey et Ané, Paris, 1953.

Piveteau, Jean, *Images des mondes disparus*, Masson, Paris, 1951.

Radin, Paul, *Primitive Religion, its Nature and Origin*, Viking Press, New York, 1937.

Salvador, Joseph, *Histoire des Institutions de Moïse et du peuple hébreu*, Ponthieu et Cie, Paris, 1828.

Sayce, Archibald Henry (editor), George Smith, *Assyria, from the Earliest Times to the Fall of Nineveh* and *The History of Babylonia*, Society for the Promotion of Christian Knowledge, London.

Schmidt, Wilhelm, *Der Ursprung der Gottesidee*, W. Aschendorff, Münster, 1912–55.

Sérouya, Henri, *La Kabbale*, Grasset, Paris, 1947.

Starky, J., Compte rendu sur *Le antiche divinità semitiche* (Ouvrage collectif, par J. Bottero et al., Rome, 1960), dans *Revue Biblique*, 1960.

Tresmontant, Claude, *Essai sur la pensée hébraique*, Editions du Cerf, Paris, 1953.

Vandier, Jacques, *La Religion égyptienne*, Collection "Mana," Presses Universitaires de France, Paris, 1949.

Vaux, R. P. de, *Introduction générale au Pentateuque* (dans *Bible de Jerusalem*), Editions du Cerf, Paris, 1951.

Vermès, Géza, *La Figure de Moïse au tournant des deux Testaments*, dans *Cahiers Sioniens*, Desclée, Paris, 1955.

Vincent, A., *La Religion d'Israël* (volume 4 de *L'Histoire des Religions*), Bloud et Gay, Paris, 1959.

Vuillaud, *La Kabbale juive*, Emile Nourry, Paris, 1923.

Weil, Isaac, *Le Prosélytisme chez les Juifs selon la Bible et le Talmud*, Deribaux, Strasbourg, 1880.

Weill, Raymond, *La Presqu'île du Sïnaï*, Champion, Paris, 1908.

Wolff, Werner, *Changing Concepts of the Bible*, Hermitage House, New York, 1951.

Woolley, Sir Leonard, *Ur of the Chaldees*, E. Benn, London, 1929. *Abraham (Recent Discoveries and Hebrew Origins)*, Faber and Faber, London, 1936.